NOVEL STUDY
DECODING THE SECRETS AND STRUCTURES OF CONTEMPORARY FICTION

KRISTEN TATE

Copyright © 2024 by Kristen Tate

All rights reserved.

No part of this book may be reproduced in any form or by any electronic or mechanical means, including information storage and retrieval systems, without written permission from the author, except for the use of brief quotations.

Published by The Blue Garret
www.thebluegarret.com

ISBN 978-1-7345742-4-1 (hardcover)
ISBN 978-1-7345742-3-4 (paperback)
ISBN 978-1-7345742-5-8 (ebook)

Cover design by Rachel Metzger

*For my mother, Danna,
who taught me that all things could be learned from books.
The result: a book about books.*

CONTENTS

Introduction	ix

THE DUTCH HOUSE, BY ANN PATCHETT

1. How do openings pull us in?	3
2. What are the components of a scene?	9
3. How do you use chronology for maximum effect?	20

THE CITY WE BECAME, BY N. K. JEMISIN

4. What does your cover and front matter say?	31
5. Should your novel have a prologue?	35
6. How do you balance multiple points of view?	41

THE SEARCHER, BY TANA FRENCH

7. How do you open a mystery novel?	55
8. How do you use dialogue to reveal character?	62
9. How do you use setting and character description?	69
10. Does your plot need to follow a set structure?	74

MATRIX, BY LAUREN GROFF

11. How do you establish setting in historical fiction?	87
12. How do you use omniscient narration?	91
13. How do you write resonant endings?	100

I KISSED SHARA WHEELER, BY CASEY MCQUISTON

14. How do you hook a reader before the first sentence?	107
15. How do you get the most mileage out of dialogue?	112
16. How do you add voices to a single-POV novel?	119

THE LAST THING HE TOLD ME, BY LAURA DAVE

17. How do you engage readers who know the hook?	127
18. How do you deliver plot surprises?	132
19. How do you plot a page-turner?	140

DIAL A FOR AUNTIES, BY JESSE Q. SUTANTO

20. How do you introduce a complex plot? — 149
21. How do you make a dialogue-focused scene feel active? — 154
22. How do you use subplots to add tension? — 159

BLACK SUN, BY REBECCA ROANHORSE

23. How do you lure readers into an epic fantasy world? — 167
24. How do you integrate world-building into scenes? — 174
25. How do you use time jumps to create suspense? — 180

THE MARRIAGE PORTRAIT, BY MAGGIE O'FARRELL

26. What can verbs do for you? — 191
27. How do you control omniscient narration? — 195
28. How do you make a novel feel historical? — 202

THE SECRET HOURS, BY MICK HERRON

29. How do you introduce multiple plot strands? — 209
30. How do you write an action scene? — 219
31. How do you add tension to a quiet plot? — 227
32. How do you write suspenseful endings? — 236

Conclusion: How do you read a novel? — 243

More Novel Study — 255
Notes — 257
Takeaways and Topic Index — 261
Acknowledgments — 275
About the Author — 277
Also by Kristen Tate — 279

LIST OF ILLUSTRATIONS

This book includes several full-color illustrations that I hope will be helpful for visual learners like myself (though you won't need them to follow my arguments). In many cases, my analysis of a novel started with a rough version of these illustrations as I tried to make sense of the structure of a scene or plot.

I've made the illustrations in the book as accessible as possible for a variety of different reading needs, and the ebook includes alt-text descriptions. You can also access the illustrations (with alt text) on my website, where you can increase their size:

www.thebluegarret.com/novel-study-illustrations

LIST OF ILLUSTRATIONS

Figure 1: Scene composition (Chapter 2)
Figure 2: Chronology of *The Dutch House* (Chapter 3)
Figure 3: Narrators in *The City We Became* (Chapter 6)
Figure 4: Plot structure of *The Searcher* (Chapter 10)
Figure 5: Internal versus external plots of *The Searcher* (Chapter 10)
Figure 6: Plot structure of *The Last Thing He Told Me* (Chapter 19)
Figure 7: Subplots in *Dial A for Aunties* (Chapter 22)
Figure 8: Chronology of *Black Sun* (Chapter 25)
Figure 9: Internal versus external plots of *The Secret Hours* (Chapter 31)

INTRODUCTION

We have always treated stories and storytellers with reverence—and that's as it should be given how important they are to our culture. But if you yourself are trying to become a storyteller, this reverence can make you believe that you can't tell good stories until someone inducts you into the guild and whispers the storytelling secret in your ear. The truth is—there is no secret. Stories should *feel* like magic to readers, but writers use craft, not magic, to create them.

Some lucky writers will discover when they begin that they already have many of the tools they need and are able to invent others for themselves as they gain experience. These authors can't always articulate how they do what they do. Stephen King's *On Writing* is deservedly popular because of the stories he tells in it: the hours spent writing at a cramped desk in a tiny room, the sudden success of *Carrie*, the hard-won victory over his addictions. He also has many useful things to tell us about process—for instance, his excellent advice to "write with the door closed, rewrite with the door open" and to put your first draft in a drawer for at least six weeks before you start to revise.[1] When it comes to specific craft tools, however, King has less to say.

Many writers who seem to come by their tools naturally have in

INTRODUCTION

actuality developed them from years and years of reading. They've absorbed the structures and techniques of the novels they've read and can instinctually reach for the tools they need. King knows this, advising, "Reading is the creative center of a writer's life."[2] In *Thanks, But This Isn't For Us*, editor Jessica Morrell gives similar advice—quoting this same passage from *On Writing*, in fact—and recounts a story about a memoir-writing class she once taught in which not a single writer in the room had read twenty memoirs.[3] Neither Morrell nor King, however, advise writers on *how* to read productively, and that's a gap I want to fill with this book. I do believe, like them, that if you read enough, you will absorb quite a bit without having to work at it. But I also believe that doing the kind of analysis I'm going to demonstrate in this book will get you there faster and more effectively.

I'll guide you through ten novels in different genres, analyzing how they work and excavating each author's tools along the way. At the end of each chapter you'll find a list of takeaways that will help you apply these tools to your own work. You can find all of the takeaways, grouped by topic, at the end of the book. In the conclusion, you'll find tips and tools to help you conduct your own novel studies, so you can go out and excavate the tools that are best suited for your story. If you want to learn from King, you should certainly read *On Writing*, but you should also use the techniques I'll show you to analyze *Carrie* and find out exactly how it works. King doesn't tell you, but the novel will.

I didn't set out to find the 'best' or most popular novels to use for my analysis. Instead, I followed my own tastes, choosing books I was excited to study and happy to read multiple times over. I've chosen recent books, all published within the last five years, because style is always shifting and I want to bring you the latest, most innovative tools I can find. I picked books by experienced authors rather than debut novels, and I tried to cover a range of styles, genres, and perspectives. I strongly believe that authors can benefit from reading not just within their chosen genre but outside it too, so don't skip chapters focused on novels that aren't what you usually read or write. You

INTRODUCTION

never know where you will find the tool or technique that will unlock a problem you encounter in your own work.

You don't need to have read the novels I discuss in order to benefit from my analysis (although I do encourage you to read them because you'll learn even more!). In chapters where I discuss the overall structure of the book, I sometimes reveal important plot points. I've added spoiler warnings to these chapters in case you want to read the book yourself first. That said, novels offer many pleasures beyond plot suspense, and knowing the plot outline might in fact make you a better reader, able to pick up foreshadowing and other nuances you would have otherwise missed. I can tell you that I read all of these novels at least twice and was just as enthralled the second time through as I was the first.

Many chapters include charts or diagrams to illustrate the structure of a novel or the components of a scene. These charts are largely subjective rather than objective; a different reader might do the same analysis and come up with a different result. Novels are not math problems, and there is no magic formula for writing a good one. There are as many ways to write a good novel as there are ways to make a good plate of pasta—the possibilities are endless, and writers show us new ones every day. That's part of the excitement for both writers and readers.

To help you do your own novel study analysis, I've provided templates and worksheets, which you can download for free from my website:

www.thebluegarret.com/novel-study-downloads

THE DUTCH HOUSE, BY ANN PATCHETT

STATS

I wrote this book, got all the way to the end, read it, hated it, threw it away and started over.
—Ann Patchett[1]

Published in 2019 by Harper
337 pages, approximately 84,250 words
The author's eighth published novel

GENRE

Literary Fiction

AMAZON CATEGORIES

Coming of Age Fiction, Family Life Fiction, Literary Fiction

AWARDS

Finalist for the Pulitzer Prize for Fiction

CHAPTER 1
HOW DO OPENINGS PULL US IN?

Having edited hundreds of novels by this point in my career, I can tell you that the opening is the most challenging section for most writers. You have to walk a narrow path between revealing too much information about your characters and not enough. A successful opening draws readers in, gives them an inside peek at some crucial element of the novel, and raises questions interesting enough to make them *want* to keep reading in order to get the answers.

Because openings are so important, I'm going to examine the opening of every novel I discuss in this book. You'll see a range of examples and learn something new from each one. Here are the questions I'll be asking:

- How does the opening pull us into the world of the novel?
- What do we know? What's implied? What's left as a mystery?
- What makes us want to keep reading?

As we take these questions to our first book, *The Dutch House* by Ann Patchett, let's start with what the cover and title tell us, for they are indeed part of the meaning of the book. The cover of *The Dutch*

House features a painting, complete with gilt frame, of a girl wearing a red dress with belled sleeves. Her gaze is level and direct, her facial expression serious. Her hands are open in her lap, partially cradling one another, as if she is holding a precious but invisible object—an unusual pose. The background, with its patterned wallpaper and vase of fresh flowers at her elbow, implies wealth. Who is the girl? What is her relationship to the Dutch House of the title? And what *is* the Dutch House, anyway?

The first paragraph of the novel gives us another clue, but also raises more questions:

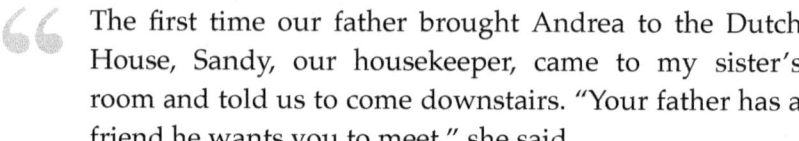
> The first time our father brought Andrea to the Dutch House, Sandy, our housekeeper, came to my sister's room and told us to come downstairs. "Your father has a friend he wants you to meet," she said.

In addition to having a name, the Dutch House has a housekeeper, confirming the impression of wealth. What do we learn about the cast of characters from these lines? We understand intuitively that we are with an older narrator who is inhabiting a younger self. This narrator knows that the "friend" is named Andrea and this is not the last time she'll be at the Dutch House. The so-far unnamed narrator is close to their sister, signaled by the immediate use of "our" and by the fact that they are together in this moment when Sandy comes to find them. Sandy tells rather than asks them to come downstairs, implying that these siblings are on the young side and also that Sandy has some measure of authority over them. Notice how much of this information is hinted at rather than told to us outright.

After this opening paragraph, we continue with the scene Sandy's dialogue line has activated:

> "Is it a work friend?" Maeve asked. She was older and so had a more complex understanding of friendship.
>
> Sandy considered the question. "I'd say not. Where's your brother?"
>
> "Window seat," Maeve said.

> Sandy had to pull the draperies back to find me. "Why do you have to close the drapes?"
>
> I was reading. "Privacy," I said, though at eight I had no notion of privacy. I liked the word, and I liked the boxed-in feel the draperies gave when they were closed.

Patchett trickles out a few more details in this exchange: Maeve is the older sibling; our narrator is an eight-year-old boy. We still don't know his name or anything about his appearance—details beginning novelists often feel they must deliver to readers right away. What readers are really interested in is the question Maeve is pursuing for us: Who is Andrea and why is she at their house? Sandy's considering pause, her use of the anodyne word "friend," which Southerners of my mother's generation still use to refer to unmarried romantic partners, only heightens our curiosity. Where is the mother of these two children in the Dutch House? Why does their father want them to meet Andrea? Will Andrea become their stepmother? Maeve, it is hinted, with her "more complex understanding of friendship," may be alert to this possibility. The purpose of her question is to rule it out. If Andrea is a work friend, then perhaps she is not romantically involved with their father.

The last paragraph quoted above gives us our most direct view yet of our narrator, and immediately we are allied with him: Like us, he is reading. The "I" in the sentence "I was reading" is the first "I" voiced by the narrator, the first action he relates of himself. Readers may hear echoes of Charlotte Brontë's *Jane Eyre*, which opens with the orphaned Jane tucked away in a curtained window seat of her aunt's lavish but lonely house, reading a book, before she is violently interrupted by her abusive cousin. The overall message we have received so far is that the Dutch House is not a warm, embracing, nurturing place.

Patchett quickly gets the children into the drawing room. Their father and Andrea don't notice them yet, focused instead on two formal portraits hanging on the wall. Our narrator goes on to give us a lengthy description of these portraits of Mr. and Mrs. VanHoebeek, "both dressed in black and [standing] with an erect formality that spoke of another time," but first we get a single dialogue line:

"It must be a comfort, having them with you," Andrea said to him, not of his children but of his paintings.

Notice how much meaning is layered into that single sentence! Andrea believes, or at least says, that the children's father must be in need of comfort (and we wonder again, why?). And she is oriented to believe that physical objects, not human relationships, bring comfort. Or does the narrator, relating this remembered scene from his childhood, attribute this belief to her? A few paragraphs later, the narrator confesses, "I will always believe that Andrea's face fell for an instant when she looked at Maeve and me." The sentence makes us curious to see how this unpromising relationship between Andrea and the children will unfold. At the same time, the phrase "I will always believe" makes us wonder about the narrator's reliability; it's the phrasing of someone who has been presented with evidence to the contrary that he doesn't wish to accept.

As the scene goes on, the relationships between these characters start to unfold. Finally, on page six, we learn the name of our narrator—Danny—when his father addresses him. The father is, as Patchett primes us to expect, cold and distant, giving Danny attention that is overly critical and ignoring Maeve altogether as far as possible. Woven into the scene, which continues on with a brief discussion about the house and its former acreage, is a great deal of backstory, most of it focused on the Dutch House but also sneakily revealing important details about the family: that Danny's father bought the house and everything in it, including the paintings, after the VanHoebeeks fell on hard times; that Danny and Maeve's mother has "left" the family, though we don't know why; that the father does marry Andrea; that there is long-standing tension between Maeve and Andrea, which some people (but not Danny) believe stems from this very first meeting between the two.

Patchett often launches this backstory material from a specific setting detail, keeping us tethered to the scene unfolding in the drawing room of the Dutch House. For example, we learn more about the portrait we encountered on the cover of the book. It portrays

Maeve at the age of ten and was painted by a famous artist brought in from Chicago:

 As the story goes, he was supposed to paint our mother, but our mother, who hadn't been told that the painter was coming to stay in our house for two weeks, refused to sit, and so he painted Maeve instead. When the portrait was finished and framed, my father hung it in the drawing room right across from the VanHoebeeks. Maeve liked to say that was where she learned to stare people down.

Here is a clue to the mother's absence—and more evidence of the father's domineering attitude toward his family—as well as insight into the character of Maeve, who refuses to be dominated.

Later in the scene, Andrea gazes at the huge panes of glass surrounding the glass front doors and asks, "Don't you worry about people looking in?" In response, Patchett, via Danny, offers up a setting description that turns out to be much more than simple description:

 Not only could you see into the Dutch House, you could see straight through it. . . . From the driveway you could let your eye go up the front steps, across the terrace, through the front doors, across the long marble floor of the foyer, through the observatory, and catch sight of the lilacs waving obliviously in the garden behind the house.

We understand, intuitively, that what Patchett is offering in this novel is a chance to see through this house and its inhabitants as she holds them up for scrutiny, like insect specimens pinned against illuminated glass. Readers (like us!) alert to theme statements might highlight the first sentence of that passage. We'll have to keep reading, however, to learn how this observation relates to the novel as a whole.

TAKEAWAYS

- Use your first lines to make readers curious (who is Andrea?) rather than establish basic information (the narrator's name).
- Don't reveal too much in your opening paragraphs: Give your readers space and time to make guesses you later confirm.
- Make setting details do double duty, like evoke a theme of the novel or reveal backstory.
- Introduce your theme subtly in the opening chapters through symbolic details, character actions, or setting descriptions, allowing readers to gradually recognize the underlying ideas.

CHAPTER 2
WHAT ARE THE COMPONENTS OF A SCENE?

Now that we've done a close reading of the opening of *The Dutch House*, let's anatomize a later scene from the novel in the way a lepidopterist might anatomize a butterfly. When we look at the parts of the scene, what do we find? How can we categorize them? Most importantly, how do these components function in the larger organism of the story?

One of the risks of this kind of analysis is getting too caught up in the categories themselves, creating classifications so specific that we spend more time defining them than analyzing them. So I've stuck to broad categories and tried to give them labels that are as clear as possible. We'll drill down into the nuances as we explore the scene, but let's start with some basic definitions:

- **Action:** a movement or change of state of someone or something in the scene—usually something visual and concrete that you could film
- **Dialogue:** words spoken out loud by a character, usually to another character
- **Interiority:** the internal thoughts and feelings of the point-of-view character, including internal monologue

- **Setting:** the environment of the scene—generally something that can be perceived by sight, sound, or smell
- **Character:** physical descriptions, but also information about characters' personality, psychology, habits, etc.
- **Summary:** a compressed recounting of action or dialogue
- **Backstory:** summary focused on events or information outside the timeframe of the novel

Other writers (or you yourself!) might come up with different categories or define them differently. You'll also see when we get into the details that some sentences do double duty or could fall into multiple categories. Remember that we're not labeling and counting for the sake of creating a rigorous taxonomy or performing data analysis, but rather so we can see what components Patchett is using and how she is using them. I'll repeat this analysis for other novels, so we'll get a chance to compare how different writers make use of the same set of components.

After all of those disclaimers about the numbers, let's look at a few of them. We'll be examining chapter five, scene one, which has about 5,100 words. Roughly a third of the scene is composed of action and dialogue—the two primary components of what I call a 'live scene,' the sections you could visualize or easily translate into a screenplay. Another third is interiority, what the point-of-view character is thinking or feeling. The final third is setting, character description, backstory, and summary—the muscles, bones, and sinews connecting everything together. See Figure 1 at the end of this chapter for a comparison of the scene composition of *The Dutch House*, *Dial A for Aunties*, and *The Secret Hours*. (You'll find my analysis of *Dial A for Aunties* in Chapter 21 and my analysis of *The Secret Hours* in Chapter 30.)

The scene is built around two important action sections: Danny's father showing him the Brooklyn neighborhood where he and Danny's mother grew up, and then Danny taking his sister Maeve back to the same spot, where they rehash what they know about their mother and her disappearance. But despite most of the action taking place in New York City, the scene both begins and ends at the Dutch House, a clever illustration of the gravitational pull of the house on Danny, who narrates the novel. These beginning and ending pages are largely summary and interiority, with a few snippets of action and dialogue to give them energy. There are a few large chunks of summary and a chunk of backstory in the scene, but Patchett is careful to position these around the more dynamic live action sections. Interiority is the only element that appears on every single page.

Before going deeper with our analysis, let's start by thinking about the overall purpose of the scene. Why is it here? How are the characters, especially our protagonist Danny, different at the end of the scene? These are questions I encourage authors I work with to ask of every scene in their manuscript, to make sure each one is pulling its weight.

So what is Patchett trying to accomplish here? By this point in the novel, she's opened three sets of story questions, focused on three different points in time: How does the family unit in the Dutch House, especially Danny, respond to the introduction of Andrea and her daughters? Why did Danny and Maeve's mother leave? And how do all of these events shape the adult Danny becomes? Even in the early chapters of the book, we get glimpses of the older Danny in scenes that jump forward in time. By chapter five, we've had two of these scenes and we're about to get another one immediately after the scene I analyze here. (In the next chapter, I'll be saying a lot more about why and how Patchett uses these time jumps.)

In the scene we are examining, Patchett zeroes in on the second question: Why did Danny and Maeve's mother leave? The event itself took place long before the novel opens—so long ago, in fact, that Danny has no memory of it. Other characters around him, of course, do remember it: his father, Maeve, and the servants Sandy and Jocelyn. Patchett could answer the question via dialogue; we could imagine a scene where Sandy sits Danny down at the kitchen table and tells him everything she knows about what happened. But Patchett wants to maximize the mystery and drama surrounding the question—she wants to show it rather than tell it, in other words.

I think chapter five is her solution: She puts her characters in motion, via the trip from Philadelphia to New York, and she adds a layer of tension by making Danny and his father the two actors in the scene. Danny's father is allergic to emotion and habitually unwilling to communicate anything personal. The few crumbs of information he drops are gathered up carefully by Danny, who then must go over them with Maeve in order to properly understand them. So in addition to the information we get about the missing mother, we get a much richer understanding of Danny's relationships with his father and with Maeve, and how these relationships are shaping him. The framing scenes at the Dutch House inject a further layer of tension, showing us the ways in which the relationships between Andrea and Danny's father, as well as Andrea and Danny himself, are poisoning the already frigid atmosphere of the family home.

Now it's time to zoom in and look more closely at a few sections of the scene so we can see these components at work. In the beginning of chapter five, Patchett uses summary mixed with action and dialogue to cover a lot of set-up work in a compressed space. We learn that Maeve has left for college in New York, and Danny is lonely without her, even with a stepmother and two stepsisters now in the house. Maeve invites him to visit over Easter break; to Danny's surprise, his father decides to drive him there and take him to lunch with Maeve. At this point we get a line of interiority that operates like a gut punch: "It sounded so nostalgic when he said it, *the three of us*, as if we had once been a unit instead of just a circumstance." After this line, a bit of action and dialogue flicker to life:

Andrea caught wind of the plan and announced at dinner that she would ride along. There were plenty of things she needed in the city. But after she thought about it some more she said the girls should come too, and that after they dropped me off at Maeve's, my father could take them sightseeing. "The girls still haven't been to New York, and you're from there!" Andrea said, as if he'd conspired to keep New York from them. "We'll take the boat out to see the Statue of Liberty. Wouldn't that be something?" she asked the girls.

We've already heard about the formal dining room in the Dutch House, with its ornate ceiling of carved and gilded leaves "more in keeping with Versailles than Eastern Pennsylvania," so Patchett doesn't spend any time on setting. We get an action from Andrea (that announcement) followed by a summary of her reasons for wanting to come along, seasoned by a couple of dialogue lines. There is only one snippet of interiority from Danny, his interpretation of Andrea's line about the girls never having been to New York, but it's enough to help us see how self-centered Andrea is—and also how narrator Danny's feelings about her may be coloring his summary of her dialogue. The next two paragraphs operate the same way, before this miniature scene is closed off by another, longer passage of interiority: "It didn't matter. I was only missing lunch, that ridiculous notion of the three of us. . . . Disappointment comes from expectation, and in those days I had no expectation that Andrea would get anything less than what she wanted." In roughly six hundred words, Patchett shows us the state of affairs at the Dutch House and sets the stage for the next burst of action.

That occurs the next morning, when Danny's father rushes them out of the house, not even giving him time to pack in his hurry to escape Andrea. Patchett stretches the moment out using setting details (the cereal bowl Danny leaves on the table, the wisteria not yet blooming on the trellis along the walk to the garage), action (Danny running to keep up with his father's long strides), and this dramatic bit of interiority: "all the way to the garage I thought, *Escape, escape, escape.* We beat the word into the gravel with every step." Once in the car, Danny's father surprises him once more by offering to show him around the Brooklyn neighborhood where he grew up. Danny's surprise at his father's offer and the reader's curiosity about what he'll reveal gives Patchett the room to deliver a big chunk of character study. We get a physical description of Danny's father for the first time (his height, his rust-colored hair, his weathered skin) as well as some important psychological details, conveyed through a chunk of backstory—Danny recalling the time he'd asked his father whether he planned to vote for Eisenhower or Stevenson for president.

 My father clicked the point of his knife against his plate and told me I was *never* to ask a question like that, not of him, not of anyone. . . . "[T]o ask an adult such a question is to violate a man's right to privacy." In retrospect, I imagine my father was horrified that I might think there was any chance he'd vote for Stevenson, but I didn't know that at the time. What I knew was that you had to touch a hot stove only once.

Patchett delivers this information right at the moment readers need to understand the finer dynamics of Danny's relationship with his father in order to interpret the scene that comes next, the tour of Brooklyn. We need to understand why Danny is so hesitant to push or question, why he regards his father as a hot stove—one that burns rather than warms.

Before analyzing one more section of this scene, I want to say a few words about the familiar bit of writing advice to show rather than tell. As Lisa Cron points out in *Wired for Story*, this "might just be the most woefully misunderstood writing maxim on the books." She argues that 'showing' in this sense is figurative rather than literal. If you want to show rather than tell your readers a character is sad, in her example, the solution isn't to show the character crying but rather to show us *why* they are sad.[1] That might mean a live scene, with action and dialogue. But I also think that all of the components we've been tracking in this chapter—not just action and dialogue—can be used to show rather than tell.

Danny's backstory about his father's vote is a good example. Patchett might have included his private nature in the list of details she gives us just before the voting anecdote (my addition in italics): "He smoked Pall Malls, put milk in his coffee, worked the crossword puzzle before reading the front page. He loved buildings the way boys loved dogs. *He valued his privacy.*" But the backstory anecdote—essentially Danny telling us something his father told him—serves to show us this important psychological insight instead. At the same time, the details we are merely told are useful too. One of them—his love of buildings—is also something we are shown in different ways throughout the novel. Others simply round out our picture of the character and serve to make him feel more distinct and real. The art comes not from converting every 'telling' moment to 'showing' but in being deliberate in your mixture.

Let's now look at the second half of this scene, which takes us from Maeve and Danny's lunch with their father through their own pilgrimage to Brooklyn. There is more action and dialogue in this half of the scene, but Patchett continues to use other components, especially interiority, at strategic moments. There's a chunk of summary in which they say goodbye to their father and go down into the subway. Maeve plans to take Danny to the Metropolitan Museum, but Danny has been waiting to tell Maeve about his morning and it all spills out:

> Maeve stopped and gave me a hard look just before we got to the turnstile. She might have thought I was going to throw up, which wouldn't have been a bad guess. "Did you eat too much?"
>
> I shook my head. "We went to Brooklyn." There must have been some better way to tell her this but the morning was more than I knew how to shape into words.

This is a good example of creative showing. Patchett doesn't tell us that Danny feels overwhelmed; instead she shows it through his lack of words and by whatever physical signs make Maeve think he doesn't feel well. As so often with Patchett's writing, the sequence does double duty in showing us how well Maeve knows Danny, how motherly her relationship is to him, and how much attention she's paying to him in this moment.

As the scene continues, Patchett uses a mix of components to show us a rounded picture of a highly charged moment, one that could easily fall flat in less-skilled hands:

> There was a black metal gate in front of us, and on the other side of the gate was the platform for the train. The train came up and the doors opened and the people got off and got on but Maeve and I just stood there. Other people rushed past, trying to get through the turnstile in time. "We left too early. I think he and Andrea must have had a fight because she was going to come with us, Andrea and the girls, and then Dad came down alone and he was in a huge hurry to leave." I had started to cry when there was nothing to cry about. I was long past the age anyway. Maeve took me to a wooden bench and we sat there together and she fished a Kleenex out of her purse and handed it to me. She had her hand on my knee.

Remember Cron's advice to tell us *why* a character is crying rather than just show him cry? Here Patchett dramatizes Danny's precise predicament. Not only does he not fully understand why he's crying, he also believes it is wrong for him to be doing so at all. Our narrator here is a much older Danny, looking back on his younger self. Twelve-year-old Danny knows that his mother's choice to leave the family is "the central question of his life," but he's also just heard his father tell him, standing outside the building where she grew up, that "Everybody's got a burden in life and this is yours. She's gone. You have to live with that." Danny knows the loss of his mother has wounded him deeply, but he's being told to just get over it, without being given any tools for doing so—this tension explains a lot of adult Danny's choices, as we'll see in Chapter 3.

After another paragraph of interiority in which Danny again downplays his pain (which boils down to the possibility or even probability that his mother is dead, just like all of her relatives), Patchett restarts the action: "Maeve was very close. She'd eaten a peppermint from a bowl by the door in the restaurant. We both had. Her eyes weren't blue like mine. They were much darker, almost navy. 'Could you find the street again?'" Here the details take us very deep into Danny's point of view, helping us feel how physically close he is to Maeve. Patchett begins the paragraph by telling us they are close, giving us an interpretive slot for the details she then shows us. Maeve's dialogue line launches them on their journey back to Brooklyn, where Patchett uses summary to cover the literal ground Danny walked with his father.

The conversation they have in a coffee shop after the tour is an important one because it shows that there are some differences between them—in what they feel both about their mother and about the Dutch House—and these differences will continue to resonate throughout the book. Danny, for example, understands why his father told Maeve to think of her mother as dead: He wanted to stop Maeve from leaving for India to try to find her. Danny also realizes he's allied with his father in believing there to be "no better house" than the Dutch House, which, he is now learning from Maeve, also puts him at odds with his mother, who hated it. It's the only reason Maeve has to propose for why their mother left. Danny tries, in twelve-year-old style, to make the contradiction vanish:

"Maybe you misunderstood her."

"She said it more than once."

"Then she was crazy," I said, but as soon as I said it I was sorry.

Maeve shook her head. "She wasn't crazy."

That's the end of the conversation—in this scene at least. The last few pages consist of a summary of the rest of Danny's time in New York, and then a brief scene back in the dining room of the Dutch House, where we see him lie to Andrea about having seen a play she'd wanted to see and search, fruitlessly, for any signs of a deeper connection with his father: "I kept waiting for my father to catch my eye, to give me some small signal that things had changed between us, but it didn't come. He never asked me about my time with Maeve or the play I hadn't seen, and we never talked about Brooklyn again." By the next chapter, Danny's father is dead, the repeated "never" here operating as a foreshadowing death knell.

TAKEAWAYS

- Use the mix of components (action, dialogue, interiority, etc.) best for *your* specific scenes—there is no ideal mixture that works for every scene.
- Make sure your scene has a purpose and that at least one character is changed in some way by the end of the scene.
- Compress less important details of a scene using summary.
- Stretch out the most important moments of your scene, using setting details and interiority, in addition to action and dialogue.
- Position long sections of summary, character description, or backstory immediately before or after more dynamic action sections to vary the pacing of the scene.
- Show the why: Rather than telling the reader how a character feels, show us *why* they feel this way.

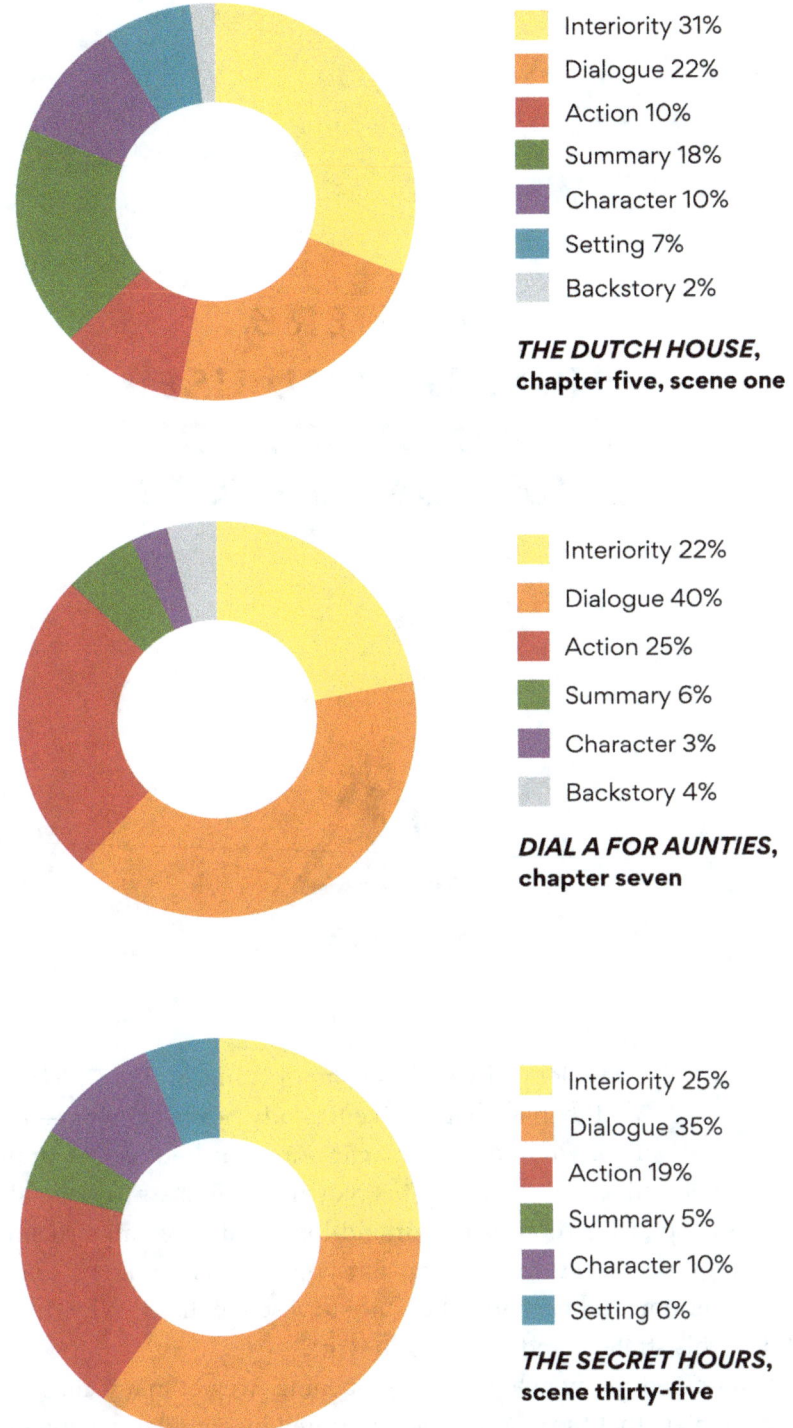

Figure 1: Scene composition. These scenes differ in purpose and pacing, but interiority is an important component in all three.

CHAPTER 3
HOW DO YOU USE CHRONOLOGY FOR MAXIMUM EFFECT?

SPOILER WARNING

We've looked closely at the opening of *The Dutch House* and then at chapter five to study how they work—examining what tools and tactics Ann Patchett uses to draw us into the narrative and then keep the plot and characters moving along. In this chapter I'll zoom back out and look at the overall structure of the plot, specifically at the way Patchett uses chronology, jumping around in time rather than telling the story sequentially. Why does she choose this strategy and how does it work?

As I noted in my analysis of the opening, we get many clues in the first chapters that the story is being narrated by an older version of our protagonist, Danny. Just how much older we don't know until the very last chapter of the book, at which point he has returned to the Dutch House, now owned by his twenty-something daughter, May. Early in the novel, in chapter six, Danny was kicked out of the Dutch House by Andrea, his stepmother, following his father's death, and one path of the book is to take him full circle back to the house, to give him a new relationship with it. *The Dutch House* is about inheritance in all its forms—houses, yes, but also stories and our other frameworks for making sense of the world.

How does the loss and restitution of the Dutch House happen? And how does Patchett control the way Danny narrates the story? At almost precisely the midpoint of the book, Danny muses, "In retrospect, it looked perfectly obvious, but at the time I might as well have been standing with my back to a craps table, throwing dice over my shoulder." He's talking about a lucky real estate deal that marks the beginning of the small empire he builds to replace his lost inheritance from his father, who made a fortune in real estate and raised Danny to believe he'd take over the business one day, but the first part of the sentence could be the tagline to the whole book, to his whole life. *In retrospect, it looked perfectly obvious.*

Let's take a quick look at the chronology of the novel. See Figure 2, at the end of the chapter, for a visual snapshot. The events chronicled in the book span roughly fifty years, from 1957 to the early 2000s, with roughly equal periods dedicated to various epochs in Danny's life. The book order follows the general trajectory of Danny's life; he's eight years old when we first meet him and in his fifties in the final scene. But along the way, Patchett jumps forward in time for select scenes to give us a glimpse of an older Danny and occasionally reaches backward in time as well. What's happening in those scenes and why does she position them where she does? Let's take a look at a few of them to see how they work.

Right away, Patchett establishes a rhythm that will become familiar in the first half of the novel. After the opening scene introducing Andrea and the Dutch House, the second scene jumps forward in time by several years. Danny is now fifteen, home on spring break from his first semester at Choate, an expensive New England boarding school. The scene is set not inside the Dutch House, however, but outside it, the two siblings watching from Maeve's car as the house lights up when evening sets in. They remember the scene we've just examined in Chapter 1—Andrea's concern about the grand front windows not providing privacy. "Sure enough," Danny thinks now, "you could see right into the house, through the house, not with any detail of course but memory filled in the picture."

At this stage, early in the novel, Patchett is drawing us in by opening a series of story questions, primary among them why Maeve and Danny are outside the Dutch House rather than inside. Chapters two and three fill in our picture of what is happening inside the house—and the family—immediately before and after Andrea marries Danny's father. Our next chronology break comes after the brief first scene of chapter four, showing the wedding itself, and places us a decade later. Danny is now in medical school in New York; he and Maeve still park outside the Dutch House when he visits Philadelphia. Danny asks Maeve, "Do you think it's possible to ever see the past as it actually was?" Maeve says she does. Danny responds, "But we overlay the present onto the past. We look back through the lens of what we know now, so we're not seeing it as the people we were, we're seeing it as the people we are, and that means the past has been radically altered." Danny is in his twenties at this point, parroting something he's learned in his Intro to Psych class. He doesn't truly understand yet how his own past—and the stories he and Maeve tell about it—are shaping his present choices, including his decision (or, more correctly, Maeve's decision for him) to attend medical school.

We get a couple more clues too: A brief conversation with a former neighbor reveals that Andrea is unfriendly and seems sad, that Maeve often parks in front of the Dutch House, and that Maeve and Danny haven't seen Andrea or their stepsisters in years. But this discussion about memory is, I think, the purpose of the scene itself—an opportunity for Patchett to plant a theme touchstone she'll return to in the next scene out of chronological order, which comes in chapter five. I analyzed the first scene of that chapter—Danny's childhood trip to Brooklyn with his father—in Chapter 2. In the second scene, Patchett takes us to 1977 or thereabouts. Danny is still chewing over the question of memory and how reliable it is. He seems to be starting to understand the impact of the stories he and Maeve have been telling themselves about their early lives:

> There was no extra time in those days and I didn't want to spend the little of it I had sitting in front of the goddamn house, but that's where we wound up: like swallows, like salmon, we were the helpless captives of our migratory patterns. We pretended that what we had lost was the house, not our mother, not our father. We pretended that what we had lost had been taken from us by the person who still lived inside.

And yet despite this insight about the patterns of the past, we later discover that right about this same time, chronologically, Danny unwittingly reenacts two stories from his father's life: He marries a woman who has fundamentally different goals than he does, and he buys her, as a surprise, a house she doesn't want.

Chapters six and seven finally reveal the mystery of why Danny and Maeve are parked outside the Dutch House: Their father died without a will, leaving Andrea with control of everything except for a trust established for the education of Danny and his stepsisters. (The one avenue for revenge open to Maeve is to make sure Danny liquidates this trust, which is why he goes to Choate and medical school despite not wanting to do either one.) Part one of the book ends here.

Part two, chapters eight through fifteen, focus on Danny's young adulthood, as he finishes medical school, embarks on his real estate business, marries Celeste, and starts a family—including a daughter, May, who looks so much like Maeve that, we are told, the portrait on the cover of the book could just as well be a portrait of her. In chapters eight through ten, Patchett is still hopping around in the chronology, now weaving in scenes set backward in time as well as forward. In the second scene of chapter ten, Maeve tells Danny the full story of the first time she ever saw the Dutch House, and their mother's horrified reaction.

It's after this scene, right at the midpoint of the novel, that the book pivots. Having already closed most of the story questions opened by the early chapters, Patchett introduces some new ones, heralded by the first sentence of chapter eleven: "It fell to Sandy to call and tell me Maeve was in the hospital." From the midpoint on, the chronology of the book moves almost entirely forward rather than looking back, and that's because the past—first in the form of Maeve and Danny's mother, and then in the form of Andrea—returns to the live narrative. The second half of the novel untangles and retells the stories, now lore, of the first half of the novel. The one big time jump, in chapter sixteen, takes us back twenty years, but to a moment of prescience about the future from Maeve. The siblings are sitting outside the Dutch House once again, this time discussing death. Maeve, a diabetic since childhood, correctly foretells her own death; Danny, characteristically, isn't willing to contemplate it.

Finally, in the last chapter of the book, we think we are encountering our narrator in close to real time: "The story of my sister was the only one I was ever meant to tell, but there are still a few things to say." Those few things bring us quickly and steadily forward in time, past Danny's divorce from Celeste, through the years required for him to forgive his mother for leaving and then for returning, past Andrea's death to May's purchase of the Dutch House. Patchett leaves us with the image of the beautiful house lit up for a fabulous party attended by May's glamorous friends, and Danny leading his daughter into the house—the inheritance restored.

Yet there's a hole here in these last two chapters, one I think Patchett leaves on purpose to complicate the tidiness of the ending. Danny may have indeed integrated the stories from his past that haunted him for so many years, but if it is his sister's story he thinks he is telling, there are parts he doesn't yet know, hasn't yet explored. Patchett reveals this subtly. Maeve is such a focus of the book, such an anchor for Danny, that her death at the end of chapter eighteen hits hard for us, just as it does for Danny. It's easy to miss, in the swirl of emotions, the odd, brief little chapter nineteen that follows. It is only a few sentences:

 I remember very little about the time just after Maeve died, except for Mr. Otterson, who sat with the family at her funeral Mass and covered his face with his hands as he cried. His grief was a river as deep and as wide as my own. I knew that I should have gone to him later, I should have tried to comfort him, but there was no comfort in me.

Do you see the story buried here? What Patchett is suggesting, I think, is that the work of integration, of continually sifting the stories we tell ourselves, isn't finished for Danny but will go on. A decade later or maybe two, he'll come back to this blank spot and try to fill it in, to understand why Mr. Otterson, the man he's known only as Maeve's boss for many years, is so grief-stricken.

Our retellings last our whole lives; they are messy and out of order, like a deck of shuffled cards. But we can lay out the cards in front of us and look at them again. Each time we do, another part of the story might emerge. As a young man, Danny thinks he's already learned, as he says to Maeve early in the book, that "we overlay the present onto the past." But Patchett shows us it isn't until the end of the novel, decades later, that he perhaps is beginning to understand the words he himself has spoken.

Patchett uses a baking metaphor to describe her writing process:

> I think of writing and editing in terms of folding, like you would fold in egg whites. You've got your egg whites beaten and you take a third of them and you lighten the batter by folding it in, and then you take a little bit and you fold it in, you fold it in—I don't feel like writing is linear as much as it is circular. There is this stirring movement of taking the story around in a circle, which means I am always writing back into it.[1]

This process of writing back into the book is the work of revision, not the work of drafting. A complex chronology such as the one we've analyzed here is something that can be constructed only after you know each part of your story and your characters thoroughly. At that point you can think about how you want your reader to experience the story. The reading process unfolds in time, and you, the author, get to control your reader's experience of the time of the novel. If you want to read more about novels with complex chronologies, see Chapter 18, on Laura Dave's *The Last Thing He Told Me*; Chapter 25, on Rebecca Roanhorse's *Black Sun*; and Chapter 31, on Mick Herron's *The Secret Hours*.

Before we leave *The Dutch House* and turn our attention to another novel, I want to point out that Patchett—already an experienced author, with seven novels behind her—threw away an entire early draft of this novel and started again. In an interview, she returns to a baking metaphor in talking about that decision:

> It was a funny thing to throw a book out. People seemed much more upset about it than I was. Some people said, *It must be like a death!* It was nothing like a death. It was like burning a cake. You know that feeling? Oh, hell, I burned the cake. Then you cut the cake open and eat the little pieces in the middle that aren't completely ruined, then you bake another cake. It's not what anyone wishes for, and it's hardly the end of the world.[2]

I hope you never reach that point with one of your own drafts and decide you need to start wholly from scratch—but I think it's important to remember that you can.

TAKEAWAYS

- Decide *when* in time to locate the story's narrator. Use chronology jumps to raise questions, control what you reveal and hide, and provide additional layers of meaning with the benefit of hindsight.
- Consider using time jumps to reveal backstory gradually,

allowing readers to piece together the past alongside the characters.
- Use a character's reactions to past events to show their growth or stagnation over time, demonstrating how their history shapes their present actions and decisions.
- Experiment with chronology jumps during revision, not drafting, once you thoroughly know the characters and events.
- Use a spreadsheet or notecards or a graph to see your chronology visually and experiment with mixing it up.

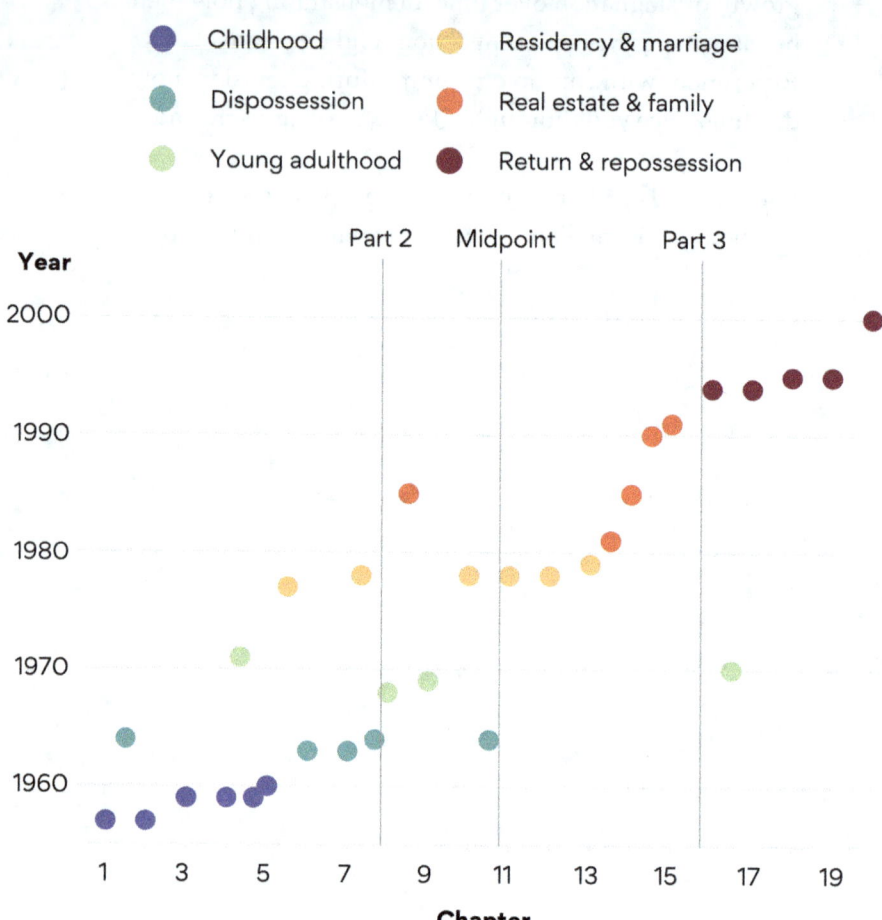

Figure 2: Chronology of *The Dutch House*. Time jumps stoke suspense, generate dramatic irony, and underscore themes.

THE CITY WE BECAME, BY N. K. JEMISIN

STATS

*[Y]ou'd be surprised by how often I encounter up-and-coming writers who start fretting about revisions (or the finished product!) long before they even have a manuscript done. This is revision anxiety, and it's bad for you! Get rid of it! Take a deep breath, touch some grass, and remember that **you can fix nearly everything in revision**, so don't worry about how the raw draft looks. Just get it down first.*
—N. K. Jemisin[1]

Published in 2020 by Orbit (Hachette)
434 pages, approximately 108,500 words
The author's tenth published novel

GENRE

Urban Fantasy

AMAZON CATEGORIES

Fantasy Action & Adventure, Paranormal & Urban Fantasy, Literary Fiction

AWARDS

Nominated for the Hugo and the Nebula Awards

CHAPTER 4
WHAT DOES YOUR COVER AND FRONT MATTER SAY?

To kick off my analysis of our next book—N. K. Jemisin's *The City We Became*—I'm going to start even before the opening lines. I did a brief analysis of the cover and title of *The Dutch House* in Chapter 1, but let's take that examination a little deeper and look at all of the front matter—everything we encounter before the first sentence—in *The City We Became*.

Let's start with the title. The cover art tells us that the city of the title must be New York. But it's an off-kilter New York with an impossible collage of a view that makes it look as if the city's iconic buildings and monuments (the Chrysler Building, the Empire State Building, the Flatiron Building, and the Statue of Liberty) are massed on the East River around the Williamsburg Bridge, ready for an attack coming by way of Brooklyn. The title and some of the other graphic elements are given an electric, jittery color treatment that make them look like an anaglyph, one of those composite images meant to be seen through stereoscopic glasses. Something is slightly off, slightly on edge in this New York City, the cover tells us.

And what about the rest of the title? Who is "we" and how does this personified group become a city? Jemisin's choice to use the past tense verb "became" is important too, signaling that the story is over and finished (the becoming is completed) but we are going to be told how it happened. The title is also in first person, not third: not "The City *They* Become" but the more dynamic, energetic, and inclusive "The City *We* Became."

Let's see how these initial impressions and questions develop as we start turning pages. First, we get an epigraph, a quote from novelist Thomas Wolfe: "One belongs to New York instantly, one belongs to it as much in five minutes as in five years." The primary purpose of an epigraph is to hint at the theme of a book. In this case, the epigraph builds on two elements of the title: It personifies New York City, casting it as a social entity like a family or a team, and it also includes the reader. You, the reader, are included in the "we" of the title, and you belong to New York, Wolfe tells us, even if you don't know it yet.

A secondary function of an epigraph can be to signal that other authors have found your theme or topic to be worthy of study, and to signal that your book is part of that conversation in the larger world of ideas. Thomas Wolfe, author of *Look Homeward, Angel* and *You Can't Go Home Again*, is known for writing about place, so Jemisin is joining that thematic conversation. Note that the epigraph is quite short. I think that's the best choice for fiction: You don't want readers to get bogged down in the rhythms and ideas of another writer before they get to your words.

Next up: a map! I do love a book with a map in the front. Right away it signals adventure, travel, new places. As a practical matter, a map orients readers to the geography of the novel and gives us a place to return to if we get lost. What clues about the story does this map in particular give us? The map is styled as a photograph of what looks like a simplified, 1950s-era map of the five boroughs of New York City, printed on heavy paper that has been neatly folded and reopened.[1] The map itself reminds us how small Manhattan is in comparison to Brooklyn and Queens, and also how the boroughs seem to share allegiances with other land masses—the Bronx being pulled north to upstate, Staten Island sidling over next to New Jersey, Brooklyn and Queens locked into the larger entity of Long Island.

Laid on top of the map is a business card for an entity called the "Better New York Foundation." The card has a notation that the foundation is "a subsidiary of Tmw. Inc." and the tagline "Prosperity and Progress," the kind of bland corporate jargon that makes you wonder what sin it is covering up. The business card overlaps a magnet or sticker shaped like one of the big old taxicabs that roamed mid-century New York City and advertises a business called "Checker Cab Dream Weddings." It includes a phone number too (the business card does not), which caught my eye immediately because it is standard copy-editing advice not to include a real phone number, email address, website, etcetera in a novel unless you are prepared to create it in the real world. Well, guess what? Jemisin—or her publisher—has done just that. When you call 212-816-7469, you get a message informing you that "City" is unavailable and urging you to try an "alternate contact method." Ominous! Where is "City" and how else can I reach them?

Also pictured on top of the map is a pen, which has been used to make handwritten notes. There is a list of cities at the bottom with two, New Orleans and Port-au-Prince, crossed out. A note under Long Island reads "HERE THERE BE DRAGONS." Studying the map more closely, we can see that the Williamsburg Bridge is crossed out and there are creepy tentacles emerging from various spots across the city and jellyfish-like creatures poised over others. What is happening in this New York?

Do you see just how much information you can convey about your book before the reader encounters the first words of the story?

TAKEAWAYS

- Spend time playing around with your title. What would be the effect of including a verb? Adding a pronoun? Changing the tense or shifting to a different pronoun?
- Consider how your novel's title and cover design can introduce your themes before the reader even begins the story.
- Choose an epigraph (if you include one) that connects to the

themes of your novel—think of your book as joining a conversation started by the work you quote from.
- Use a map or frontispiece illustration to drop hints or to illuminate contrasts or connections between story or setting elements.

CHAPTER 5
SHOULD YOUR NOVEL HAVE A PROLOGUE?

Before I became an editor, I didn't fully understand how many feelings people have about prologues. Agents have feelings! Readers have feelings! Writers most definitely have feelings! As a freelance editor, my job is to provide advice; it is the job of the authors I work with to decide whether or not to take it. To help you make that decision, let's walk through the benefits and drawbacks of prologues in general and then turn to *The City We Became* to analyze one prologue in detail.

Let's start with the potential weaknesses of prologues. I think the biggest is that they often slow down the start of the book and prevent readers from becoming immediately engaged with your protagonist and encountering the all-important plot hook that will make them keep reading. This is a particular problem for first-in-series books from debut authors. You are asking readers to commit hours of their time to your series. If you've managed to win their attention through your book description or a recommendation or savvy marketing, you want to make sure that your first pages deliver on what the book promises.

Authors sometimes want to include a prologue that is set long before the main action of the book or is told from the point of view of a minor character. Prologues like these often contain backstory information that helps readers understand the motivations or challenges of the protagonist or perhaps an antagonist. The problem isn't with the material itself, usually, but with its placement. It's almost always better to introduce us to your protagonist first and show us the problem they are going to have to solve over the course of the narrative before you deliver this backstory element. In other words, deliver the *what* before the *why*. If you start with the *why*, you require readers to carry that material forward with them into the narrative until they can make sense of it.

This kind of prologue is very tempting! If you are using it to showcase a point-of-view character who isn't going to feature in your main narrative, the prologue might feel (rightly!) like the only place you can give readers access to the character's internal thoughts and feelings. Backstory characters can be like metaphorical sirens for authors, pleading for their feelings to have a chance to shine, for their motivations to be revealed. In many cases, exploring this material can help you fully understand your story world and your characters, and yet often it's better to put the material aside and consider it as exploratory writing rather than part of your final manuscript.

Another reason authors might start with a prologue is to introduce readers to a broader conflict or theme that undergirds the book or perhaps even carries across an entire multi-book series. This strategy can often be successful, especially for books in action-oriented genres. For example, George R. R. Martin starts the *Game of Thrones* series with a scene featuring the white walkers, introducing the "winter is coming" theme that drives the big-picture conflicts across the series as a whole. And N. K. Jemisin, as we'll see, does the same in *The City We Became*.

Both writers, however, are careful to inject plenty of suspense and action into their prologues. If a prologue in a manuscript isn't working, it's usually because it's big on atmospherics and short on drama. Authors often want to offer up small clues but hold back bigger revelations until later in the narrative. That may be the right choice for the main plot but, again, can make for a prologue that is static and slow. It can be hard for an author who has been living with this story world for months or years to judge how a reader will process the information given to them in a prologue. What seems to you like a bright flashing beacon of a clue might be forgotten immediately by a reader who is looking for a character to latch onto.

Let's look now at a prologue that works and find out why and how it functions. In Chapter 4, I discussed the questions Jemisin's title opens up: Who is the "we" and how does a city "become"? Her prologue answers the second question and partially answers the first. By the end of the prologue we understand the underlying premise of the whole series: that great cities are literally alive. After centuries of gestation they have a chance to be born as an entity with agency and power, but that moment of birth is also a time of great vulnerability as "the Enemy" is waiting to attack. (The prologue also answers a smaller question raised by the illustration we looked at in that chapter: New Orleans and Port-au-Prince are crossed off because they have been stillborn, defeated by the Enemy before they had a real chance to thrive.)

Jemisin, however, dramatizes this premise in her prologue. In other words, she *shows* it rather than *tells* it. The point-of-view character of the prologue turns out to be the avatar of New York City—a role that he himself doesn't know he inhabits at the beginning of the prologue. Readers are along for the ride as he learns what it means to be the city's avatar and confronts the Enemy's initial attacks.

The prologue as a whole operates as a story, with a beginning, middle, and end—in fact, Jemisin first published it as a standalone short story.[1] We see the avatar, a young Black street kid, at first ignore the call to action presented to him by his guide Paulo (the avatar of São Paulo, the most recent city to have been born) until his instincts teach him that he is indeed part of something bigger.

We watch him run from the Enemy (personified first by two cops that merge into one "Mega Cop") and defeat its first attack by leading it into the traffic of the FDR Drive, nimbly navigating through the cars, letting the city do the work of smashing the creature to smithereens. Right after that dramatic battle comes the labor scene as the avatar both births the city and becomes one with it, then immediately reengages with the Enemy and seems to defeat it with his newfound power. Paulo arrives to congratulate him, to admire "all the bright light and bluster" of the city and its avatar.

In the short story version, we then jump forward in time fifty years and see New York's avatar in LA, preparing to assist with that city's birth just as Paulo did for him. But—and this is a crucial but!—in the novel version we instead get dropped off a new roller-coaster of suspense, sending us hurtling into the novel proper. These are the last words of the prologue:

> I live the city. It thrives and it is mine. I am its worthy avatar, and together? We will
> never be
> afr—
> oh shit
> something's wrong.

This brief snippet gives you a sense of another attraction of this prologue: Jemisin pulls out all the stops when it comes to the writing. The avatar channels the voice of New York: sharp, informal, profane, funny. Here, for example, is how the avatar describes the underlying premise of the whole series:

> This is the lesson: Great cities are like any other living things, being born and maturing and wearying and dying in their turn.
>
> Duh, right? Everyone who's visited a real city feels that, one way or another. All those rural people who hate cities are afraid of something legit; cities really are *different*. They make a weight on the world, a tear in the fabric of reality, like . . . like black holes, maybe. Yeah. (I go to museums sometimes. They're cool inside, and Neil deGrasse Tyson is hot.)

I'm going to talk more about voice in future chapters, but this passage is a good example of what people mean when they use the term. The rhythms of the sentence, the word choices, the references all feel distinctive. The avatar also has a different register—one that is lyrical and metaphorical, deliberately evoking Walt Whitman's great poem "I Sing the Body Electric" in the very first line of the prologue, "I sing the city," which is echoed in later lines—"I paint the city" and "I run the city" and, finally, after the birth, "I live the city."[2]

Let's also admire and examine the way Jemisin uses stream-of-consciousness narration to bring us right into the climactic moment when the avatar defeats the Mega Cop:

> I go
> over the barrier and through the grass into fucking hell I go one lane silver car two lanes horns horns horns three lanes SEMI WHAT'S A FUCKING SEMI DOING ON THE FDR IT'S TOO TALL YOU STUPID UPSTATE HICK screaming four lanes GREEN TAXI screaming Smart Car hahaha cute five lanes moving truck six lanes and the blue Lexus actually brushes up against my clothes as it blares past screaming screaming screaming
> *screaming*
> screaming metal and tires as reality stretches, and nothing stops for the Mega Cop; it does not belong here and the FDR is an artery, vital with the movement of nutrients and strength and attitude and adrenaline, the cars are white blood cells and the thing is an irritant, an infection, an invader to whom the city gives no consideration and no quarter
> screaming, as the Mega Cop is torn to pieces by the semi and the taxi and the Lexus and even that adorable Smart Car, which actually swerves a little to run over an extra-wiggly piece.

Do you see how the repeated word "screaming" anchors the sections of the passage and keeps us oriented amidst the deluge of details and metaphors? If you are able and willing to write a stylistically show-stopping prologue (and if that fits your novel) then you have more leeway to include one.

If you decide to remove a prologue from your manuscript, what can you do with the material? First, look for places where you can work the best details into the main strand of the plot. Can it become backstory? Can a character discuss the events of the prologue with another character, in a way that has emotional charge and relevance to the primary plot? Second, save the original prologue as a reader bonus or extra you can feature on your website or include in a blog post or newsletter. Readers who become fans love seeing cut scenes of this sort, especially if they are from the point of view of a character not featured in the novel itself.

TAKEAWAYS

- Inject suspense and action—not just atmospherics—into the prologue, if you include one.
- Save important backstory information for later in the novel, after we've met your protagonist and understand their current problem and what's at stake.
- Dramatize the novel's premise through a mini-story that functions as the prologue.

CHAPTER 6
HOW DO YOU BALANCE MULTIPLE POINTS OF VIEW?

One of the pleasures of rereading is holding your memories of a book up alongside the reality and seeing where the gaps are. Often the mismatch will lead to valuable insights about the writer's craft. I picked N. K. Jemisin's *The City We Became* to include in this book in part for the author's deft use of multiple third-person narrators. In my memory of the book, there were five narrators (for the five boroughs of New York City) and they had roughly equal page time. It turns out, my memory was wrong—though I could see why I'd remembered it incorrectly and I could also see why Jemisin made the choices she did.

Authors must make three key decisions when it comes to point of view (POV):

1. Will you write about your protagonist (and possibly other point-of-view characters) in first person (I) or third person (he/she/they)?[1]
2. Will you primarily use past tense (I said) or present tense (I say) to tell the story?
3. Whose inner thoughts and feelings can readers access? If we see the interior thoughts and feelings of only one or a

handful of characters and only one at a time, then that's limited narration. If we have access to the interior thoughts of any character in the novel at any time, then that's omniscient narration.

The City We Became is somewhat unusual in using multiple tenses and mixing first and third person narration, but all of these narrative flavors are limited rather than omniscient.

Before we dig into the details of how Jemisin uses multiple narrators, let's spend some time talking about *why* she does so. I'm going to avoid major spoilers in this chapter, but let's pinpoint the starting premise, which we learn in the prologue of the novel, discussed at length in Chapter 5. New York City, as other great cities have done before it, is emerging—being birthed—as a live entity. But it is vulnerable in its newborn state, and it has an Enemy. It also has an avatar—in this case a young Black street kid—to both embody the city and fight for it. However, the Enemy has developed new tactics the avatar is unprepared for and manages to damage him. The newly awakened avatars of the five boroughs (Manhattan, Brooklyn, the Bronx, Queens, and Staten Island) must come together to fight off the Enemy and heal the primary avatar if the city is to survive.

The prologue is written in first-person present from the point of view of the unnamed primary avatar, and shows him awakening to his power and fighting the first battle with the Enemy. First-person present is as close as authors can take readers to a character, which is why it's often the choice for young adult (YA) fiction, which prizes the reader–character connection. But Jemisin can't stick with this narration choice because the plot of the book requires that this first narrator be forced off stage until the end of the novel.

After the prologue, we encounter a chapter that is titled "Interruption," narrated in third-person past from the point of view of Paulo, the avatar of São Paulo, the most recently born city, whose job it is to help the avatar of New York City through its own birth. Paulo knows the rules of this fantasy world, and that's what Jemisin needs readers to have access to. But she's smart about what she delivers here. Paulo, through his own observations (the avatar disappears in front of him) and a terse phone conversation with an unnamed person, reveals the stakes (there have been "postpartum complications") and the quest, but only obliquely:

"Like London, then," says Paulo.
"Hard to be sure. But yes, so far, like London."
"How many, do you think? The greater metropolitan area crosses three states—"
"Don't make assumptions. Just 'more,' as far as you're concerned. Find one. They'll track down their own." A pause. "The city is still vulnerable, you realize. That's why it took him away, for safekeeping."

The person on the other end of the phone warns Paulo to watch his back and advises, "Make them work fast. Never good to have a city stuck halfway like this." As readers, then, we have a broad sense of the quest and the stakes from this "Interruption."

Now, why doesn't Jemisin stick with Paulo as her narrator through the action that follows? I think there are two answers. First, Jemisin knows that she is writing a high-stakes, high-suspense story. The closer the readers are to the action, the more intensely they'll feel the heat of that suspense. Paulo is invested in the outcome, but only at second hand. This is not his city, after all. The consequences are not life and death *for him*.

The second answer has to do with theme: One of the themes of the book is the power of discovering and owning your identity. For that theme to fully land, we need access to the inner lives of the avatar characters. Paulo has already passed through his dramatic moment of calling and acceptance. By deploying a classic assemble-the-team trope, Jemisin is able to show us a group of characters—with different backgrounds, motivations, strengths, and weaknesses—confront the call to action and make their own decisions.

Before we move on, let's examine another option open to Jemisin: omniscient narration. In omniscient narration, the (usually unnamed) narrator is like a god, able to dip into the interior thoughts of any character at any time. This is the narration style of *Lord of the Rings*, for example. I'll explore omniscient narration in depth in Chapter 12 on *Matrix* and Chapter 27 on *The Marriage Portrait*. For our purposes here, I think it's enough to say that Jemisin wants us to step into the lives and minds of her characters as fully as possible, and limited point of view allows her to achieve that goal better than omniscient narration.

Now, how do you balance multiple narrators? If you've read the novel, take a moment to guess how many scenes each character narrates before you look at Figure 3 at the end of the chapter. As I noted earlier, in my memory, each avatar had roughly equal 'page time,' though I remembered Manny, Brooklyn, and Bronca as carrying more weight in the novel than Padmini and Aislyn. (I had not remembered that the NYC avatar and Paulo were point-of-view characters at all.)

As you can see from Figure 3, I was right that Manny and Bronca carry more weight in the narrative. But I was shocked to see that Brooklyn—who feels like a guiding, grounded force throughout much of the book—has only one POV chapter, though it is placed right at the heart of the novel. I was equally surprised to find that Padmini, the avatar for Queens, has only one POV scene, and that Aislyn, the Staten Island avatar, has so many.

Note too that Paulo's "interruptions" stop appearing midway through the book. This is, in part, because his narrative role as knowledge-bearer is partly taken over by Bronca, who—as the oldest character and also the one with the longest connection to the land, thanks to her Native American heritage—is given the knowledge of how this multiverse works when she steps into her role as avatar for the Bronx. Paulo also becomes more directly entwined in the action rather than following a step behind the avatars, so when we see him appear in the second half of the book, it's through the point of view of another character.

Now let's analyze how Jemisin uses her multiple narrators. If you choose to use a multi-POV narrative structure, how do you decide which parts of the plot each character will narrate? How do you manage to show a character arc for each one? *The City We Became* offers up clever solutions to both problems.

Generally, you do want each of your point-of-view characters to have a well-developed arc because otherwise what is the point of having access to their internal thoughts? That said, in a book like this one with multiple POV characters, some of those arcs can be truncated or flat. John Truby presents a useful formula for character arcs in *The Anatomy of Story*:

$$(W)eakness \times (A)ction = (C)hange^2$$

In other words, your character starts from a state of weakness, lack, and unrealized goals, then is forced to confront and resolve their inner conflicts in order to take an important action that will fundamentally change them, allowing them to end the novel in a state of strength, fulfillment, and realized goals. Ideally, the action the character must take has a big impact on the plot of the story, becoming the linchpin that connects the external plot (what happens in the novel) and the internal plot (character growth).

Let's look at how Jemisin varies the kinds of arcs she gives her characters and also how she layers them together to create an immersive, engaging story. The first borough avatar we meet is Manny, which feel natural given the geographic centrality as well as the power and prestige of Manhattan amongst the boroughs. Manny's character arc also takes the longest to develop because he begins the novel with almost no identity at all: He has been struck with an odd form of amnesia as his train enters Penn Station. He knows he is from somewhere else and is moving to Manhattan, but he has only a few external clues and vague internal instincts about his identity. He accepts his new role as avatar for Manhattan without knowing exactly what he's doing, and in part because he has been emptied of his former identity first.

We first meet Brooklyn in chapter two, while we're still in Manny's POV, and this is where we see Jemisin being particularly smart and strategic about how she balances these multiple POVs and character arcs. Rather than keeping these character arcs separate, she layers them. And that's why I remembered Brooklyn having such a major role in the book. She does, in fact, have a lot of page time, but much of it is not from her POV.

Why is that? Jemisin makes another smart choice here to vary the kinds of character arcs we see. She avoids any feeling of repetition that way but, more importantly, she gets to show us many different forms of what it looks like to accept a call to action and claim your identity. Like Manny, Brooklyn accepts her role as avatar right away (before we even meet her). Unlike Manny, Brooklyn is supremely confident in her identity—it's no accident that she is the only character whose name is exactly the same as the borough she represents. And she literally represents her borough too, as an elected city council member.

When she steps onto the page in chapter two, Brooklyn first rescues Manny from the Enemy's minions and then confidently guides them to the aid of Padmini, the avatar for Queens, educating Manny about New York City along the journey. But Brooklyn does have an alternate identity, a past life as MC Free, one of the most popular female rappers in the early days of the form. She doesn't hide that identity, but she doesn't embrace it either, and that is the focus of her single POV chapter in the middle of the book. The last element of her character arc —seeing the other boroughs as allies rather than competitors—is shown through oblique touches in chapters narrated by Bronca and Manny. Compared to Manny, who has to evolve quite a bit, Brooklyn's character arc is flatter, less dramatic.

So, by the end of chapter two, we've met Manny and Brooklyn and left them on their way to find Queens. We then move to Staten Island, to meet its avatar, Aislyn. I'm not going to say much about her character arc to avoid spoilers, but as soon as I saw how much POV time she gets, I understood immediately why Jemisin needed to give her that much page time and also why I hadn't quite remembered it accurately. I'll just say that it's easy to identify with Manny and Brooklyn and to understand their motivations and choices. It's harder to understand Aislyn's, and yet it's crucial to the story Jemisin is telling that we do.

After Aislyn's first chapter and another interruption from Paulo, we meet Bronca. She too, after an initial confrontation with the Enemy, steps into her role as avatar for the Bronx without resistance. Where she resists, however, is in joining the fight to save the city as a whole, focusing first on her beloved Bronx, the art center she helped build, and her coworker Veneza, who is a daughter figure to her. Jemisin cleverly deploys a suspenseful subplot involving a group of white supremacist artists, emissaries of the Enemy, that Bronca must solve before she can turn her attention to the overall quest she is being asked to join.

Because Jemisin has so many POV characters to introduce and because, unlike Patchett in *The Dutch House*, she is telling a fast-paced, suspenseful, future-oriented story, she has to be very efficient with backstory. She still needs it to establish the inner motivations for her characters, but she uses it sparingly and weaves it subtly into quiet pockets in the narrative. Manny, for example, gets flashes of intuition about the person he used to be. After getting some access to his mind during a shared vision of the NYC avatar, Brooklyn probes for information. She's still wary, after all, and uncertain how far to trust him. Manny tells her he knows he "used to hurt people" but doesn't remember why:

"Mmm," she says, taking a deep breath. "Serial killer?"

"No." He doesn't remember feeling pleasure in the things he did. But he does remember that causing pain and fear was as easy for him as terrorizing Martha Blemins had been, in the park. Meaningless. He's not sure that's any better than being a serial killer. "It was… a job, I think. I did it for power, and maybe money."

But somewhere along the way, he'd chosen to stop. He clings to this proof of his humanity as if it is the only thing that matters. Because it is.

"Well, that's pretty damn fitting, for Manhattan."

Notice just how much Jemisin accomplishes in this short exchange. Manny shows that he has made a decision to leave his past self behind; in other words, his character arc has advanced. And Brooklyn's responses display her habit of confronting truths head on, her brutal honesty, and her belief that her values aren't entirely aligned with Manhattan's. After this snippet of conversation, Padmini rejoins them and they are on their way again on the next step of their quest. Jemisin never lets the forward action pause for long.

Aislyn's backstory is given more extended page time than the others, especially in an important conversation with her mother in chapter ten, for the reasons already explored: Jemisin wants us to truly, deeply understand this complicated, and damaged, character.

Let's dive down one more level now and look at how Jemisin signals to readers whose point of view we are in. First, note that she never mixes two points of view within the same scene. In omniscient narration, this kind of slide can be fine, but it requires that we have a narrator whose voice and thoughts are guiding us. (We'll see an example of this in Chapter 12 on Lauren Groff's *Matrix*.) In third-person limited, where we dispense with that narrator figure and are brought right inside each character's head, it can feel jarring to move from one character's perspective to another—a problem many editors call "head-hopping."

You can avoid this, as Jemisin does, by using a scene or chapter break as the switching point. Jemisin generally uses chapter breaks to change POVs. The one notable exception is in chapter fifteen when we toggle between the POVs of Manny and Aislyn as the battle with the Enemy proceeds on two different fronts. It is possible to do POV hand-offs within a scene in third-person limited narration, but it has to be done quite carefully and sparingly.[3]

Second, Jemisin uses her clever chapter titles to provide clues about whose POV we are in. For example, "Our Lady of (Staten) Aislyn," the title of chapter three, prepares us to step into the point of view of Aislyn, with the knowledge that she is likely the borough's avatar. Some authors of multi-POV novels use character names in place of chapter titles or as subtitles to guide readers.

Third, Jemisin is careful to orient us in the first lines of the chapter. Here's the opening of chapter three:

NOVEL STUDY

 It's time.

Aislyn Houlihan is at the St. George Terminal of the Staten Island Ferry, trembling. She's been here for twenty minutes, trembling. There are open seats because it's early enough in the day, just before the start of rush hour, that the ferry won't be anywhere near full—but she's opted to pace in front of the glass window-wall instead of sitting. The better to tremble while she paces.

Jemisin starts with a propulsive, italicized action beat, then immediately answers the questions it raises: Time for who to do what? By the end of the paragraph we know the POV character's name, where she is, and what time of day it is. We can intuit, based on her location, that she's going to take the ferry to Manhattan and, thanks to the pacing and the trembling, she is deeply anxious about doing so.

As so often with Jemisin's writing, I also have to stop to admire what she achieves through repetition and variation. Let's take a moment to analyze what she's doing in this passage. Here are the sentences again, with key words bolded:

1. Aislyn Houlihan is at the St. George Terminal of the Staten Island Ferry, **trembling**.
2. She's been here for twenty minutes, **trembling**.
3. There are open seats because it's early enough in the day, just before the start of rush hour, that the ferry won't be anywhere near full—but she's opted to **pace** in front of the glass window-wall instead of sitting.
4. The better to **tremble** while she **paces**.

In sentences 1 and 2, Jemisin uses parallel structure, with the gerund "trembling" punctuating the end of both sentences. The parallelism and repetition create a pleasing rhythm and subtly emphasize Aislyn's anxiety. Sentence 3 is much longer, with a complex structure: two independent clauses, the first with an embedded dependent phrase ("just before the start of rush hour"), joined by an em dash and coordinating conjunction "but." This sentence also introduces the verb "pace," which then gets paired with "tremble" in the short sentence fragment that concludes the passage. Sentence 4 feels extra snappy and punchy because it follows the very complex Sentence 3: This is what we mean when we talk about the effectiveness of sentence variety. If your sentences are this dynamic and clever, it's almost impossible for readers to be bored, even when we are being fed ordinary information: An anxious woman is waiting for a ferry.

As the scene continues, every bit of the action is filtered through Aislyn's point of view. We are not seeing it from a bird's-eye perspective, perched above the ramp to the ferry, but from within Aislyn's mind:

> Her thoughts ignite—GET AWAY GET OFF ME DON'T TOUCH ME GET ME OUT OF HERE—and her body contracts without any conscious input. Now she is moving against the flow (with the island's wishes, though, at last), lurching from one stranger's horrifying touch to another and wondering the whole time who's screaming with such an ear-piercing pitch. Only belatedly does she recognize her own voice. People around her freeze or jerk away from the crazy lady, but they're still too close. Crushing her.

In this passage, notice the vividness of Jemisin's verbs: ignite, contract, lurch, scream, freeze, jerk, crush. These verbs communicate Aislyn's abject panic, as does her moment of depersonalization when she doesn't recognize her own voice screaming.

Before getting to our takeaways, I want to briefly discuss the last two scenes of the novel because I think they are supremely successful pieces of writing. As noted above, Jemisin toggles between the POVs of Manny and Aislyn in the climactic chapter fifteen. The battle with the Enemy continues in chapter sixteen, with Bronca taking up the narrator's role, and then, with the battle over, the final scene of that chapter moves to a collective "they" narration that widens out even beyond the avatars: *"They* are New York. *They* are the single titanic concussion of sound from every subwoofer and every steel drum circle that has ever annoyed elderly neighbors and woken babies while secretly giving everyone else an excuse to smile and dance." The italicized *they*'s are in the original text; Jemisin wants us to take notice of this narrative shift, which modulates to "we" at the very end of the chapter.

At that point, we move to the Coda, where we meet again the first-person present-tense narrator who opened the book—the primary avatar of New York City. I analyzed the way the prologue works in Chapter 5, so the only thing I'll add here is that this feels like the perfect choice at the end, allowing Jemisin to leave us with his lyrical, profane first-person voice—the voice of New York City.

TAKEAWAYS

- Use your POV choices to control the distance between reader and narrator(s), as well as the pacing and suspense of specific scenes.
- Choose a narration style that underscores your theme. Jemisin's multiple voices emphasize her message that healthy cities function by housing many different voices and perspectives.
- When developing multiple point-of-view characters, ensure each has a distinct voice, perspective, and character arc that contributes uniquely to the overall narrative.
- You don't need to give each POV character equal page time: Choose the balance based on the needs of your plot and theme.
- Provide only the amount of backstory you need in order to make each POV character's motivations clear—a character with a flatter arc needs less backstory.
- Use scene or chapter breaks to move between narrators, or carefully (and rarely!) do a POV handoff within a scene.

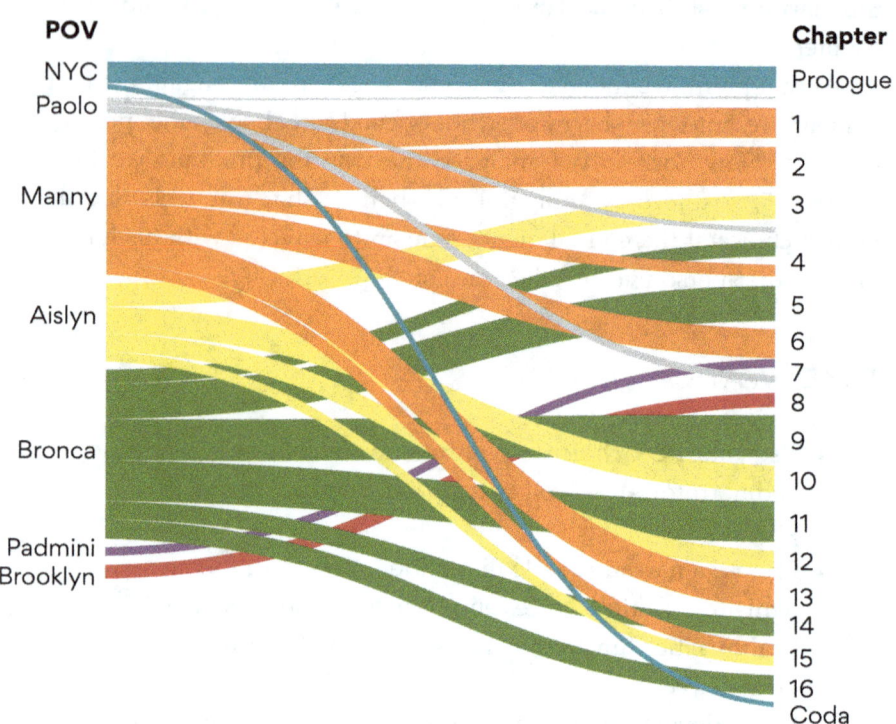

Figure 3: Narrators in *The City We Became*. POVs are not evenly distributed and do not follow a set pattern. Narrator switches serve the needs of the story and shape the reading experience.

THE SEARCHER,
BY TANA FRENCH

STATS

Usually, the mystery structure starts out with a dead body, and then you gradually unravel, going backward. But I think that if you get people deeply engaged with the characters, you can sow all the seeds that lead to murder; build out all the threads being intertwined until the murder happens. If your readers are involved in these characters and care about them, they are fascinated in the factors that lead to the murder.
—Tana French[1]

Published in 2020 by Viking
451 pages, approximately 112,750 words
The author's eighth published novel

GENRE

Mystery

AMAZON CATEGORIES

Police Procedurals, Literary Fiction, Suspense Thrillers

AWARDS

New York Times Best Book of 2020 list

CHAPTER 7
HOW DO YOU OPEN A MYSTERY NOVEL?

This is the first installment of our analysis of Tana French's *The Searcher* so, as always, let's start at the beginning. I took the time to examine covers, front matter, and prologues in Chapters 1 and 4, so this time I want to get straight to French's first chapter and dig into the questions we've been asking of all openings:

- How does the opening pull us into the world of the novel?
- What do we know? What's implied? What's left as a mystery?
- What makes us want to keep reading?

Because this is a mystery novel, we are also going to be wondering what *is* the mystery? French is slower to answer that question in *The Searcher* than in her previous novels, which follow the more typical pattern of murder mysteries in providing a body within the first chapter or so of the book. Let's walk through the first chapter of *The Searcher* and see what French delivers instead of a body.

Here is the first paragraph of the novel:

> When Cal comes out of the house, the rooks have got hold of something. Six of them are clustered on the back lawn, amid the long wet grass and the yellow-flowered weeds, jabbing and hopping. Whatever the thing is, it's on the small side and still moving.

French plays with our expectations here, letting us think that we've got our dead-body moment right in the first sentence before disillusioning us at the end of the paragraph. Instead, all we can do is pay attention to Cal. We are drawn so deeply into his point of view that we don't have another choice. Let's look more closely at the structure of that first sentence. Why, for example, didn't French choose a more straightforward way to establish these two unremarkable pieces of information—that Cal has walked out of his front door and there are birds in the yard? Compare this stripped-down version to the original:

> Cal comes out of the house, and the rooks swoop down to cluster around something on the back lawn.

By adding "when" to the first clause, French shifts the emphasis of the sentence. "When Cal comes out of the house" is now a dependent phrase, which could be stripped off the main clause but cannot stand on its own as a sentence. The weight and attention of the sentence then falls on the rooks and whatever they've gotten hold of.

Notice also what French is doing with the tense. Cal's action ("comes") is in present tense and is finished as soon as it starts, but the rooks' action is more complex. The rooks don't "swoop down" at the same time Cal comes out of the house; rather, they already "have got hold of" whatever it is they are pursuing. The rooks' action extends backward into the past and is still ongoing.

Note too that French has stripped out all filter words.[1] The sentence doesn't read: "When Cal comes out of the house, he **sees** the rooks have got hold of something." As readers, we automatically assume it is Cal who is doing the seeing; by stripping out the verb, French takes us deeper into his point of view. It is like we are inside Cal's mind as he processes what he sees when he steps outside.

On the surface, the paragraph seems like just a setting detail, but underneath it is doing quite a lot of work. Intuitively, the reader understands that the story is going to be told through Cal's point of view and that the action is going to take place in Cal's immediate present (signaled by the verb tense). On a metaphorical level, French establishes Cal as an outsider who comes across an ongoing conflict involving creatures who were here before him. The grammatical structure of that first sentence, which gives the rooks rather than Cal the starring role, hints at Cal's tendency to recede into the background. He wants to be a passive viewer not an active participant in the scenes in front of him and will have to be dragged into the action of the story.

In the next paragraph, we learn that he understands his role as an outsider:

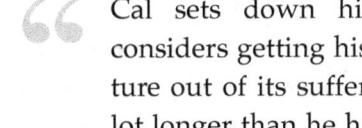
> Cal sets down his garbage bag of wallpaper. He considers getting his hunting knife and putting the creature out of its suffering, but the rooks have been here a lot longer than he has. It would be pretty impertinent of him to waltz in and start interfering with their ways. Instead he eases himself down to sit on the mossy step next to the trash bag.

Rather than interfere, he sits down to observe.

As the scene progresses, with Cal continuing to watch the rooks kill and then eat what turns out to be a young rabbit, French trickles out a few more details: Cal has been in this place for three months; he is doing renovation work on his house, which makes him feel "old and fat"; he used to be married to someone named Donna; he's applied for a license for a firearm, which he plans to use for hunting, a skill his grandfather taught him.

On the second page we finally learn where he is, in a passage that gets full-dress treatment from French:

> Away to the north, a line of low mountains rolls along the horizon. Cal's eyes are still getting used to looking this far, after all those years of city blocks. Landscape is

one of the few things he knows of where the reality doesn't let you down. The West of Ireland looked beautiful on the internet; from right smack in the middle of it, it looks even better. The air is rich as fruitcake, like you should do more with it than just breathe it; bite off a big mouthful, maybe, or rub handfuls of it over your face.

The wonderful fruitcake metaphor and the sensory details that come with it are the stars of the show, but French continues to deliver bits of backstory in this passage: Cal is from a city (Chicago, we learn on the next page) and he decided to move to the West of Ireland without ever having set foot in it first. Note too how French weaves in Cal's voice, especially his pragmatic informality—the "right smack in the middle," the "bite off a big mouthful, maybe."

After this passage, Cal stands up to take his garbage bag down to the trash pile at the edge of the yard, stopping to inspect the remains of the rabbit (which tells us he's not the squeamish type), and here's where the chapter pivots: Someone has been watching Cal, and that someone is in the yard again, their presence signaled by the rooks kicking up a fuss. Immediately after this pivot, we get another key piece of information: Cal is a retired cop, having spent twenty-five years in the Chicago PD, and he moved to this out-of-the-way place in part to switch off "his mental alarm systems."

By this point we've got a few intriguing story questions pulling us into the novel:

- What happened to Cal's marriage?
- What happened in his career as a cop that made him want to turn off that mental alarm system?
- Who is watching Cal and why?

Note that the first two are backstory questions: Cal already knows the answers to them, and presumably we readers will find out in due time. But that last question—who is watching and why—is the one that really stokes the suspense because neither the readers *nor Cal* know the answer yet. A character can't transmit a sense of suspense about a question he already knows the answer to, and suspense is what, more than anything else, pulls a reader into a story. What will happen next?

I often work with writers who are so enamored with their protagonist's complex and emotionally resonant backstory that they want to deliver it to the reader first—which also makes intuitive sense because it happens first chronologically. However, backstory is essentially old news to the protagonist and to readers, even though they are encountering it for the first time. Readers want to see your protagonist encounter a suspenseful question they don't know the answer to yet either. Backstory can be snuck in along the way—tripping up your protagonist just as our unprocessed emotional baggage does to us in real life.

What happens next in this chapter is that Cal walks back into the house and begins making dinner. French keeps us lightly tethered to the present action, showing Cal turning on a burner under a frying pan in one paragraph and putting bacon in the pan a page later. But the real purpose here is summary: Cal is sifting through the incidents before this one, the other times he felt he was being watched during his short time living in this house. And he's also considering other details that have triggered his "cop sense":

> Engines revving, three a.m. down faraway back roads, deep-chested bubbling snarls. A huddle of guys in the back corner of the pub some nights, too young and dressed wrong, talking too loud and too fast in accents that don't fit in; the snap of their heads towards the door when Cal walks in, the stares that last a second too long. He's been careful not to tell anyone what he used to do, but just being a stranger could be plenty, depending.

Let's take a moment, before moving further into the scene, to admire the sentence-level writing in this passage. The first two sentences are, technically, not sentences at all but fragments, without the anchor of a verb. (To 'unfragment' these sentences, you'd do this: "Engines **rev** at three a.m. . . . . A huddle of guys **sit** . . .") By withholding the verbs, French helps that last, quieter sentence land harder, carry more gravity and weight. What would those loud guys do if they did know he was a cop?

Cal, still cooking his dinner, recalls the long-simmering, intergenerational feuds he's heard about from his next-door neighbor, Mart, who has given him "an inkling of how tangled up things get around here, and how carefully you have to watch where you put your feet." Now he's worried that he's already made a wrong step and doesn't know enough about the community to understand what he might set in motion if he deals aggressively with whomever is watching him. He ponders a theory that it has something to do with the house, which had stood vacant for many years before he bought it. This allows French to catch us up on the state of the house when he found it and the work he's been doing to slowly restore it, building in more details about Cal's past along the way.

Then, as Cal is eating the dinner we've seen him make, we get another punch of action in the present tense of the scene: Cal hears a noise outside, sneaks out his bathroom window, circles the house, and grabs the lurker. This turns out to be an adolescent boy, who bites Cal's hand and gets away.

So we (Cal and the reader) know the answer to *who*, but we still don't know the answer to *why*. Cal attempts to dismiss his mental alarm system, telling himself it's just a bored kid, but his deeper sense tells him that the kid wasn't there for kicks. "He was here for a purpose. He'll be back." The chapter ends on the same ominous note with which it began, Cal "listening to foxes fighting somewhere out across the fields," under a sky full of "cloud-patched stars." This piece of West Ireland where Cal is attempting to make a home for himself is wild, untamed, and he is, at least at the moment, unable to see it clearly.

TAKEAWAYS

- Use grammar and syntax to direct your readers' attention where you want it. Sentence fragments can build suspense as readers wait for a sentence anchored by a verb.

- Use metaphor and setting to suggest the theme and mood of the story.
- Make sure that your first chapter launches 'live' story questions—questions your characters don't know the answers to—in addition to backstory questions.
- Anchor summaries or extended internal reflections to the present moment by occasional references to an easy-to-understand action, like making a meal.
- Build momentum and suspense by answering one part of a story question but leaving another part open. If you answer a *who* question, leave open a *how* or *why* follow-up question to pull readers forward.
- Don't feel like you need to tell readers everything at once—start with the familiar ("village"), then add specifics ("Ardnakelty") later.

CHAPTER 8
HOW DO YOU USE DIALOGUE TO REVEAL CHARACTER?

Now that we've looked at how Tana French pulls us into *The Searcher* in her first chapter, let's step just a little further into the novel and examine how she uses dialogue. Like interiority and point of view, dialogue is a big topic and one I'll return to in future chapters (see, in particular, Chapter 15 on *I Kissed Shara Wheeler* and Chapter 21on *Dial A for Aunties*). To start, let's zero in on the two components of dialogue: first, the dialogue line itself, which should reveal story information and also display the voice and personality of the speaker; and, second, the dialogue tag, which identifies the speaker but can also convey tone, emotion, and even action.

Let's look at chapter three of *The Searcher* to see how French uses these two components. At this point in the book, readers have a few key story questions to focus on: Why is Trey, a young local kid, sneaking around Cal's house? And what happened in Cal's past life in the Chicago police department to make him want to move to a remote Irish village? We are also in pursuit of the usual question at the heart of a mystery novel: Who committed the murder? As readers, we've now modulated that question into two others: Who is going to be murdered, and when is it going to happen? Because we still don't have our dead body.

French puts us on alert at the beginning of chapter three when she has Cal recall a conversation he had with the bartender at the local pub about the gun license he'd applied for:

"Sure, they oughtn't to give you a gun anyway," Barty the barman told him, when he pointed this out.

"Why not?"

"Because you're American. Ye're all mental with the guns, over there. Shooting them off at the drop of a hat. Blowing some fella away because he bought the last packet of Twinkies in the shop. The rest of us wouldn't be safe."

"What would you know about Twinkies?" Mart demanded, from the corner where he and his two buddies were ensconced with their pints. Mart feels a responsibility, as Cal's neighbor, to defend him against a certain amount of the ribbing he gets. "It's far from Twinkies you were reared."

"Didn't I spend two year on the cranes in New York? I've et Twinkies. Horrible fuckin' yokes."

"And did anyone shoot you?"

"They did not. They'd better sense."

"Should've done," one of Mart's buddies said. "Then we might have a barman who could put a dacent head on a pint."

First, I want to draw your attention to how few dialogue tags French uses, even in a conversation that expands to multiple speakers. We can easily understand from context how the conversation shifts, after Mart's initial intervention, from Barty and Cal to Barty and Mart. Note too that French takes the opportunity with Mart's dialogue tag to stitch in a character observation—that he feels obliged to defend Cal, or at least this is Cal's interpretation of what Mart feels.

Second, let's talk about dialect and accent. This is a topic I've tackled often with authors who want to give their work a historical or regional flavor. The key is to be restrained, particularly when it comes to changing the spellings of words, and to lean instead on word choice and syntax—the order of the words in a sentence. For example, Barty's use of "sure" as a sentence-opener, his verb construction "oughtn't to," and his use of the words "packet" (rather than the American "pack") and "yokes" (an Irishism for "things") all give his speech an Irish flavor. An Americanized version of his initial dialogue line might read, "Well, they shouldn't give you a gun anyway." These are all word-choice examples. As for syntax, Mart's line is a perfect example: "It's far from Twinkies you were reared." All of the words in this sentence are in common usage by Americans, but they would never be arranged in this order in casual conversation.

French also uses a non-standard spelling for three words in order to suggest the sound of the Irish accent: *ye're, et,* and *dacent*. Note how sparsely they are sprinkled through the passage and that they all involve tiny vowel substitutions: y**o**u're > y**e**'re, e**a**t > **e**t, d**e**cent > d**a**cent. In a set of 898 characters, French has altered precisely six, all of them vowels.

Be aware that using non-standard spellings and speech takes you into tricky territory in which you need to be alert to the power dynamics operating between your characters and between you and your characters. Enforcing standard pronunciation and spellings can be a tool of oppression and cultural erasure; noting non-standard speech for certain characters can mark them as "other" in ways you must be alert to and use deliberately.[1] This scene is filtered through the point of view of Cal, an American, so it makes sense that he hears "dacent" when Mart's buddy says "decent." Mart, if he were transcribing this bit of dialogue, would use the standard spelling.

As we move further into the scene, we watch Cal try to decode what he is seeing and hearing. Returning to the substance of the scene at hand, the discussion about guns reminds readers that we haven't yet encountered the expected dead body and makes us wonder if Cal is going to need to use the gun he's applied for. French is, effectively, saying to us, "Don't worry—the dead body is coming. Be patient." The passage also strikes a note we've already seen in the opening chapter: Cal's awareness of his own cultural difference and just how much he doesn't understand. When Mart asks him why he walks to the pub rather than driving, Cal cites his gun license application, not wanting to risk a DUI while his application is pending. He's smart enough not to say he doesn't want to drive drunk given that's exactly what many others in the pub that night, including Mart, will do.

After the recalled dialogue above, we get some additional detail about the pub itself and what's going on during this particular night: "Seán Óg's is, by its own standards, buzzing tonight. Mart and a couple of his buddies are in their corner, playing cards with two unprepossessing young guys in tracksuits whom they've acquired somehow." We learn that Mart's group plays for money, and we readers peg that table as a potential source of conflict as the evening unfolds.

A middle-aged woman, whom Cal has slowly come to understand is a sex worker, is sitting on a banquette, and a group in the corner is listening to a man playing the tin whistle. Cal plans to sit at the bar and relax, enjoying the music and his lack of responsibility. Readers might be on alert, but Cal is not: "after twenty-five years of maintaining an intricate mental database of everyone he met on the job, Cal enjoys the lackadaisical feeling of not bothering to remember whether Sonny is the one with the big laugh or the one with the cauliflower ear."

But his attention is drawn to an argument between a group down the bar from him:

> "There's no dog could do that," the guy at the end of the bar is saying stubbornly. He's little and round, with a little round head perched on top, and he tends to wind up on the wrong end of jokes; generally he seems OK with this, but this time he's turning red in the face with vehemence and outrage. "Did you even look at them cuts? It wasn't teeth that done that."
>
> "Then what d'you think done it?" demands the big bald slab of a guy nearest to Cal. "The fairies?"
>
> "Feck off. I'm only saying, it was no animal."
>
> "Not them fecking aliens again," says the third guy, raising his eyes from his pint. He's a long gloomy streak

with his cap pulled down close over his face. Cal has
heard him say a total of about five sentences.

Again, we see French using word choice and syntax to give flavor to the dialogue. But what I want to draw your attention to here is the absolute mastery of French's descriptions of these speakers. They are filtered through Cal's knowledge—he doesn't remember the name of the little, round guy, but he knows he's often the butt of jokes just as he knows the "third guy" rarely speaks. French's physical descriptions are particularly vivid and distinct: "big bald slab of a guy" and "long gloomy streak."

Cal is drawn into the conversation, and there is an undercurrent of tension now, both because of the topic and because they are challenging Cal, testing his knowledge and thus his right to be sitting in this pub and, by extension, living in this village:

"Come here," he says, shifting his bulk around on the bar stool to face Cal. "Listen to this. Night before last, something kilt one of Bobby's sheep. Took out its throat, its tongue, its eyes and its arse; left the rest."

"*Sliced* out," Bobby says.

Senan ignores this. "What would you say done it, hah?"

"Not my area," Cal says.

But, when pressed, Cal passes the test, relying on the hunting knowledge his grandfather passed down to him. The mystery of what happened to the animal is left behind when the table French wanted us to peg as trouble at the beginning of the chapter does finally erupt. One of the young guys, named Donie, is accused of cheating, challenges Mart to a fistfight, and is thrown out of the bar by Barty, who asks Cal to help. Cal goes back into cop mode briefly, asking questions of Barty and then insisting on accompanying Mart home to make sure Donie hasn't turned up there to continue the fight. He hasn't, but as readers we are on alert: Is this the clash that is finally going to kick off the murder mystery? And what about that mauled sheep? But French leaves those questions hanging in the air, using the end of the chapter instead to delve into a bit more of Cal's backstory via a phone call between Cal and his daughter Alyssa, who lives in Seattle.

In this conversation, it's the in-between spaces, not the words themselves, that are important:

"How's work?" Alyssa works for a nonprofit in Seattle, something to do with at-risk teenagers. Cal missed the ins and outs of it when she first told him she was applying for the job—she applied for a lot of jobs, and work and Donna were taking up most of his mind around then—and it's gotten too late to ask.

"Work's good. We got our grant—big relief—so that should keep the show on the road for another while."

This is a clever strategy for delivering character description or backstory information. Tucking the material in between two dialogue lines means that the pace of the scene still feels fast. If this were an actual conversation, there would be only a tiny pause between the question and the response. Because the dialogue lines themselves are less important, French keeps them short. Notice how the phrase "big relief" has been shorn of the "which was a" that would usually precede it.

At each turn of the conversation, Cal feels his insufficiency, feels the distance between them. French underlines this distance in a passage of interiority:

When Cal hangs up he has the same empty feeling he always gets after talking to Alyssa these days, a sense that somehow, in spite of having been on the phone for all that time, they haven't had a conversation at all; the whole thing was made of air and tumbleweed, nothing solid there.

The subtext, the unspoken thoughts, carry more meaning than anything that has been said during the conversation. This is a form of earned telling—French shows us a snippet of conversation along with Cal's commentary to tell us what it really means beneath the surface.

TAKEAWAYS

- Look for places you can either strip off or enrich dialogue tags (for example, "he says").
- Rely mostly on word choice and syntax to give dialogue a historical or regional flavor. Use non-standard spellings sparingly, and be alert to the power dynamics involved in those choices.
- Take advantage of the space in between dialogue lines to deliver a snippet of character description, backstory, or interiority.
- Use subtext—the difference between the surface meaning of dialogue and the feelings underneath—as a way to show the stakes of a conversation or the tension in the relationship between the speakers.

CHAPTER 9
HOW DO YOU USE SETTING AND CHARACTER DESCRIPTION?

One of the great pleasures of Tana French's novels is her descriptive writing, and she pulls out all of the stops in *The Searcher*, in part because the setting—the tiny West Irish village of Ardnakelty and the mountains behind it—is a key part of the plot. I touched on her descriptions briefly in my analysis of the opening chapters of the novel, but I think the topic warrants further exploration.

Cal is unusually alert to setting details because he is working to decode his new surroundings, and he still hasn't been able to leave behind the cop radar honed over years on the job. Nothing is ordinary background noise to him. Take, for instance, this passage in which Cal is high up on the mountain, outside an abandoned house that a missing teenager, Brendan, had been using:

> Up here has a silence that separates it from the lowlands. Down below, there's always a lavish mix of birds fussing and flirting, sheep and cattle conversing, farmers shouting, but up here the air is empty; nothing but the wind and one small cold call like pebbles being tapped together, over and over again.

Cal is alert to the possibility that Brendan has been killed, perhaps at this very spot, and also that he and Trey—Brendan's younger sibling, who has led him there—could be under surveillance by whomever caused the teen to go missing. The texture of the description establishes this spot as barren and dangerous: "empty," "wind," "cold," the repetitive tapping of the birdsong. The words associated with the lowlands, on the other hand, are vibrant, alive: "lavish," "fussing," "flirting," "conversing," "shouting." This passage is strategically placed after Cal has scanned the abandoned house for traces of blood and before he begins combing the exterior yard for clues—perhaps even a body. The description is bracketed by action, so the pace of the scene doesn't flag, and its tone heightens the suspense.

Here's another example, where French uses setting details to give a quick car trip an ominous flavor:

> The road up into the mountains feels different in a car, rockier and less welcoming, like it's biding its time to puncture Cal's tire or send him sideslipping into a patch of bog. He parks outside the Reddys' gate. There's no shoulder, but he's not too worried that another car will need to get by.

Note how French personifies the road, giving it the possible agency to harm Cal. The detail about the lack of shoulder is a more interesting way to emphasize the loneliness of this spot than stating it plainly.

French also regularly uses description to establish character—both Cal's, since he is always our observer—and the character described. For example, while Cal is interviewing Eugene, a friend of Brendan's, he notices the boy's "features are finely modeled enough that plenty of people, himself included, probably consider him good-looking, but he's got a skimpy jaw and no chin." This description reinforces other details that establish Eugene as a self-centered narcissist; the details also convey Cal's distaste for a young man he finds unserious and insubstantial.

Let's look at one more example, of another minor character:

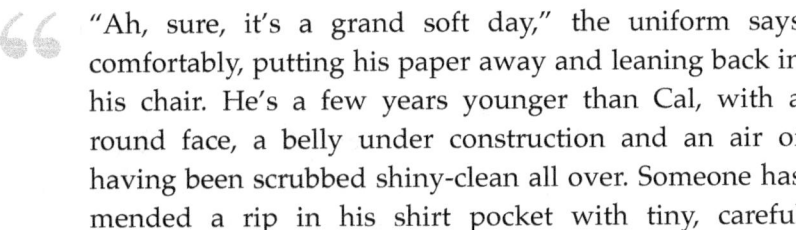

"Ah, sure, it's a grand soft day," the uniform says comfortably, putting his paper away and leaning back in his chair. He's a few years younger than Cal, with a round face, a belly under construction and an air of having been scrubbed shiny-clean all over. Someone has mended a rip in his shirt pocket with tiny, careful stitches. "What can I do for you?"

This is the first time we've seen this character, a police officer in the nearby town. We don't even have a name for him yet; he is just "the uniform." French weaves the description between two dialogue lines that get us into the scene. The dialogue lines are standard enough that they fade into the background, allowing the descriptive details to stand out. These details convey the sense that the police station is a calm backwater; this officer, with his fresh-scrubbed shine and carefully mended shirt, is not accustomed to seeing rough action—and likely not inclined to jump into it if called. Through this subtle bit of description, French is showing us that if—*when*—Cal runs into a sticky situation, he's probably going to be on his own to get out of it.

One last technique I want to call your attention to is French's recurring strategy for opening chapters in a way that reveals the day and time, while also layering on character and setting details. Here's a typical example, from the opening of chapter nine:

Cal has always liked mornings. He draws a distinction between this and being a morning person, which he isn't: it takes time, daylight and coffee to connect up his brain cells. He appreciates mornings not for their effect on him, but for themselves. Even smack in the middle of a temperamental Chicago neighborhood, dawn sounds rose up with a startling delicacy, and the air had a lemony, clean-scoured tinge that made you breathe deeper and wider. Here, the first light spreads across the fields like something holy is happening, striking sparks off a million dewdrops and turning the spiderwebs on the hedge to rainbows; mist curls off the grass, and the first calls of birds and sheep seem to arc effortless miles. Whenever he can make himself, Cal gets up early and eats his breakfast sitting on his back step, enjoying the chill and the earthy tang of the air. The doughnut Trey brought him yesterday is still in pretty good shape.

What French needs to establish here is that it is the morning of the next day. The last sentence alone would have done most of that work, but the additional details tell us that Cal understands how his brain works and that his own sharpness is a matter of importance to him. We also see how sensitive he is to his surroundings. If he was able to find delicacy in "the middle of a temperamental Chicago neighborhood," it's not surprising that the beauty of his current surroundings feels like "something holy." French has embedded a clue here about how Cal's well-trained radar for people—and what they are capable of—has been dazzled and misdirected by this West Irish village. Cal comes to this recognition much later in the novel, but French is tipping her hand here so that the later revelation lands as certainty for the reader.

TAKEAWAYS

- Be alert to the connotations of words when writing description and use them to establish mood.
- Description is a place to pull out all of your specialized writer tools, like simile, metaphor, and personification.
- What your point-of-view character notices—and doesn't notice—can reveal just as much about that character as it does about whatever they are observing.

- Weave snippets of description in between more active aspects of a scene—between a series of actions or in the white spaces of dialogue lines.
- Use description to foreshadow future plot developments or character arcs.
- Chapter and scene openings are opportunities for description that also establishes setting, date, and time.

CHAPTER 10
DOES YOUR PLOT NEED TO FOLLOW A SET STRUCTURE?

SPOILER WARNING

If you pull out your writing craft books and look for advice on plot structure or search the internet for plot templates, you'll find an enormous variety. (I've discussed many in my previous book, *All the Words*, including Shawn Coyne's *Story Grid*, Jessica Brody's *Save the Cat! Writes a Novel*, James Scott Bell's *Write Your Novel from the Middle*, and John Truby's *The Anatomy of Story*.) I've spent time mapping them out against one another, seeing if I can spot commonalities. I've tried applying them to my clients' work. I've even considered their structures as I developed the plot of my own novel. Each time, however, I find that whatever template I'm trying to apply doesn't naturally fit the work I'm trying to apply it to—like I'm trying to fit a tiny, exquisite doll's coat onto a toddler having a tantrum.

One writer or editor might be able to distill the story structure that works for them into a generalized template, but that structure might not be workable—or even comprehensible—to another writer. This is true even within genre fiction. Outside genre fiction, I'm seeing more interest in non-Western story structures or structures that follow shapes that aren't an arc.[1]

The truth is, I think every story has its own unique rhythm and structure. Rather than rely on story templates, I lean on my reader sense to tell me when a manuscript I'm editing drags when it should fly or zigs when it should zag. I map out the plot as it unfolds, scene by scene, and see what it has to tell me. I zero in on those areas that feel weak or wrong and try to figure out where the story has departed from its own specific, individual plot logic. I consider which strands from within the story might be moved, bolstered, or invented to fix the problems. While this doesn't lead to a neat template you can apply to many books, it does lead to a method you can use to study your own work and the work of others.

Let's apply this technique to Tana French's *The Searcher* and see what we discover. As usual, I started my analysis by charting the details of each scene on a spreadsheet. (You can download my spreadsheet template at www.thebluegarret.com/novel-study-downloads.) I then zeroed in on the plot until one underlying structure stood out to me. While I organized the structure into three distinct movements, they don't follow all of the rules of the traditional three-act structure.

See Figure 4 at the end of the chapter for a visual overview of the movements: "Setup," chapters one through five; "Slow build," chapters six through thirteen; and "Action cascade," chapters fourteen through the end. I've assigned each chapter an intensity score for both the internal and the external plots. The internal plot is another way to think about the character arc—the psychological and emotional change within the protagonist over the course of the novel. The external plot is the action—the answer to the question "What happens?" Figure 4 shows the total intensity score for each chapter, which will give you a sense of the overall pacing and action levels of the novel. Figure 5 shows the comparative intensity of the internal and external plots.

As we've seen in previous chapters, *The Searcher* builds slowly. We don't get a page-one murder; what we get instead is a jumpy retired cop from Chicago, Cal Hooper, who needs to find out who is lurking around his house so he can put his cop radar to rest. French also launches a backstory question that is gradually answered over the course of the book: What happened in Cal's professional and personal life that brought him to this remote Irish town where he has no connections?

Through the first four chapters, French doles out hints that partially answer the backstory question: Cal is divorced, and he isn't as close to his adult daughter as he'd like to be. He left policing because everyone involved—cops and community alike—seemed angry and unable to communicate effectively.

French continues to add new story questions in each chapter, to draw us deeper into the novel. We're introduced to a character named Lena who shares Cal's wry manner and practical bent: Will they become romantically involved? Cal identifies his lurker—an adolescent kid named Trey—but what does Trey want? Cal wonders about his tenuous place in Ardnakelty: Has he already put a foot wrong, perhaps just by buying the abandoned house he's fixing up?

Cal tries to decode the meaning of other events around town: the mauling of a sheep, and the dispute between his neighbor, Mart, and a young local, Donie. He tells himself these problems are not his responsibility any longer but fails to fully shut off his cop radar. Finally, in chapter five, we come to the question that drives the main action of the book: Trey has heard Cal was a cop—a fact Cal thought he had carefully hidden from his new neighbors—and wants him to find Trey's older brother, Brendan, who disappeared several months earlier.

This, then is our dead body moment—marked on Figure 4 by a cross symbol—except it arrives later in the story than is usual in the genre and in a way that is less clear-cut than usual. Brendan certainly isn't in Ardnakelty, but we don't know for sure that he is dead, much less that he has been murdered. Many characters in the novel insist that he has simply run away, but Trey refuses to believe it.

Starting with chapter six, then, we enter what I'm calling the slow build section. Cal is reluctant to get involved but finally does so, finding that the investigation makes his restlessness disappear. We learn that his ex-wife accused him of being addicted to lost causes; he thinks she might be right. This section of the novel mostly involves Cal traveling around Ardnakelty and the neighboring town of Kilcarrow to interview Brendan's friends and ex-girlfriend, but French deploys two punches of action to increase the pace. In chapter eight, another sheep is mauled—this time one belonging to Cal's neighbor, Mart, who plans a night-time stakeout to catch whomever or whatever is doing the killing. And in chapter eleven, Cal is invited to the pub to sample poteen, the potent local moonshine. He understands from the start that he is being tested, but the test morphs into something between a warning and a threat. I'd be curious to know if French added one or both of these scenes during revision, seeing that this stretch needed some additional action.

Chapter fourteen launches the final part, what I'm calling the action cascade, a relentless crescendo of revelations, followed by a spurt of violence, and finally a tense, suspenseful resolution that feels like it could spiral back into violence at any moment. Chapter fourteen is, like chapter five, a pivot point in the book—it's marked by another cross on Figure 4 because the focus is on what happened to Brendan, the central question of this mystery novel. Trey leads Cal to an abandoned house in a remote spot far up the mountain (the scene whose setting details I analyzed in Chapter 9), and Cal discovers Brendan had equipped it as a meth lab. French uses interiority to make sure we understand the importance of this discovery:

Cal's heart zigzags. For a second he can't move. He wanted something that would burn off all the hazy possibilities and show him the solid thing in their midst. Now that he's got it, he finds he doesn't want it one bit. . . .

A half-cocked kid in a huff can get himself into plenty

of shit. A kid with method is less likely to get himself into shit, but if he does, the shit is a whole lot deeper.

Cal is sure now that Brendan has been killed; he doesn't say as much to Trey, but he begins scanning the floor for bloodstains, then searching the brush outside the house.

Immediately after this chapter, French detonates a major plot twist: Mart informs Cal that Trey is a girl, not a boy as he'd thought, and warns him that the village will be up in arms if it becomes known how much time they are spending together. Cal understands it as another warning to leave the investigation alone as well—but he doesn't correctly interpret Mart's motive in making that warning. Regardless, he feels he doesn't have any choice but to comply.

This pair of chapters—fifteen and sixteen, marked by diamonds on Figure 4—leave both the external and internal plots on a precipice. Cal hasn't answered the central question of what happened to Brendan, and he is forced to violate his own moral code in lying to Trey. French uses a classic best-bad-choice scenario here: Cal can tell Trey the truth and risk that she continues to investigate and come around his place, endangering both of them, or he can lie to her about what happened to Brendan and about his own emotional investment in her, perhaps driving her off. Lying seems like the best option, but it leaves his already wavering moral compass spinning wildly.[2]

In this same pair of chapters, we get two pieces of backstory that help us make sense of Cal's choice. First, the event that triggered his retirement from the police force was his partner almost killing a young, unarmed suspect they were pursuing. Second, the event that triggered the dissolution of his marriage was Cal's response to the violent mugging of his daughter. Rather than spend time nurturing her, he helped the local police track down and arrest the perpetrator. His ex-wife makes it clear to him that his daughter would have preferred his presence to his action. His daughter needed comfort; the justice turned out to be important only to Cal. These two pieces complicate the understanding we had in the slow build section of the novel about why Cal left policing—and the United States.

These chapters are the high point of the internal plot of the novel.

Why didn't French deploy these stories earlier in the book, using them to raise the temperature while the external plot was still slowly coming to a boil? Saving them gives her two advantages: First, she can gradually raise the suspense about what happened over the course of the novel. We are told just enough to know that there are dark stories lurking in Cal's past, but we don't know what they are or how they might alter our perception of him. Are we sure we can trust this narrator? We can't know until he has revealed more. Second, the revelations hit harder at this spot, two-thirds of the way through the novel. We know Cal better, and we also know the stakes, both internally and externally, if he walks away from this investigation. If you look at the external plot, you'll also see that the high-intensity internal scenes give additional fire to external scenes that are a lower temperature. (You can see the juxtaposition quite clearly in Figure 5.)

Chapter seventeen raises the intensity sky high again. When Trey doesn't accept Cal's lie and starts searching for answers herself, she is severely beaten by her own mother—who has been warned that worse than a beating will come if she does not compel the girl to stop asking questions. Because we've just read about two vulnerable people whom Cal has failed in some way—the young, unarmed suspect Cal and his partner were chasing, and Cal's daughter—we know instinctively that helping Trey offers Cal a chance for redemption.

Cal, resuming the investigation into Brendan's disappearance, uses physical force to get Donie to reveal what he knows about Brendan's ties to the Dublin gang that controls the drug trade in the village. Cal himself is then attacked, which makes him only more resolute. Before he can track down the leader of the Dublin gang, however, he discovers in chapter twenty that Mart was involved both in the attack on him and in the death of Brendan.

French has been careful to lay out the background pieces so we understand the motivations at play. Mart and his fellow entrenched, aging bachelors are obsessed with keeping the village protected from outside forces—in this case the corroding effects of meth, but also, more broadly, the effects of cultural change. (Mart has some inkling that this resistance to change is not an unalloyed good. One of his brothers was gay and left for America decades earlier. Even with gay marriage now legal in Ireland, a measure he voted for, Mart realizes the village wouldn't welcome his brother back.)

The resolution of the novel hangs on the question of how the violence of Brendan's death, and the further violence triggered by Cal's investigation, can be laid to rest. Earlier in his life, Cal's first instinct would have been to call in the Guards, but he now understands that official justice isn't always the same as moral justice, nor does it always serve the victim or the community. The justice that Cal could expect from police intervention would not bring Brendan back and would almost certainly result in Trey being sent into foster care away from the village—worse than a mother who loves her and is making her own best bad choices to keep her alive. Mart and his cronies did not mean to kill Brendan—only to beat him badly enough to abandon his meth scheme—and they have no motive beyond covering up the death to continue their violence unless provoked by some new outrage. (Cal has reason to believe that, even then, their response will be measured. The English fairy-hunter who moved to town has been judged ridiculous but harmless; the English writer who objected to badger baiting was run off but not killed.) Cal brokers a tentative peace: He will bring Trey evidence of Brendan's death, and she won't pursue the matter further.

The final chapter of the novel, the longest of the book, is a kind of self-contained quest. Cal is guided up the treacherous mountain by Mart, unsure the whole way whether he will come back alive. Mart shows him the spot in the peat where Brendan's body was buried, and Cal laboriously uncovers it. French has cleverly reversed the standard trope of the mystery novel, finally showing us the dead body in the last chapter, not the first. When Cal returns with Brendan's watch, the proof of death Trey needs, it seems he has found the magic talisman that will restore peace to the community—perhaps even allowing him to build a new life in Ardnakelty and support Trey in the way he now knows he should have supported his own daughter.

This is, in essence, a three-act structure, although French's first two acts are perhaps slower than is typical. The setup section is roughly 80 pages; the slow build and action cascade sections are about 180 pages each. (At approximately 112,750 words, *The Searcher* is also longer than many mysteries and thrillers; 70,000 words is a typical length.) The effect, for the reader who sticks it out, is an intense, immersive roller-coaster of action in the last third of the novel. Could it work for your book? Certainly it might if you have a slow-developing plot with lots of action at the end. Will it work for every book? It will not.

TAKEAWAYS

- Use plot templates as a way to generate ideas or to spot missing pieces, but don't feel that you need to cram your plot into a template that wasn't designed for it.
- Map out and study novels in your genre so you can see a variety of approaches. Then go back to your own novel and do the same mapping. What stands out now?
- Use structure to help you decide where to place key plot moments or important pivot points.
- Vary the intensity of your internal and external plots—they can ebb and flow at different times to create a range of effects.
- Position backstory strategically to heighten suspense or provide context for key revelations in the plot.
- Use interiority to reveal a character's biases or preconceptions, showing how these influence their interpretations of events and other characters.

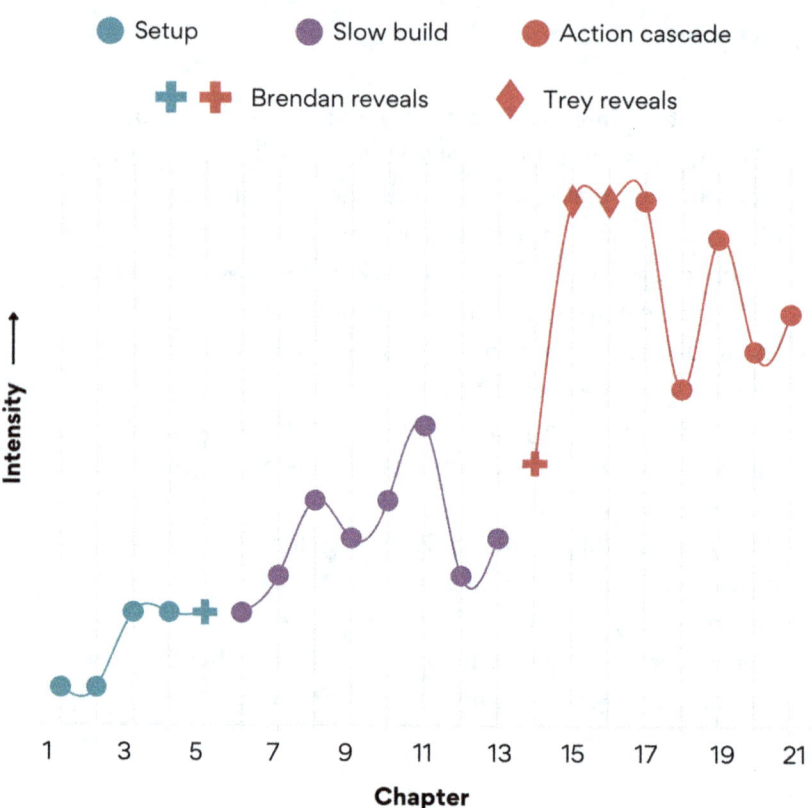

Figure 4: Plot structure of *The Searcher*. The novel has an idiosyncratic structure and pacing that exists alongside a traditional three-act structure.

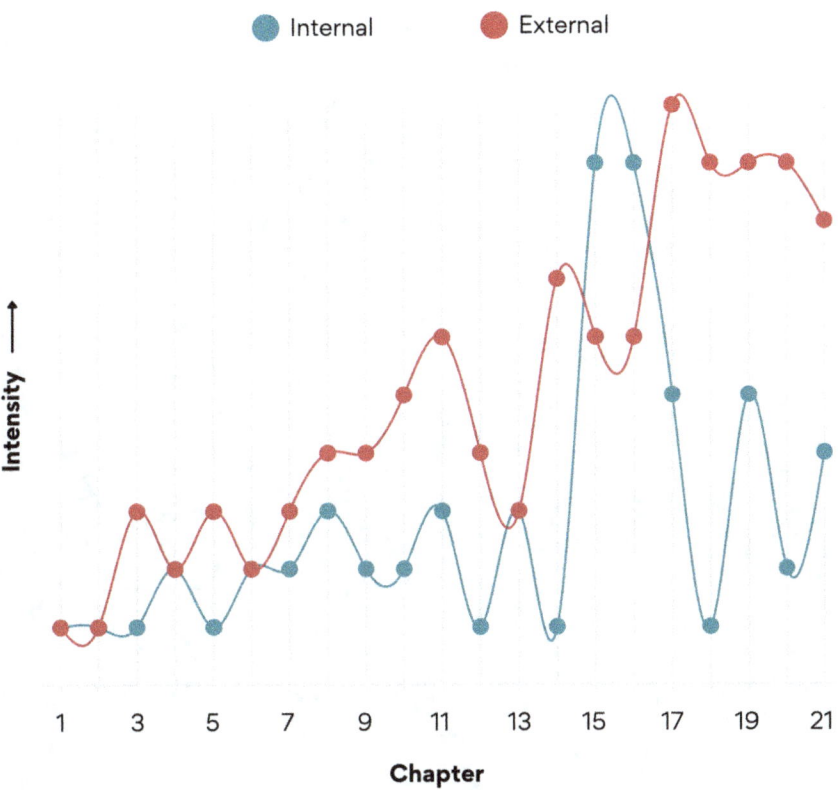

Figure 5. Internal versus external plots of *The Searcher*. The novel slowly builds in intensity; the emotional arc and the action arc peak at different times.

MATRIX,
BY LAUREN GROFF

STATS

Everything that I write, I write in longhand. And I do the first complete draft, throw it out, start over again, throw it out, and I don't reread the things that I've done. . . . And the beautiful thing is, if I get a few drafts into this process of writing, throwing out, writing, throwing out, suddenly I start to think in very different ways about the story that I'm writing.
—Lauren Groff[1]

Published in 2021 by Riverhead Books (Penguin Random House)
257 pages, approximately 64,250 words
The author's fourth published novel

GENRE

Historical Fiction

AMAZON CATEGORIES

Medieval Historical Fiction, Literary Fiction, Women's Literature and Fiction

AWARDS

Shortlisted for the 2021 National Book Award for Fiction

CHAPTER 11
HOW DO YOU ESTABLISH SETTING IN HISTORICAL FICTION?

Historical fiction and speculative fiction both require authors to introduce readers to unfamiliar worlds alongside their characters. A skilled author can make this orientation feel both seamless and dynamic; examining their strategies can teach writers in any genre how to improve setting and world-building. Let's take a look at the opening of Lauren Groff's historical novel *Matrix* to see how one author meets the challenge.

Here is the first paragraph:

> She rides out of the forest alone. Seventeen years old, in the cold March drizzle, Marie who comes from France.

The first sentence is short and active, placing us immediately in a present-tense scene. The second sentence supplies more context, leaning on the unusual sentence structure to give interest to details that are fairly ordinary. The sentence—which is a fragment, without an anchoring verb—drapes lightly over the scaffold of the prior sentence. The "she" now has a name, an age, and an origin. The "ride" is now both out of a forest and into a rainy March day.

After this short first paragraph, we get a long paragraph full of setting details, including the key information that we are in the year 1158 and that Marie's destination is an abbey, which she is seeing now for the first time. Our narrator is focused on Marie but not entirely subsumed in her point of view—there are shades of distance. Take these sentences:

> She sees for the first time the abbey, pale and aloof on a rise in this damp valley, the clouds drawn up from the ocean and wrung against the hills in constant rainfall. Most of the year this place is emerald and sapphire, bursting under dampness, thick with sheep and chaffinches and newts, delicate mushrooms poking from the rich soil, but now in late winter, all is gray and full of shadows.

Marie has no experience yet with summer in this place, but the narrator establishes in these sentences that we are not entirely limited to Marie's experience. Readers are watching Marie; we are not ourselves Marie. Groff even dramatizes this relationship between protagonist and reader a few lines later: "The wind hushes. The trees cease stirring. Marie feels that the whole countryside is watching her move through it." Groff positions readers as voyeurs and Marie as a subject worthy of and equal to being observed. (I'll discuss Groff's narration style more thoroughly in the next chapter.)

Groff also stitches in tiny details that convey the twelfth-century setting: Marie's Angevin face, sealskin cloak, and green headcloth; her warhorse and the falcon shivering in its wicker enclosure. At the same time, Groff is careful to also weave in details that are more familiar: seeds unfurling in the cold ground, Marie's height and ungainly build, the wind and trees.

We also start to get some hints about who Marie is as a person—clever and passionate—and why she is on this journey. We are told, "She has yet to cry for having been thrown to the dogs." Notice how much meaning is packed into that short sentence: We get not just Marie's characterization of what has happened to her, but also a hint that she feels deeply and yet is strong and stubborn enough not to let those feelings loose.

Next, we move back in time to the scene that launched this lonely ride:

 The queen said that she had news, oh what delightful news, what relief, she had just now received the papal dispensation, the poor horse had exploded its heart it had galloped so fast to bring it here this morning. That, due to her, the queen's, own efforts over these months, this poor illegitimate Marie from nowhere in Le Maine had at last been made prioress of a royal abbey. Wasn't that wonderful. Now at last they knew what to do with this odd half sister to the crown. Now they had a use for Marie at last.

Note how even the queen's dialogue is filtered through Marie's point of view. In other words, we get the feel of the queen's language, especially in phrases like "Oh what delightful news, what relief" but there are no quotation marks, and the passage feels like someone—Marie—reporting what they remember of the queen's words. Yet our omniscient narrator is still with us here as well, telling us, for example, that Marie's half sister, "a bastardess sibling of the crown just like Marie," will one day become a Welsh princess—not a fact that Marie herself could know at this point in the narrative. We understand that perhaps if Marie were more like her half sister—this "simpering creature" who understands "the uses of popularity in the court"—she also might have been a princess. Instead, she is destined for the abbey, despite her protest to Queen Eleanor that she "had no godly vocation whatsoever in any way." Here our narrator steps in again, with an oblique glimpse into Marie's future, the future we are following her into: "Her faith had twisted very early in her childhood; it would slowly grow ever more bent into its geometry until it was its own angular, majestic thing." Marie will not be a princess but, our narrator hints, she will achieve her own kind of majesty. That is the story we are promised.

By the end of this backstory excursion, we understand that Marie lost her mother early, at age twelve, and then spent two years running the family estate in France herself before having to flee to England; that she has fallen in love with Queen Eleanor, wife of her half brother; that she is not technically alone on her journey, for which she has a royal escort, but feels herself alone because the servant, companion, and lover who has been with her from childhood has refused to go with her to the abbey to, in her words, "be buried alive forever with a bunch of dead-eyed nuns."

We then return to the present, to Marie riding closer to "the buildings clenched pale atop the hill," past "fourteen fresh black graves" of nuns who have recently died of a terrible sickness, and finally to the abbey itself, where, numb with cold and her long ride, she falls in the mud before the abbess and subprioress. As Marie enters the abbey, Groff continues the pattern of interspersing unfamiliar words and details (medlarfruit, windowpanes made of horn, the order of prayers) with familiar ones (the feeling of hunger, the motivations of jealousy), guiding us with a sure hand into the world of this twelfth-century abbey.

TAKEAWAYS

- Tie setting description to action: Make sure that your characters are moving, interacting, remembering, not just staying in place to be described.
- You likely need fewer details than you think to establish the historical feel of a book, but make sure those details are both specific and vivid. (A falcon is a memorable detail!)
- Intersperse historical or fantasy details with familiar ones, like descriptions of time, nature, human emotions.

CHAPTER 12
HOW DO YOU USE OMNISCIENT NARRATION?

SPOILER WARNING

I've been wanting to write about the way Lauren Groff uses point of view in *Matrix* since I first read the book—it may even have been one of the inspirations for the original Novel Study blog series. What Groff pulls off in *Matrix* is a version of omniscient narration that feels modern and self-aware, and still brings us as close to her protagonist as we might be with third-person limited point of view. (See Chapter 6 for an explanation of the different kinds of point of view.)

The heyday of omniscient narration was also one of the heydays of the novel as a form: the nineteenth century. Here's the opening of

George Eliot's *Middlemarch* (1872) to give you a sense of the nineteenth-century style of omniscient narration:

> Miss Brooke had that kind of beauty which seems to be thrown into relief by poor dress. Her hand and wrist were so finely formed that she could wear sleeves not less bare of style than those in which the Blessed Virgin appeared to Italian painters; and her profile as well as her stature and bearing seemed to gain the more dignity from her plain garments.

This passage positions the reader as the observer of Dorothea Brooke, with a chatty narrator acting as a kind of museum docent, directing our attention to certain details and telling us what we should think of them. If we have access to a character's inner life, it isn't direct—it's filtered through our omniscient narrator, as in this passage from later in the same paragraph:

> She was enamoured of intensity and greatness, and rash in embracing whatever seemed to her to have those aspects; likely to seek martyrdom, to make retractations, and then to incur martyrdom after all in a quarter where she had not sought it. Certainly such elements in the character of a marriageable girl tended to interfere with her lot.

Right there in the opening paragraph is the central question of the novel: How is a woman like Dorothea—a woman of intense faith and feelings—going to find a place in a world in which marriage is one of the few options available to her?

Groff's protagonist in *Matrix*, Marie, is living in medieval England, a time in which choices are similarly constrained for most women. In Marie's case, the decision has already been made for her, and we meet her at the moment when she has been deemed unmarriageable and dispatched from the court of Queen Eleanor of Aquitaine to become prioress of an impoverished abbey. Unlike Dorothea, Marie has no stirrings of faith—all she wants at the beginning of the novel is to remain in the orbit of Eleanor, with whom she has fallen hopelessly in love.

Groff's novel, it seems to me, is a deliberate contrast to *Middlemarch* and not just in the path taken by her protagonist. Groff's use of omniscient narration is also a considered departure from Eliot's style. Where Eliot gives her omniscient narrator authority, Groff tends to make hers more neutral. Eliot's narrator is an active interpreter; Groff's narrator is a more detached researcher.

In *The Art of Perspective*, Christopher Castellani argues—correctly, I think—that omniscient narration has fallen out of favor because it is "too old-fashioned for a fractured world that distrusts authority, has abandoned God, and has little faith in any absolute truth put forth by an individual. . . . Who is [the author] to speak for anyone or anything other than herself and her own experience?" Groff solves this dilemma by creating a narrator who speaks for herself only very rarely and who, instead, gives us access to points of view that provide counterpoints—and sometimes correctives—to Marie's point of view.

The narration remains closely focused on Marie through part one of the novel as she moves from grief to acceptance. As soon as Marie accepts her fate, she begins to grasp her power and take action to improve the condition of the starving nuns. She goes to the cellar, where she discovers the cellatrix (what a word!) has put aside food for her own use, a practice she tries to defend as ordinary in other abbeys. Marie's response is decisive:

> Ah. Do other cellatrices keep food to themselves despite their sisters starving? Marie asks, and Ruth would later recount that Marie's face was terrible, granite, inhuman in this moment; that the cellatrix, a stout and loud woman prone to slapping the servants and lesser nuns, cowered in fear. Marie does not shout, though she demotes the cellatrix to work in the fields, though the field nuns are mostly drawn from the English, and certainly not the French of bluest blood.
>
> She promotes to the cellatrix position noseless Sister Mamille, who has not felt hunger since her nose was

bitten off and who has a mind that slides only along lines of justice and fairness. She would prove a most excellent and thoughtful cellatrix even to the last days of Marie's own abbacy.

Groff's researcher-biographer narrator inserts herself here in two places, informing us of what Ruth would "later recount" and showing us the future, revealing that Marie will eventually be abbess and hinting that her tenure in that office will be a long and prosperous one. These revelations remind us that Marie is not our only touchpoint through the novel and prepare us for part two, in which Groff begins to move rapidly through time, jumping to Marie's second year at the abbey, then her third. By the end of part two, thirty years have passed; the "grief-blasted" seventeen-year-old of the opening paragraphs is now a forty-seven-year-old about to step into the full power of her role as abbess.

In part three of the novel, Groff's narrative choices bear their full fruit. We are still most closely allied with Marie's point of view as she begins to take dramatic steps, guided by visions that tell her to build a labyrinth to protect her nuns from the outside world, to create a dam from a marshland, and, most controversially, to take on the offices of the mass and confession—traditionally reserved for male priests.

Part of the drama in this last part of the novel comes from the reader's shifting relationship to Marie. It's easy to cheer the demotion of the greedy cellatrix in part one; Marie's choices in part three are more complicated. Groff wants us to question whether Marie has overstepped her authority, become too drunk on her own power to consider the negative consequences of her actions. To do that effectively, she needs to give readers access to viewpoints outside of Marie's. I'm going to walk you through the second chapter of part three to show you exactly how Groff pulls it off.

In this chapter, Marie has summoned her four closest advisors to share with them her vision for creating the enormous labyrinth that will encircle the abbey, preventing all access except through hidden tunnels that will be known only to the nuns. To start, we see the four through Marie's eyes:

> The new prioress Tilde, twitchy and scrupulous, with the sweet, startled face of a dormouse. Oh how the girl loves god, hungers for god, believes in the goodness of all things with a kind of rigorous simplicity. Such knowing simplicity in this complex world takes great intelligence, Marie finds. She envies the girl, admires her.

We get similar introductions to Sister Asta, who has the mind of an engineer; Sister Ruth, who was a novice with Marie; and Wulfhild, whom Marie brought to the abbey as a young child and employed as bailiff when she wanted to marry rather than take orders.

After these introductions, the narrator pulls back from Marie to show us the scene from a neutral position, seemingly hovering above all of the characters:

> It is deep in the night when all are assembled in Marie's chambers. Marie's kitchener brings up cheese and bread and pies of fruit and good sweet wine carried over from Burgundy. With the arrival of the food, the women mind less missing their sleep.

In that last line we move a step closer in, seeing the collective state of mind of all the women in the room except Marie.

In the next paragraph, the narrator takes us into the mind of another character, looking at Marie: "Ruth thinks with wonder that she glows with a light that is not of fire. She tells them slowly of her vision in the fields that day, and of her plan." Next, we see the internal reaction to Marie's plan from Tilde, who is "frightened of Marie, how swiftly her mind leaps and turns," then Asta, who is thrilled by the challenge: "she calculates swiftly and says that it can be done in two years, perhaps, if all hands inessential to the abbey's urgent needs are used." We then return to Ruth for two paragraphs as she wrestles with her unease and doubts until "she at last arrives at the understanding that Marie's will is stronger than any practical impossibilities." The next paragraph moves us a step away from Ruth's consciousness, externalizing her worry by making it perceptible in her voice rather than just in her mind: "She lowers her head and prays and raises it and says yes, though in a voice thick with worry when the vote is called."

Only Wulfhild resists Marie, and at this point the narrator keeps us in that pulled-back position, watching the exchange from above but loosely allied with Ruth, Tilde, and Asta. When Wulfhild begins her intervention, we learn a wealth of details about her, but they are all external:

> Twelve years now the abbey's bailiffess, in her strange leather tunic and skirt, shining with the tallow she rubs on to make them impervious to the weather. She is a dark-haired, sunbrowned woman who gives the impression of boiling turmoil held in check by willpower alone, smaller than Marie but like Marie holding a kind of natural authority in her shoulders thrown back.

When Wulfhild votes no, "the other women in the room hold their breath." This clearly excludes Marie, who "asks very quietly if Wulfhild does not love her." Groff is careful to use very specific rather than generalized language in Wulfhild's response, to make it clear that we are hearing the words unfiltered from the points of view of others in the room:

> Wulfhild says she loves her so much that she dares to tell Marie when she is making a mistake and that not all even in this room can boast of such honesty when Marie puts on her murderess face, which she is wearing right now. But the abbess doesn't scare her, Wulfhild.

However, the narrator now tells us, "It is clear by the rapid pulse twitching in Wulfhild's neck that the abbess does in fact scare Wulfhild." This is an external cue, visible to all the women except

Wulfhild, though she herself must feel it. The passive voice construction ("It is clear . . .") means that Groff doesn't have to name who exactly notices this rapid pulse. Just Marie? Or do the other women notice it as well? The next line—"The silence stretches on and it is horrid"—similarly sidesteps subjectivity, but we can guess that it includes all of the women in the room except for Marie, who is the one prolonging the silence. That intuition is confirmed by the next sentence:

> In a voice so soft that all the women lean forward to hear, Marie says that when Wulfhild speaks, she speaks in the voice of Marie's own authority, which she has only lent to the bailiffess. But Marie herself speaks with the authority of the Virgin Mary who has bestowed upon her a great vision that very day.
>
> Surely, she says, Wulfhild would not dare to contradict the Virgin Mary.

It is only at this point that we make a step closer inside Wulfhild's consciousness, but it is so small as to be barely perceptible: "And so Wulfhild's resistance is overrun. She sighs. She adjusts. With burning eyes she bends over the table where Asta has already in excitement begun sketching her plans." Wulfhild's adjustment is internal, as is her sense of the tears burning in her eyes, but the scene closes with Asta's plans, leaving the readers positioned again at that ceiling-level view, looking down at the group of women gathered around the table.

In order to establish whose point of view we are in, Groff uses filter words like "sees," "thinks," "hears," "feels." In limited point-of-view narration, we don't need these words because we already know which character's mind we're inhabiting; eliminating filter words closes the gap between character and readers. In omniscient point of view, however, they are crucial anchors. (See Chapters 7 and 18 for more about filter words.) Groff also uses a technique I've seen frequently in recent literary fiction, like Sally Rooney's *Normal People* and Weike Wang's *Joan Is Okay*: As we saw in Chapter 11, she removes quotation marks from dialogue, which removes the reader's direct access to it.

Instead, it feels as if all dialogue is filtered through the consciousness of our point-of-view character or presented to us by the omniscient narrator.

Once Groff has established this technique of shifting points of view and walked readers through it slowly, she can use it more economically at later points in the novel. Marie's next vision tells her it is time to build a grand abbess house and shows her how she will fund it. In chapter four of part three, Groff leads us, one by one, through the internal reactions of the same group of women: Tilde weeping in her bed at night at the thought of the work she will have to undertake, Asta dreaming of buttresses, and Wulfhild swallowing her exhaustion and resistance, knowing Marie's visions will win out.

We are still in Wulfhild's point of view when she comes to Marie to explain how she will bring in stonecutters to do the work but keep them away from the abbey, and in this remarkable passage, we get a short glimpse into three points of view, moving from Wulfhild to Marie to Asta:

> She will work out a system of blindfolds to bring the strangers in, give extra pay for swifter better work. She will take it on herself to keep trouble from imposing itself on Marie's tender nuns.
>
> Practical Wulfie, Marie says aloud. Inside, she says: heart of my heart.
>
> Done in a year, perhaps, Asta believes, having her own glorious visions.

Because Groff has thoroughly established her omniscient narrator's range of movement and repeatedly demonstrated the presence of that narrator, we can easily follow these shifts without feeling disoriented. Omniscient narration is an advanced technique and offers greater flexibility along with higher risks than limited narration. If writing in limited point of view is like driving on a controlled-access highway, then writing in omniscient point of view is like taking an all-terrain vehicle off-road. You will be able to find less-traveled spots—and you also run a good chance of losing your readers along the way unless you proceed carefully.

TAKEAWAYS

- Be deliberate about your point-of-view choices. Know why you are making your overall choice, as well as the effects of choices in individual scenes.
- Establish omniscient narration early by providing details your point-of-view character or protagonist cannot know.
- To make omniscient narration feel fresh, give readers close access to the protagonist, moving away only for select moments.
- Use filter words to identify whose experiences and thoughts we are seeing when using omniscient narration.

CHAPTER 13
HOW DO YOU WRITE RESONANT ENDINGS?

SPOILER WARNING

I've analyzed a number of openings so far in this book, but we haven't yet discussed endings. In many ways, endings should be harder to execute than openings, right? The entire weight of the novel is flying through the air, and the novelist must bring it safely to rest, making the reader feel they have completed a journey. In my decade of experience working with writers, however, I've learned that it is much harder to get the plane off the ground than to bring it in for a landing.

By the end of the novel, after all, the writer knows the entire shape of the story; the decisions have been made and the landing can happen almost on autopilot. Readers too will generally have an intuitive sense of what the ending will deliver, especially in genre fiction—order restored, love won, victory secured. Unlike in the opening, when readers must meet all of a novel's characters and learn about the setting—be persuaded to walk onto the plane and take the journey—by the end, the story world will be almost as familiar to readers as it is to the writer.

The plot requirements of the ending are fairly obvious: Answer all open story questions, weave loose plot threads into the story, and show that your characters have learned their lessons and completed the arcs that will leave them at rest—even if it is just temporary rest. But there is one further, less obvious step: Ring the gong of your central theme one last time so it can continue to resonate for the reader even after they've closed the book.

Let's look at how Lauren Groff accomplishes these steps in *Matrix*. The last chapter of the novel is broken into two scenes, which are stylistically very different from one another. In the first, we are with Marie on her deathbed, where we'd left her at the end of the previous chapter. The first line of the chapter orients us immediately: "Marie sickens deeper." The point of view is tightly focused on Marie, though in the first paragraphs of the scene she can still hear the voices of the nuns around her: "Someone is saying now that the poor abbess has been ill longer than she has admitted. She has been gasping in her pain and pressing her hand to the space between her breasts for years. Feel now. There is a rock in there." Marie can still respond in her thoughts if not out loud and muses about the deaths of her grandmother and mother before her from the same disease. "It will be soon now," she thinks.

After that moment, the scene modulates into stream of consciousness as we track Marie's last moments—her struggles for breath, her desire to warn her nuns about the last judgment, then her release of responsibility. The last movement of the passage is to take Marie from body to spirit, carrying readers with her over that gulf:

 My vineyard, which is mine, is before me.
>
> Marie longs for it, longs for it, her whole body reaches for it, the gold, the heavenly music, the release. To see god, who is not split in three, but singular. God,

sole, female. She has had an eternity of community, it has been enough.

Make haste, my beloved.

So be it, she thinks. And it is.

The stripped-down sentences allow readers to stay focused on interior emotion rather than external details, and Groff gives them plenty of white space to resonate. The last words of the scene echo the first chapter of Genesis: "Then God said, 'Let there be light'; and there was light." The language has the richness and allusiveness of poetry, allowing readers to linger with Marie in her final moments.

From a plot standpoint, ending the novel with Marie's death feels natural. The novel opened with her journey to the abbey where she completed her life's work, bringing an impoverished community into health and power. This last scene also finishes her character arc, which leads her from faithlessness to a kind of faith that centers female power—note her final vision of God as "sole, female."

But Marie's death is the climax, so let's look now at the falling action in the last scene of the chapter. Here is the opening paragraph:

> The funeral is solemn and the feast is large; the mortuary roll will return so thick with their sewn-on tituli of praise for Abbess Marie that it becomes quite clear that no other woman of the realm could be remembered with such veneration. Marie was majestic; great, still, in death, and her renown struck fear in the hearts of even those who had never known her.

Note the sharp stylistic change. We are in a distanced point of view, focused on external details conveyed in long, complex sentences. The older nuns, those few who are old enough to remember the dire straits of the abbey when Marie came to it, tell their stories of hunger, plague, and hopelessness. In contrast to the spare writing in the final scene in Marie's point of view, here we get lush detail, as in this one long sentence heaped with nouns:

> But the novices, thinking now of the summer gardens overgrown with vegetation and the honeybees darting through the flowers and the grapevines under their singing sculptures and the pigs and sheep and goats and chickens and cows and the apple trees heavy with fruit, give little smiles, knowing these nuns to be holy and truthful yet not quite believing their tales.

Slowly the point of view of the scene comes to focus on Tilde, now abbess in Marie's place. Plagued by dreams after Marie's death, she goes to the chapel to pray and sees a shimmer she believes to be Marie's spirit. The shimmer leads her to a small volume she remembers seeing Marie writing in; when she opens it she discovers records of Marie's visions—those that led to the building of the labyrinth and to Marie hearing confession, but others too, of a kiss between Eve and the Virgin Mary, of god as an egg-laying hen.

Tilde wrestles with what to do with the book. She knows just how dangerous it is: "had such visions as these seeped into the world during her lifetime, Abbess Marie would have been burned a heretic at the stake and all the sisters in the abbey would have been scattered." Even keeping the book, letting alone revealing it, feels dangerous to Tilde. After hours of reading and deliberation, she hears Subprioress Goda coming to reprimand her for missing services and, in a moment of "thoughtless panic," she tosses the book into the fire.

Here the omniscient narrator we've encountered at many significant moments in the novel steps in again, bringing us forward into our present moment so we can feel the significance of this loss:

> Tilde is not blessed with mystical sight, she cannot see . . . the visions that might have shown a different path for the next millennium. . . . How slow the final flowering of good intentions can be, the poisonous full bloom taking place centuries beyond the scope of the original life.
>
> The abbey crumbling, the earth warming, the clouds

abandoning this place, and the newts and birds vanishing, and in the new dryness of the hot world, the traces of the old dead abbey's buildings are thrown up in seared brown lines upon the grasses of the strange changed place absent of holy women, the lines of the labyrinth buried under the roads and houses of later, even more ravenous people.

As readers, we recognize that *we* are the ravenous people living in the hot world. The shock of seeing ourselves named in a novel set in this faraway time closes the distance, making us want to reach back in time and rescue Marie's visions from the fire to help us build a different kind of future. Marie's death concludes the plot; the job of this passage is to make the plot continue to resonate after we close the book.

TAKEAWAYS

- Use your ending to not only resolve plot threads but also reinforce your central themes.
- The falling action or resolution of the novel (everything after the climax) is your opportunity to reveal what it all meant—why you wrote the novel and what you want readers to take away with them.

I KISSED SHARA WHEELER, BY CASEY MCQUISTON

STATS

Shara is everywhere, all the time . . . . The hardest part of that was striking a balance between making her overwhelming presence known and still keeping her an unattainable enigma that the reader (and the characters) wants to unravel. So I'd say that was the challenge: crafting a character who's everywhere and nowhere at the same time.
—Casey McQuiston[1]

Published in 2022 by Wednesday Books (St. Martin's)
351 pages, approximately 87,750 words
The author's third published novel

GENRE

YA Romance

AMAZON CATEGORIES

Teen & Young Adult LGBTQ+ Romance, Teen & Young Adult LGBTQ+ Fiction, Teen & Young Adult Contemporary Romance

AWARDS

Stonewall Book Award, #1 *New York Times* Bestseller

CHAPTER 14
HOW DO YOU HOOK A READER BEFORE THE FIRST SENTENCE?

Casey McQuiston's first novel, *Red, White, and Royal Blue*, published in 2019, was a massive bestseller, sparking what the *New York Times* called an "LGBTQ romance boom."[1] It's a hilarious, joyful, page-turner of a book that showed readers a female president with an openly gay son living in the White House—a fantasy many readers needed after living through years of a Trump presidency. For our Novel Study analysis we're going to examine McQuiston's 2022 novel, *I Kissed Shara Wheeler*, which is billed as a YA romance. The tagline for the novel is featured on the cover and hints at yet a third genre: "To get the girl, first you have to find her." A mystery!

Before we get to the first words of the novel, we get three bits of text to interpret. First is an address to the reader, which turns out to be a content warning that the novel "includes elements of religious trauma and homophobia." McQuiston softens this warning by telling us that Chloe Green, their point of view character, *isn't* an Evangelical Christian and that the topic will be "approached with humor, because sometimes you really do have to laugh." I like this solution, which honors the reader while also staying lighthearted.

After the content warning is an epigraph, a line from a song by the Killers: "It started out with a kiss . . ." This clever once-upon-a-time alternative gestures at the inciting incident referred to in the title, though it turns out that's not what McQuiston is going to show us first.

Our last bit of information is the time stamp after the chapter header:

> HOURS SINCE SHARA WHEELER LEFT: 12
> DAYS UNTIL GRADUATION: 42

We don't yet know who Shara Wheeler is, but the title tells us someone has kissed her, and now we know she is missing. These two time stamps—one in the past and one in the future—establish the timeframe of the novel. Even without having read the first sentence of the novel, we are mid story, between these two events. In addition to being a clever hook, the time stamps generate steady suspense. Watching the hours Shara Wheeler has been missing tick up as the days to graduation tick down generates a charge each time we reach a new chapter.

Before we get into the story proper, let's explore the topic of time stamps in more detail. Traditionally, a time stamp is used in stories with complex timelines, like a plot that jumps forward or backward in time. These preliminary lines can also include things like a location or a character name—again, useful for any book that covers a lot of territory or stories that are told from multiple points of view. Do you have to use them? Certainly not, even in narratives that jump around in time. As we saw with Lauren Groff's *Matrix*, it isn't hard to use internal references to keep readers oriented. Groff jumps years and even decades between chapters and uses her protagonist's age as a subtle time marker.

Returning to *Shara Wheeler*, look at this first line: "Chloe Green is going to put her fist through a window." Fabulous, right? We know whose point of view we are in now, and we know she is worked up. The use of the near future tense ("is going to") gives a charge to the narrative and, just like the time stamp, tells us we are diving straight into the action.

The next paragraph gives us a character insight and also the setting: "Usually when she has a thought like that, it means she's *spiritually* on the brink. But right now, squared up to the back door of the Wheeler house, she's actually physically ready to do it." Before giving us the details of Shara's disappearance, McQuiston tells us how Chloe feels about it. The disappearance has already happened, so it's backstory, but Chloe's feelings are about to propel her into an action—breaking into the Wheeler house to look for Shara.

When we do get more details, they are filtered through Chloe's point of view, telling us as much about her as about Shara:

> It has to be an act, is the thing. Obviously, Shara Wheeler is fine. Shara Wheeler is not missing. Shara Wheeler is doing what she does: a doe-eyed performance of blank innocence that makes everyone think she must be so deep and complex and enchanting when really, she's the most boring bore in this entire unbearably boring town.

Notice how distinctive the voice is—a hallmark of YA as a genre. McQuiston's use of repetition and parallel structure in this passage is masterful: the angry drumbeat of "Shara Wheeler is . . .", the repetitive drone of variations on the word "bore."

The next paragraphs follow the same pattern. We find out first what Chloe had planned for *"her* perfect prom" (not *"the* perfect prom")—a dress that made her look like "a sexy vampire assassin," screaming to Lil Yachty, going to Waffle House—before we learn the specifics of what happened to Shara. She walked out the door before she was announced prom queen and hasn't been seen since. Knowing the basic facts only generates more questions in our minds, and Chloe is so busy pursuing her own theory (that Shara is fine), she's not in a hurry to answer all of the questions we want answered.

Chloe is convinced Shara is simply skulking inside her house while her family is in church, so she casually breaks in. As she wanders through the house, we start to get a sense of how closely she's paid attention to Shara. She's shocked, for example, to find a scrunchie in the bathroom because Shara has never been known to wear her hair back. When she reaches Shara's room, she feels a frisson of excitement to discover "what sort of perfection incubator Shara Wheeler climbs inside when she goes home every day." Here McQuiston sneaks in an important theme question: "Who is she when, for once, nobody is looking?"

Buried in the many specific details about the objects in Shara's room are more clues to the relationship between these two girls: Chloe considers Shara to be popular, while she is part of the "weird and queer" crowd in their small Alabama town. She thinks that perhaps Shara disappeared in order to frame her, Chloe, for her murder. Another mystery!

We're just about to learn more about the mystery embedded in the title and epigraph—that kiss between Chloe and Shara—when Chloe's reverie, brought on by the smell of a lipstick she finds in the trash can, is interrupted by a new character, Rory Heron, coming through the window. Chloe gives him the kind of hyper-precise social label used only by teens and Real Housewives: "Willowgrove's answer to every brooding bad boy from every late '90s teen drama. The most eligible bachelor amongst the stoners-skaters-and-slackers rung of the social ladder."

It's only then, when Rory asks why Chloe even cares why Shara is gone, that we understand the relationship between the two girls:

> Why does she care? Because she and Shara have both spent every day of their high school careers dedicated to the singular goal of graduating valedictorian, and the only thing Chloe has ever wanted as much as that title is the satisfaction of knowing Shara Wheeler can't have it. Because Shara Wheeler has everything else.
>
> Because if Shara's really gone, that's a forfeit, and Chloe Green does not win by default.
>
> Because two days ago, Shara found her alone in the B Building elevator before fifth hour, pulled her in by the elbow, and kissed her until she forgot an entire semester of French. And Chloe still doesn't know why.

At this point, romance readers will know exactly which classic trope McQuiston is engaging: enemies to lovers. The tension of this trope, already quite high, is heightened in this case by the YA setting and by the questions around Shara's sexuality. She has a boyfriend, Chloe has told us (the football quarterback, *of course*), but then there was that kiss . . .

The final twist of the chapter is that Rory has recently been kissed by Shara too. This turns out to be enough of a bond to unite Chloe and Rory in trying to discover what happened to Shara—not so much because they are worried about her (she is perhaps too perfect for them to believe something bad could happen?) but because, as Chloe puts it: "What if she ghosts everyone forever? What if you spend the rest of your life wondering why, in the name of God, Shara Wheeler kissed you?"

And that is how to create an effective hook. McQuiston doesn't rely just on a missing prom queen to draw in readers. That story, after all, has a few known endings. What McQuiston is offering instead is a less predictable mystery: Why did Shara go out of her way to entangle weird-and-queer Chloe and stoner–bad boy Rory in a quest to figure out where she went, awakening them each with a kiss before disappearing, like a reverse Sleeping Beauty? We'll have to read to the end of the book to find out.

TAKEAWAYS

- If you include a content warning, make sure it matches the tone of the novel and the voice of your primary narrator.
- Time stamps keep readers oriented in place and time, but they can also be used to build suspense by establishing a timeline and ticking clock.
- The job of your first chapter isn't to tell readers everything they need to know about your protagonist or story world; its job is to hook readers so they will keep reading.
- Hook readers by jumping straight into a dramatic situation, withholding key details, twisting familiar genre tropes, and establishing a strong narrative voice to help readers identify with a protagonist narrator.

CHAPTER 15
HOW DO YOU GET THE MOST MILEAGE OUT OF DIALOGUE?

As I read through the books I selected for Novel Study, one question I kept asking is this: What is new in fiction these days? It's the reason I focused only on books that have appeared in the last few years. So far, we've seen evidence of a tempering of the show-don't-tell maxim (Chapter 2), a fresh new way to use omniscient narration (Chapter 12), and now, in *I Kissed Shara Wheeler*, some clever dialogue tricks. Let's take a close look at how Casey McQuiston uses dialogue so you can apply the techniques to your own work.

Chapter two of the novel starts with a chunk of backstory telling us how Chloe ended up in the wonderfully named False Beach, Alabama. McQuiston wisely chooses to orient even this backstory around the mystery of the missing Shara Wheeler (already top-of-mind due to the new time stamp). Chloe remembers that the first thing she saw in False Beach was an enormous billboard featuring Shara as part of an advertisement for Willowgrove Christian Academy, the high school both girls attend. McQuiston livens up this backstory by grounding it in a specific scene—the moment Chloe's family first drive into town—complete with a single dialogue exchange:

"What kind of name is False Beach?" Chloe asked her mom for the five thousandth miserable time that day as they glided under Shara's billboard. It was a question she'd been asking since her mom first told her the name of her hometown.

"It's a beach but it's not," her mom answered, same as always, and her other mom flipped a page in *The Canterbury Tales*, and they kept driving out of the California sunset and into the buttcrack of Alabama.

Notice how much work the space around the dialogue lines is doing. The lines themselves are quite ordinary—just a pretext for delivering details that bring both Chloe and her mothers into focus. We learn that this move from California to "the buttcrack of Alabama" is not a happy one for Chloe. (I spent a lot of time as a child with my grandparents in Decatur, Alabama, further up that buttcrack, and I can attest that I too would have been very unhappy living there as a teenager.) We can also guess that Chloe's mother may have been happy to leave the town behind, and that her other mother—the one reading *The Canterbury Tales* on a road trip—may fit in there just about as well as Chloe will.

After a few more details about the town, McQuiston brings us back to the present timeline of the novel: "It's just a town by some water where nothing interesting ever happens. And, in what Chloe has learned is the nature of small towns, when one thing does happen, everyone knows about it. Which means by Monday morning, all anyone wants to talk about is where Shara could have gone." And here's where McQuiston does something very interesting—they give us examples of the town talk, without identifying it as such:

 Shara Wheeler's so *pretty*. Shara Wheeler's so *smart*. Shara Wheeler has *never* been mean to *anyone* in her *life*. Shara Wheeler has the voice of an angel, actually, but she's never auditioned for a spring musical because she doesn't want to take the spotlight away from students who need it more.

The effect is almost like Chloe is parroting these lines back to us, putting mocking emphasis on certain words. It's an Austen-esque technique, akin to the much-discussed free indirect discourse, in which dialogue is implied rather than quoted and filtered through a point-of-view character who gives it her own spin. (I touched on this technique in my discussion of *Matrix* in Chapter 12.) By the end of this passage, we tilt more firmly to something we are beginning to identify as Chloe's voice: "It's a miracle nobody has put her [Shara's] likeness on like, the side of a butter container yet."

McQuiston then does start giving us direct quotations, though unattributed to specific speakers:

Today:
"I heard nobody's seen her since prom night."
"I heard Smith broke up with her and she lost it."
"I heard she ran away to build houses for the homeless."

See how different these feel from the reported lines above, delivered straight this time, without Chloe's mocking tone?

Now, get ready for the tour-de-force that comes next:

"I heard she's secretly pregnant and her parents sent her away until she gives birth so nobody finds out."
"That's literally a plotline from *Riverdale*, idiot," Benjy calls after a passing sophomore. He sighs and carefully lays his folded Sonic uniform polo for his after-school shift at the bottom of his locker.

McQuiston transitions seamlessly from backstory to 'front story,' keeping Shara Wheeler as the focus but prioritizing Chloe's voice and point of view, and then moves us into a live scene in the high school hallway so smoothly that we don't even notice they've done it unless we stop to see how it works. McQuiston has also told us a great deal about Shara's status in False Beach while making it seem as if they've shown it instead. And one more detail I want to call out: Notice how specific the detail about the Sonic shirt is and how much it reveals about Benjy's socioeconomic status. McQuiston has thought carefully about what Benjy puts in his locker (not the expected textbooks) and makes the detail count.

I've got just a few more passages from this chapter I want to show you, all of them illustrating just how much you can do with dialogue. The first comes soon after Benjy's line above. He and Chloe are standing at their lockers, and Benjy asks Chloe if she's okay. Her response:

"Of course I'm good," Chloe says, straightening her shiny silver collar pins. Georgia describes her interpretation of the uniform as "doing the most." Chloe describes it as "please let me feel one sweet hit of individuality before it's squeezed out of me by lunch." It's whatever. "Why wouldn't I be good?"

Here again, it's the in-between space that delivers the goodies. McQuiston fits in a big wedge of character description that is anchored in specific details (those shiny pins) but also tells us a lot about how this character sees herself—as a creative nonconformist. Because the details are sandwiched in between two closely related dialogue lines we imagine being spoken back to back, the pace of the scene doesn't flag.

As Chloe adds the missing eyeliner that provoked Benjy's concern, Benjy delivers the reverse effect—a wedge of dialogue absolutely packed with information:

"Anyway," Benjy says, picking their conversation back up. "I told Georgia that we have to do movie night at her place this week because Ash wants to watch that *Labyrinth* movie your mom mentioned, and if my dad walks in and sees David Bowie's junk in white spandex, he is going to have some questions that I'm not interested in answering. So, we're—" He breaks off. "Um. Why is Rory Heron coming over here?"

What can we glean from these sentences? Let's see how much: Benjy is likely gay or bi, but he's not yet out to his father; this group of friends is tight knit and has regular routines; and Chloe's mom is respected enough for the group to actually want to watch a movie she suggested (a miracle!). Once again, McQuiston keeps the pace moving by pulling us back to the plot rather than having Chloe respond. Rory Heron is there to join Chloe in the next step of their plan, which is to confront Shara's boyfriend, Parker Smith (who Chloe later describes as "victim of a tragic first-name last-name, last-name first-name situation").

The last passage I want to show you is the awkward conversation between these three characters, each of them members of such different social groups that just being seen in conversation together threatens to "rip a hole in the Willowgrove space-time continuum." Smith is reluctant to talk at first, but Chloe persists. Once again, it's the white space between dialogue lines where the magic happens. I'm going to give you the passage first with just the dialogue lines so you can see what I mean:

Smith: "Look, I had a long weekend. Can y'all just—"
Rory: "I kissed Shara."
Smith: "What?"
Rory: "I mean, uh . . . she, uh—before she left, we, um—"
Chloe: "He kissed Shara. And so did I. I mean, she kissed me, if we're being specific. But I kissed her back."

Do you see how flat and ordinary that is, even though this is a dramatic revelation? Very little of the emotions at play come through—perhaps only Rory's nervousness emerges in his hedging and pausing. Now take a look at the original:

"Look, I had a long weekend," Smith says, turning to her. This time, she can see heaviness around his eyes. She wonders how he spent his Sunday—probably cow tipping with the boys or something. "Can y'all just—"

> Rory blurts out, "I kissed Shara."
> Smith freezes. Rory freezes. Untipped cows on the edge of town freeze.
> When Smith speaks again, his voice is low. "What?"
> "I mean, uh," Rory says. It's almost funny, the way all his class-cutting, shoe-gazing edginess shrinks into nothing. Boys are so embarrassing. "She, uh—before she left, we, um—"
> "He kissed Shara. And so did I," Chloe says, stepping up like the Spartacus of people who have kissed Smith Parker's girlfriend. "I mean, she kissed me, if we're being specific. But I kissed her back."

Chloe's point of view dominates the passage, absorbing the white space even between dialogue lines that aren't her own. In the midst of Smith's first line we get a strong dose of Chloe's scorn not just for him but also for this whole town. Even though she notices the "heaviness around his eyes," she doesn't attribute it to the fact that his girlfriend is missing, but rather to some imagined late-night high jinks. Likewise, poor Rory's nervousness is an opportunity for Chloe to malign his entire gender before depicting herself as the hero.

I Kissed Shara Wheeler showcases the versatility and power of dialogue as a narrative tool, demonstrating how it can simultaneously reveal character, advance plot, deepen themes—and make us laugh. McQuiston's novels should be studied closely by any writer who wants to find new uses for dialogue in their own work.

TAKEAWAYS

- Use a snippet of recalled dialogue to liven up a backstory recollection.
- Consider using reported speech to give the sense of a community's reaction to an event. If it makes sense for your narration style, you can filter this speech through the point of view of your narrator.

- Use the white space around dialogue to reveal details about the character speaking. Bracketing those details between two dialogue lines keeps the pace lively.
- Use dialogue lines to sneakily hint at important facts about a character rather than revealing them directly.
- If you are using a limited, close narration style, you can allow your point-of-view character to take over the white space in another character's dialogue paragraph with their own thoughts and reactions.

CHAPTER 16
HOW DO YOU ADD VOICES TO A SINGLE-POV NOVEL?

In previous chapters on Casey McQuiston's *I Kissed Shara Wheeler*, I've looked at how the opening of the novel hooks readers and how McQuiston uses dialogue—especially the white spaces around dialogue—to reveal character. In this chapter, I'm going to focus on another white space McQuiston makes use of: the interstitial breaks between chapters, which they fill in with extraneous materials that illuminate corners of the fictional world that their single point-of-view character, Chloe Green, doesn't have access to.

All of these excerpts are given the heading "From the Burn Pile"—a title we don't learn the meaning of until the bonfire in the final chapter—and they are all quite short, most under a page. All of them are 'found' documents, the kind of detritus you would discover in a locker or backpack at the end of a school year: notes between characters, old homework assignments, scribbled exchanges on scripts, teacher evaluations, student council meeting minutes.

Our point-of-view character, Chloe Green, has an intense, dramatic personality, and we can hear her voice coming through on every page she narrates. Take, for example, this opening line to chapter five: "Chloe enters the choir room for lunch with a peanut butter sandwich in her lunch bag and murder in her heart." Or this showstopper of a speech she delivers at a high school party:

"One day, when Dixon's fifty and his second wife has left him because he's a balding middle school football coach with the personality of a frozen meatloaf, and his kids hate him because he's never expressed an emotion that's not impotent rage or horniness, he's gonna look back on senior year of high school and realize that being prom king was the only thing he ever achieved in his life, and that at his absolute peak, before everything went to shit, that girl from LA with the huge boobs still wouldn't have slept with him."

If you want to stand up and cheer, I think that's the effect McQuiston is going for.

But Chloe's strong voice threatens to drown out quieter characters. McQuiston uses the Burn Pile material to showcase some of those other characters, as well as to provide documentary-style clues about emerging subplots. The first Burn Pile document, a note from Chloe to her friend Georgia, keeps us in Chloe's POV but changes medium. The note—apparently sent during class because Chloe writes, "PLEASE DO NOT REACT you are calm you are a placid lake you are my moms after a pitcher of hemp tea"—delivers the news that we have already gleaned from the previous chapter: that Chloe was kissed by Shara Wheeler.

The next Burn Pile note also delivers a piece of information we already had—that Shara kissed Rory, her next door neighbor, in addition to Chloe—but this time from Rory's point of view, using a transcript of one of the tapes he uses to record his music. It's in first person and reveals his emotional reaction to the kiss: "It didn't exactly feel like the earth-shattering moment I always thought it would, mostly because I was just … confused." Without this Burn Pile material, we'd never know Rory's interior reaction to the kiss since he's established as the cool, aloof rebel, and it would be out of character for him to reveal this, especially to our point-of-view character Chloe, whom he doesn't yet trust.

A later Burn Pile document—this one an excerpt from a creative writing assignment to describe a person with one word, written by Chloe's friend Georgia—hints at a subplot that McQuiston will deploy at a dramatic moment late in the novel. Georgia writes, "There's a girl with brown eyes who reminds me of the first book I ever loved. When I look at her, I feel like there might be another universe in her." The excerpt, highlighted by Chloe's annotation, "Who is this about????," reveals that Georgia may have her own long-standing romantic obsession.

As the novel progresses, McQuiston moves farther away from the central characters in the Burn Pile documents. Showing passed notes between secondary characters and tertiary characters brings all of them to life, making the fictional world of Willowgrove Christian Academy feel layered and realistic. For example, the minutes of a student council meeting reveal the personalities and social standing of Brooklyn Bennett, the hyper-organized, micromanaging student council president, and April Butcher, a stoner friend of Rory's. The header tells us the minutes were "extracted from the back of Brooklyn's accordion folder (the pink one, not the green one)" and the minutes include these lines:

> ii. April Butcher (not a member) suggests adding more spicy items to the vending machines
>   iii. April Butcher is not recognized by the chair . . . .
>   i. April Butcher proposes *Teen Mom 2* as a prom theme
>   ii. April Butcher is again not recognized by the chair
>   iii. April Butcher is asked to leave the meeting by Secretary Bailey Hunt

It's funny, of course, but also sheds a light on the many tiny rebellions and power plays afoot at the school, which Chloe will succeed in tapping into in the triumphant conclusion of the novel.

Perhaps the most moving of these documents gives us a brief

glimpse inside the head of Mr. Truman, the longtime drama teacher at Willowgrove. Chloe, convinced he is gay, wonders why he teaches at a school that requires him to either forgo or hide any long-term romantic relationship. The discarded draft of a self-evaluation that ends up on the Burn Pile gives us a clue.

The piece starts off with his musing about the Kevin Bacon movie *Tremors*, in which the main character sees a hard hat full of brains twenty minutes into the movie. "In the real world," Mr. Truman writes, "if you happened to see somebody's brains by accident, it would mess you up. The whole movie would be about the fact that you saw somebody's brains." He notes that by middle age, it's easy to forget how your own seeing-the-brains moment felt, but when you are in high school "the brains are everything." He's concluded that God's plan for his life is for him to "keep some kids from seeing the brains. Or at least showing them something in the desert that isn't brains. A cool cactus, maybe. I don't know. Metaphors are hard. I'm not the literature teacher." This tiny glimpse into Mr. Truman's interior life allows us to imagine, then, just how meaningful it must be when Chloe, giving a graduation speech about specific moments that have shaped her sense of who she is, finds Mr. Truman in the crowd and directs this line at him: "The moment a teacher told us they believed in us." Without the seemingly extraneous Burn Pile document, the line would have much less emotional resonance.

As you are reading them, these Burn Pile documents can seem like throwaway bits of lighthearted fun, but when you sift through them and lay the contents up against the plot, themes, and narrative structure of the novel, you'll find that McQuiston has put more meaning into them than you can catch on a first read. It's a clever strategy easily adaptable to a wide range of stories.

TAKEAWAYS

- Incorporate pieces of 'primary evidence' (letters or other materials) from your story world to illuminate other POVs in a single-POV novel.

- Consider focusing interstitial material on minor characters in order to give glimpses into their internal thoughts or feelings, and to make your story world feel more rounded and realistic.
- Use interstitial material to foreshadow important plot elements or touch on the themes of your novel.
- If you try this technique, be sure to keep it limited and brief. Don't let yourself get carried away into writing books within books!

THE LAST THING HE TOLD ME, BY LAURA DAVE

STATS

I wanted to write a thriller rooted in hope. What I mean by that is I didn't want the smoking gun to be that the husband turns out to be evil, or that the main character was wrong to trust herself, or that the story would hinge on betrayal. . . . [A]s my main character (Hannah Hall) navigated the twists and turns of her dilemma, I wanted her to find her way to somewhere unexpected, somewhere better.
—Laura Dave[1]

Published in 2021 by Simon & Schuster
303 pages, approximately 75,750 words
The author's sixth published novel

GENRE

Thriller

AMAZON CATEGORIES

Family Life Fiction, Women's Domestic Life Fiction, Suspense Thrillers

AWARDS

#1 *New York Times* Bestseller, Reese Witherspoon Book Club Pick

CHAPTER 17
HOW DO YOU ENGAGE READERS WHO KNOW THE HOOK?

The first pages of all novels need to pull the reader in, but that goal is particularly pressing for a novel billed as a thriller or mystery. If, as a reader, you are looking for a book that is going to keep you turning pages, the first few chapters are a test of whether the author can create that forward momentum. In *The Last Thing He Told Me*, Laura Dave has an extra difficulty: The inciting incident is the disappearance of the protagonist's husband, so she must show us the texture of their relationship without bringing the character himself onto the page. Let's look at the opening to see how she pulls it off.

To start, Dave leans on the reader's prior knowledge of the disappearance of Owen Michaels. The book description reveals the hook, and it's hinted at in the title. Dave knows that we want to see the first dramatic moment the hook makes us envision: the moment Hannah learns that her husband is missing. How is the news delivered? How does she react? What does she already know or guess about what has happened to him?

But before we get to that scene in chapter one, Dave gives us a prologue—and this is a case where I think the book really does need one. (I discuss the pros and cons of prologues more broadly in Chapter

5.) In order for us to care about Owen's disappearance and get some sense of the relationship between him and Hannah, we need to get a glimpse of the two of them together *before* that inciting incident. Dave takes us back to the beginning of their relationship, telling the story of their second date, during which Hannah insisted on driving herself to meet him, then lost the parking ticket for her car.

It's a short prologue (which is a good choice) but accomplishes quite a bit. We learn that Hannah has a tendency to lose or forget things—a quality Owen teased her about, but which Hannah, our narrator, tells us she has left behind. As readers, we wonder, *Can we trust this narrator?* We learn that their connection was intense, immediate, even "overwhelming." Owen counters Hannah's statement during their second-date dinner that he barely knows her with the comment, "It doesn't feel that way, does it?" We learn that Owen may have more money than Hannah, based on his "fancy sports car" compared to her "rented Volvo."

And there is a slightly unsettling minor mystery in the anecdote. When he learns she has lost her parking stub and will have to pay $100, Owen smiles, "as if this were the best piece of news about me that he'd gotten all night." What are we to make of this reaction? Is it possible that Owen himself took the parking stub to put Hannah off balance, maybe even lead her to leave her car behind for the rest of the evening? The unease it generates is compounded by a dream Hannah has a week after his disappearance (reminding us again that we're going to see the dramatic ripple effects of that event very soon):

> He was wearing the same suit—the same charmed smile.
> In the dream he was taking off his wedding ring.
>   *Look, Hannah,* he said. *Now you've lost me too.*

Is someone to blame for Owen's disappearance? If so, do we think that blame belongs to Owen or to Hannah? Losing a marriage or a person is not the same as losing a parking stub—it takes more than a moment of inattention. The prologue, then, successfully adds to our questions about the inciting incident and gives us some subtle clues we can use to start making our own guesses about what has happened.

The prologue, in other words, welcomes us into the mystery and initiates us as sleuths.

Now let's go to the first chapter, where we move to present-tense narration. Here's the opening paragraph:

 You see it all the time on television. There's a knock at the front door. And, on the other side, someone is waiting to tell you the news that changes everything. On television, it's usually a police chaplain or a firefighter, maybe a uniformed officer from the armed forces. But when I open the door—when I learn that everything is about to change for me—the messenger isn't a cop or a federal investigator in starched pants. It's a twelve-year-old girl, in a soccer uniform. Shin guards and all.

Dave makes a couple savvy moves here. First, she continues to bring us, the readers, into the story: That *you* in the first sentence, watching the fateful knock-on-the-door scene on TV, that's us. She's also showing off a bit, making sure we notice that she's tweaking the trope. This novel, she's promising readers, is going to deliver exactly what you want to see but in ways that are going to surprise you.

Second, note that even though we've shifted into present-tense narration in this first chapter after the past-tense narration of the prologue, the framing of the scene is from the point-of-view of a narrator who already knows what this knock heralds. Dave knows this is the moment we want to see; by introducing the messenger, she buys herself time to build in some additional backstory, both about Hannah's marriage and about her relationship with her stepdaughter, Bailey. Before the girl at the door even hands over the note she's holding, we learn that Hannah and Owen have been married for a little over a year, that Hannah was thirty-eight when they married, and that she hasn't changed her name because she "didn't see a reason to become someone else." We also learn that Hannah and sixteen-year-old Bailey have a rocky relationship that got off to an awkward start and hasn't improved much since.

The girl hands Hannah the note but, if we've read the book description (and it's a rare reader who doesn't these days), we already know that it is from Owen and says only, "Protect her." Dave, again, uses that reader foreknowledge to her advantage, allowing the suspense to build while giving us more context (the family lives on a houseboat docked near Sausalito in San Francisco Bay; Hannah finds teen culture generally bewildering) and a few clues (Owen was in a hurry when he handed off the note; he told the girl his phone was broken).

At this point, Dave drops the advanced-knowledge framing and puts us firmly in the present-tense point of view of Hannah—the Hannah who hasn't yet read the note. She wonders perhaps if this is some kind of practical joke perpetrated by her "lovely and silly" husband. Here Dave uses dramatic irony—when the reader knows something the point-of-view character doesn't—to drag the suspense out as long as possible. Finally, eight pages into the novel, Hannah reads the note:

It occurs to me, in the quiet, how much I don't want to open it. I don't want to know what the note says. Part of me still wants to hold on to this one last moment—the moment where you still get to believe this is a joke, an error, a big nothing; the moment before you know for sure that something has started that you can no longer stop.
    I unfold the paper.
    Owen's note is short. One line, its own puzzle.
    Protect her.

And that's where the chapter ends. Dave continues the pattern in chapter two, coasting on the punchy drama of that chapter one ending to start with more backstory, telling us how Hannah and Owen met and what Hannah's pre-marriage life was like, before bringing us back to the present with a scene between Hannah and Bailey. Because Hannah is trying to pretend that nothing is wrong—calling Owen repeatedly, still hoping he'll pick up and provide an explanation—we get a good sense of the tricky relationship between stepmother and stepdaughter before it's put under additional pressure by Owen's disappearance. As Hannah puts it, "Bailey almost tries with me. That's the worst part. She isn't a bad kid or a menace. She's a good kid in a situation she hates. I just happen to be that situation." Hannah doesn't ignore the note—she assesses whether Bailey will be safe enough if she gets a ride to her play practice with her friend Suz—but she hasn't fully integrated its meaning either: Owen is gone and Bailey is in need of protection. By the third chapter, Hannah can no longer avoid this knowledge as the action shifts into high gear. We'll cover that in our next chapter, studying the timing and pace of these revelations—asking, in other words, what makes this novel a page-turner.

TAKEAWAYS

- If your reader already knows the hook of your novel, use that foreknowledge to create dramatic irony and build anticipation, while delivering important backstory information.
- Use familiar, well-loved tropes that are common in your genre but find ways to tweak them, especially if you open the novel with one.
- If you include a prologue in a thriller, mystery, or suspense novel, use it to generate new questions in the reader's mind, beyond those already created in the book description.

CHAPTER 18
HOW DO YOU DELIVER PLOT SURPRISES?

In the last chapter, I looked at how Laura Dave sets up reader expectations and then delays fulfilling them to pull us into *The Last Thing He Told Me*. By chapter three, however, she has to start delivering on the promise of the premise, showing us the aftermath of Owen Michaels's disappearance and the mysterious note he left for his wife, Hannah, telling her only to protect her stepdaughter, Bailey.

How does Dave keep us turning the pages? How does she balance filling in the backstory that will make her characters come alive and give them an arc that will deepen the narrative, while also delivering revelatory punches that answer some questions even while they raise more?

In this chapter, I'll step a little further into the novel to show you exactly how she does it. We're only going to go as far as chapter four, just thirty-five pages into the novel, so I'm not going to reveal too much of the plot—you can read on without fear of major spoilers! (Don't worry—I'll get to them in the next chapter.)

The first chapter showed us Hannah receiving the note, and chapter two is largely backstory, filling us in about Hannah's relationships with both Owen and Bailey. Dave wisely moves away from backstory in chapter three, delivering two new dramatic developments. First,

NOVEL STUDY

Hannah hears in a radio news report that the CEO of the company Owen works for has been arrested in an FBI raid. Second, Bailey emerges from her high school drama practice carrying a bag of cash and another enigmatic note from Owen.

It's a short scene, just over four pages, and Dave spaces out these two revelations. The first, the radio broadcast, is bracketed by a bit of interiority from Hannah. Before the news, she is pondering possible explanations for Owen's disappearance—all of which must be discarded after she hears the report. Afterward, she struggles to make sense of what she's heard, and we become sleuths alongside her as she sifts through what she knows: The company, called The Shop, was building software to help privatize online life; Owen had taken a salary cut to work there; he believed in his work and thought it would make a positive difference in the world. Hannah asks herself, "How could there be fraud in that?" Remember the concept of open and closed story questions we've talked about? What Dave is doing here is pointing a big flashing arrow to a new story question so readers don't miss it. In addition to wondering, more broadly, why Owen disappeared and what's going to happen to Hannah and Bailey, we also now wonder if he was involved in this alleged fraud.

The question is still hanging in the air when Bailey gets into the car, kicking off the next revelation. The actual content could have been delivered in just a paragraph: The bag is stuffed full of cash, and the note instructs Bailey to "Help Hannah. Do what she tells you" and counsels her, "You know what matters about me. And you know what matters about yourself. Please hold on to it."

But Dave draws on a number of writerly tools to slow the scene down in order to maximize the drama of the moment. Her most important tool, once again, is interiority. She's writing in deep first-person point of view. Writers are often urged to cut out filter words (as I discussed in Chapters 7 and 12)—terms like "see," "notice," "heard," "felt"—when writing in close, limited POV. Readers already know that it is the POV character experiencing whatever external details are being noticed, so you can just cut the narrator from the sentence.

What Dave does at the beginning of the bag of money sequence, however, is to lean on filter words in order to draw attention to the act of Hannah noticing:

> "Bailey?" I say.
> "I don't know," she says. "I don't know what's going on..."
> This is when I notice it. The bag she has with her isn't her messenger bag. It is a duffel bag. It's a large black duffel bag, which she cradles in her lap, gently, like it's a baby.
> "What is that?" I say.
> "Take a look," she says.
> The way she says it makes me not want to look.

Notice the impact of "This is when I notice it"? And then the sentence of interiority at the end serves to bring us into Hannah's emotion, while also delaying the moment of actually opening the bag and seeing the cash. Here, Dave speeds up again and eliminates filter words: "I pull back the zipper just a bit and money starts spilling out. Rolls and rolls of money, hundreds of hundred-dollar bills tied together with string. Heavy, limitless." After that first complete sentence, Dave eliminates a subject and verb in the next two. She's renaming the money that is spilling out of the bag in these sentences, focusing our attention tightly on the "heavy" rolls that seem, to Hannah, "limitless."

Dave adds drama to the follow-up punch, the note, by tracking Hannah's rising emotions as reflected in her physical state. After the money spills out, her heart is "starting to race." After she reads the note, the words "start to blur." Hannah pictures what must have happened, Owen running through the hallway of the high school to put the bag and note in Bailey's locker, then deliver Hannah's note to the girl who brings it to her. At this point, Dave tells us, Hannah's "chest starts heating up, making it harder to breathe." Readers might be readier than Hannah to see the appearance of the bag of money as an answer to the question of whether Owen had been involved in fraud, but Hannah's body seems to have made the connection even if her conscious mind has not. Dave then makes use of the backstory details she set up in the previous chapter: Hannah recognizes this feeling because it's what she felt when she realized her mother wasn't coming back and when her grandfather died. "How do I explain the feeling?" Hannah asks herself, then answers: "Like my insides need to get out. One way or another." At which point she vomits everywhere—interiority followed by action.

The next two scenes operate a bit differently, though in both of them Dave holds the revelations until the very end. Let's look at how they work.

In the second scene of chapter three, Hannah and Bailey are parked at the dock near their houseboat, trying to make sense of what they've learned. We get a couple more details about Bailey—she has a joint, which Hannah suspects she got from Bobby, her boyfriend, whom Owen doesn't trust—and they make a tentative plan about what they'll do next. All of this is handled fairly expeditiously. But for the last pulse of action in the scene, Dave slows down again before ending with a punch.

They've gotten out of the car but haven't yet gone into their houseboat when another car pulls up, "headlights blinking at us, bright and demanding." Notice how Dave personifies the car to add to the drama? What does the person driving this car want from them? Here Dave gives us several lines of interiority from Hannah as she thinks through who might be in the car: Owen? The police? Hannah is sure by the end of the paragraph that it is the police, then reveals: "But I'm wrong on that count too." Dave draws out the suspense of who is in the car for as long as possible, then surprises us by introducing a new character: It is Hannah's best friend, Jules, who steps out of the car. Even Bailey loves Jules, and the three characters share a group hug. "This is who Jules is to everyone who is lucky enough to know her," Hannah tells us. "Comforting, steady." Dave has surprised us, delivering comfort rather than the additional stress she led us to expect. But she has another swerve in store for us:

[O]f everything I'm guessing she'll say to me in that moment, the one thing I don't expect is what actually comes out of her mouth.

"It's all my fault," she says.

Dave ends the chapter on this small cliff-hanger. If we want to find out what Jules knows about Owen's disappearance—and how she is involved—we have to turn the page.

Chapter four does answer these questions, but Dave makes us wait for the answers, just as she made us wait to see Hannah's reaction to the first note in chapter one. Dave starts the chapter in scene: Hannah and Jules are sitting at a table, "drinking coffee spiked with bourbon." The first line of the chapter is dialogue from Jules: "I still can't believe this is happening." This is it—the conversation we are dying to see!

Not so fast, says Dave, who deploys a number of delaying strategies. First, we get backstory about the relationship between Hannah and Jules, who met at fourteen when they were both newcomers in their Tennessee hometown. Next, character description: Jules is a photo editor at the *San Francisco Chronicle*. A hint about how she might be involved in Owen's disappearance? But, Dave tells us, she focuses on sports—how could that be related to fraud at a software company?

After that, Dave leans on a subplot to delay the revelation and yet keep the scene moving. Hannah notices Bailey snuggling with Bobby on the couch in the living room. We learned in the previous scene that Owen didn't trust Bobby, which sets up her thought here: "I have no idea what harmless looks like," reminding us of how high the potential stakes are in the main plot. Bailey notices Hannah's gaze and slams the door angrily, reactivating the tension of their relationship that might have dissipated in the hug with Jules.

Only then does the conversation start up again, though Dave delays a bit longer by having them discuss Bailey and whether or not Hannah should have more whiskey. We're getting closer: Hannah recognizes that Jules is nervous, building the tension, though delaying a few more sentences to remember the time Jules had to tell her she'd seen her "quasi-boyfriend" kissing another girl. Finally, Hannah is forced to ask directly, once again using the very question the reader might be asking at this point: "So are you going to tell me, or what?"

Now we do get some fresh information. Jules explains that The Shop had been selling their privacy software before it was functional, but counting those future sales as profit in order to juice the stock price. Jules learned this from an investigative journalist at the *Chronicle* who got the scoop about the raid and couldn't resist boasting about it during the period he was required to sit on the story so the raid could be pulled off.

We see Hannah reacting to this news both internally and externally, trying to work out what it means. We also get a couple more clues to add to our store: Owen was the chief coder at The Shop and must have known the software wasn't ready for release. Avett, the CEO, had been quietly selling millions of dollars of his stock in the company, while Owen had kept and even increased his own shares. We also get a new story question to add to our list: Who tipped off the SEC, thus leading to the raid?

What we don't know yet is how any of this is Jules's fault. Dave saves this bit of drama for the end of the chapter, and she uses the answer to heighten the suspense around the story question introduced in the book description: Why has Owen disappeared and where has he gone?

Jules, we learn, called Owen to tip him off before the raid. She considers it her fault that he ran. But Jules also knows something else —Hannah can read it in her face: "I realize she isn't telling me whatever it is that is beneath that look. She isn't saying the worst of it." Here again, Dave slows down to intensify the drama. Jules demurs at first and must be pressed before she finally says, "He wasn't surprised when I told him about the raid."

Hannah doesn't process at first what this means:

> I stare at her, waiting for the rest, as something starts shifting in my head. I look through the glass at Bailey. She is lying against Bobby's chest, her hand on his stomach, her eyes closed.
>
> *Protect her.*

See how Dave is deploying filter words here to deliberately slow down the scene? She tells us the wheels are spinning in Hannah's head, but she's also showing it in her aimless gaze, which just happens to land on Bailey. Note too the emotional thrust of the remembered phrase "Protect her," from Owen's note. Dave has quoted this line four times already before this moment; it's a steady drumbeat reminding readers of the stakes.

The chapter ends, once more, on a revelation as Jules explains how she knows Owen was aware of the fraud:

> "He would have needed a lot more information about what was going on at The Shop. He'd have said something like, *Slow down, Jules. Who do they think is guilty? Does it look like Avett spearheaded the fraud alone or is the corruption more widespread? What does it look like happened, how much has been stolen?* But he didn't want to know more. Not about any of it."
>
> "What did he want to know?" I say.
>
> "How long he had to get out," she says.

Both Hannah and the reader are left asking, *Can we trust this man?* We've already become invested in what happens to Hannah and Bailey. Part of us wants, like Hannah, for there to be an easy explanation for Owen's disappearance—one that allows us to still like him as a person. With this last revelation, Dave forces us—right alongside Hannah, whom it will impact most—to confront the possibility that Hannah has married someone who would commit fraud and then run away, leaving his wife and child to pick up the pieces.

In the next chapter, we'll see how Dave keeps us guessing about Owen until the very end of the novel.

TAKEAWAYS

- Provide enough backstory for readers to care about your characters and understand how their arcs might develop,

but make sure there is also something happening in the "front story" of the scene, like an action or decision or goal.
- Be deliberate about where you place surprises or new information within a scene. Placing the surprise at the end is a guaranteed method to keep readers turning pages, but vary the rhythm—don't end every scene with a cliff-hanger.
- If you've ended a previous chapter on a cliff-hanger, you don't have to resolve it at the beginning of the next chapter as long as you start the scene in a place that makes readers believe they'll get to the revelation soon.
- Use techniques like interiority, filtering, and physical reaction to build suspense and maximize the drama of a climactic moment.
- Structure sentences to control the pacing of revelations, using longer, more complex sentences to build tension before delivering key information in short, punchy sentences.

CHAPTER 19
HOW DO YOU PLOT A PAGE-TURNER?

SPOILER WARNING

n this final chapter on Laura Dave's *The Last Thing He Told Me*, I'm going to step back and examine the overall architecture of the novel to find out how Dave handles plotting and pacing to produce a bona fide page-turner.

As I discussed in Chapter 10, most novels do not match up exactly with any of the popular story structure outlines—and this is true of *The Last Thing He Told Me* as well. Dave discusses her process in the author interview included at the end of the novel:

> For each of my novels, *The Last Thing He Told Me* included, I don't write with an outline or any involved

beat sheet. This means that writing for me is a process of rewriting. I utilize the first draft to find the characters and plumb the questions I want them to grapple with. The next draft is where I begin to solidify theme and motivations. It's usually somewhere around draft eighteen—I wish that were an exaggeration—that I find my way to the ending.

Having examined the novel closely, I'm not surprised it took Dave eighteen drafts to find her ending because it feels so completely earned. When the pieces settle into place in the final chapters, the resolution seems inevitable—we know this is where the characters have been pointing all along.

How does Dave pull it off? Part of the magic is in her plot: She offers up plenty of active puzzles for readers to try to solve alongside her protagonist. But a big piece of the magic is in her use of backstory, which she strategically stitches into the story in small, subtle patches and then bigger, showier pieces.

One classic story structure Dave does follow is to organize the plot in three acts, clearly signaled by her part breaks. Using a three-act structure allows a storyteller to provide cathartic stopping places for the story arcs. A part break signals to readers that one part of the story has concluded or resolved, and that it's going to continue in a different way on the other side of that brief pause of the blank page. Dave uses three-act structure in exactly this way.

Figure 6, at the end of this chapter, shows the three parts of the novel. Each chapter is given an intensity ranking, with backstory chapters given a cross symbol. Compared to *The Searcher* (Figure 4), Dave's novel has a fast start—Hannah's husband disappears, leaving her only with a note telling her to protect her sixteen-year-old stepdaughter, Bailey, with whom she has a fragile relationship. Part one ends with Hannah deciding that she and Bailey need to travel to Austin, Texas, following a hunch that they will learn something important about Owen's past that will tell them where he might be now.

Even in part two, which has a slower build, Dave makes sure to deliver a high-intensity scene about a third of the way through. Part two begins with Hannah and Bailey on the airplane and then plunges them right into their quest, following Bailey's hazy childhood memories around the city. Dave steers them into seeming dead ends before they finally find the right track. Hannah and Bailey realize they are close to finding the truth when a man named Charlie Smith reacts violently to being shown a photo of Owen and addresses Bailey as "Kristin"—a name she later admits to Hannah she now remembers having been called. Hannah learns that Owen changed his and Bailey's identities after his wife was murdered. Owen believed his father-in-law's mob clients were responsible for the murder, so he turned over evidence that eventually landed his father-in-law and several of his clients in jail. At this point, before Hannah can even tell her what she's learned, Bailey disappears, ending part two on a cliff-hanger and forcing us to hurry over that blank page to find out what's going to happen next.

Part three, matching the classic principles of three-act structure, is all about finding resolution and restoring the story world to some kind of order; an intense climax is positioned in the middle of the act, followed by lower intensity scenes as we move toward resolution. At the beginning of part three, Hannah must make a crucial decision: Should she follow the advice of the US marshal, Grady Bradford, who has been advising Owen since his original identity change, and accept new identities for herself and Bailey, which could someday allow them to be reunited with Owen? Or does she fight to protect Bailey's still emerging self-identity, believing that's what Owen would want, and sacrifice any chance of seeing him again? It's a classic best-bad-choice scenario, and the stakes couldn't be higher.

Hannah ultimately chooses the second option, venturing into the heavily guarded estate of Owen's ex-father-in-law, Nicholas, to broker a deal that would allow her and Bailey to continue living their current lives, protected from mob retribution, in exchange for Bailey's grandfather having contact with her again. Nicholas is adamant, however, that there will be no forgiveness or amnesty for Owen—either from him or his mob associates. The work of the end of part three is to show us this was the right choice. In the final pages of the novel, Dave shows us that the story we were reading was about the relationship between Hannah and Bailey all along.

One more thing I want to call attention to is that Dave directs us to new story questions in each of these three parts:

- Part one: Why did Owen disappear? Where has he gone? Is he guilty? How will Hannah and Bailey react?
- Part two: What was Owen hiding about his past? Who or what was he running from?
- Part three: Will Hannah and Bailey be safe? Should they change their identities? Will they ever be reunited with Owen?

Notice how those questions shift? At the beginning of part one, we think Owen's disappearance is related to the fraud charges against the startup he works for. But the importance of that aspect of the plot recedes quickly, and by the time we get to part two the questions we are asking are all about Owen's (and Bailey's) distant past. Then in part three, the questions focus more on Hannah and Bailey and their future.

No matter what structure your novel follows, take some time to think about what questions you want to be uppermost in your readers' minds as they move through the story. Where and how do you want those questions to shift? You can look to *Last Thing* to see how Dave makes us ask those questions, but one key is interiority—readers will naturally mirror the questions that are most important to the protagonist at any given moment. If you can show us what your point-of-view character is asking, we'll know what we should be asking as well.

Let's look now at an area where Dave departs a bit from standard storytelling approaches. Every novel has its own specific problem to solve, which is precisely why a single beat sheet or story structure can't work for all novels. Dave's problem, as I touched on in Chapter 17, is that in order to maximize suspense, she must make readers suspicious of Owen; however, in order for her ending to feel satisfying, she must then convince readers of his integrity and his love for Hannah and Bailey. How can she achieve this in a novel whose hook and inciting incident is the character's disappearance?

Dave finds an answer in backstory, which she weaves in liberally throughout the novel. If you look again at Figure 6, you'll see that the backstory chapters occur at regular intervals, every few chapters. There are nine of these chapters, and they move steadily further back in time; the first one shows us the day before Owen's disappearance and the last one shows us the night Hannah and Owen met. They are all short chapters, so Dave doesn't keep us too long from the "front story," and they are often positioned right before or after a particularly intense scene. These choices are part of what makes the book a page-turner. Compare, for example, my discussion in Chapter 3 of the way Ann Patchett handles backstory and story chronology in *The Dutch House*, a novel that asks readers to linger in the present and take leisurely swims in the past rather than hurry forward.

The backstory chapters in *Last Thing* have different functions in different parts of the novel. The initial backstory chapters do two things: First, they show us the closeness of the relationship between Hannah and Owen, making us believe in their love and share Hannah's fundamental trust in Owen. Second, they provide little clues for readers to gather up and use to speculate about what has happened to Owen. Because *Last Thing* only has one narrator, Dave can't easily make use of dramatic irony—when readers know something the protagonist does not—except in these backstory chapters. For example, in part two we see a scene eight months before Owen's disappearance in which someone recognizes him as a high school classmate—except that high school was in Texas, not in Massachusetts, where Owen claimed to have grown up. The reader waits for Hannah to remember this encounter and add it to her small store of clues.

Then, just before we find out Owen's true identity and start coming to terms with the fallout from what he's done, we get two backstory scenes that reaffirm that his relationship with Hannah was true and real. One is a tender scene at the end of their wedding dinner; the other is an intense conversation on the flight that marks Hannah's move from New York City to California to live with Owen and Bailey. We need the reassurance and emotional ballast of these two scenes to carry us through the tense final act.

In that final act, the backstory chapters shift again, to focus on Bailey and her relationships with both Owen and Hannah, mirroring the shift in the story questions in this part. The two backstory scenes show us that Hannah can be the parent Bailey is going to need her to be in Owen's absence, and they confirm Hannah's belief that she is making the choice Owen would have wanted for Bailey—even if it means he can't be part of her life. The last backstory scene takes us to the night Hannah and Owen met. When she asks him if there is one thing that defines him, he tells her this: There is nothing he wouldn't do for his daughter. Those words echo through the bittersweet resolution of the plot.

TAKEAWAYS

- Use beat sheets and story templates for inspiration or to diagnose plot problems or gaps, not as a set of rigid rules.
- Offer readers new story questions as your novel unfolds. If your story is organized in three acts, the primary story questions should change for each act.
- You can deliver the primary story questions to your reader by using interiority to show what your point-of-view character is asking.
- One way to use backstory is to give readers access to information the point-of-view character might not remember, creating dramatic irony.

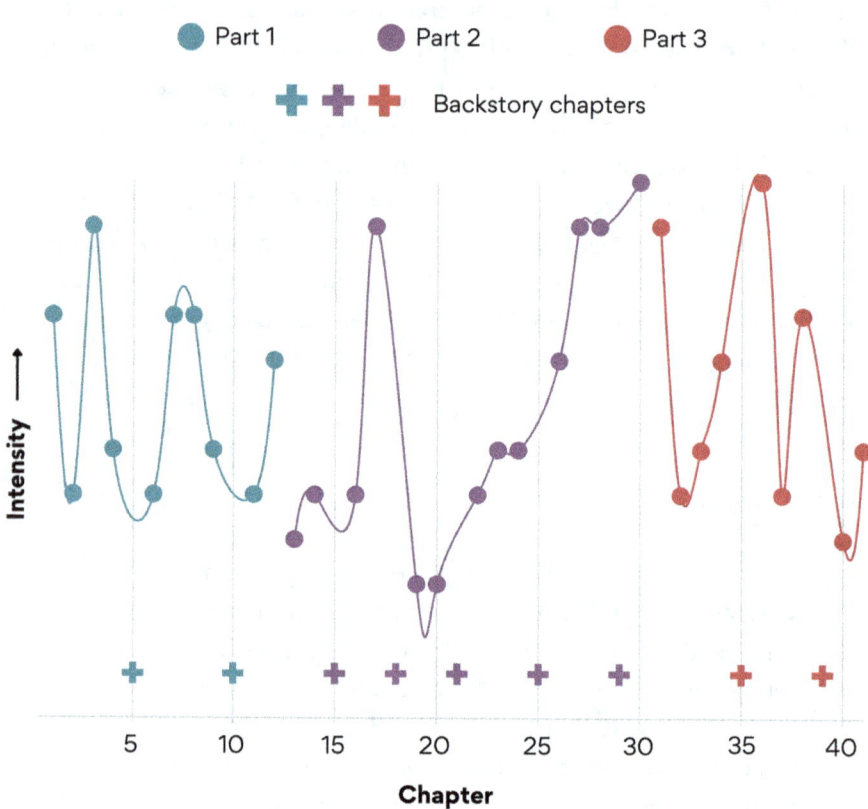

Figure 6. Plot structure of *The Last Thing He Told Me*. Frequent high-intensity scenes are undergirded by backstory chapters.

DIAL A FOR AUNTIES, BY JESSE Q. SUTANTO

STATS

I watch a lot of TV . . . and every time I watch something, my brain is toiling away in the background, going, "Ooh, does that inspire me in some way?" Same with books I'm reading. It can be a wonderful book or a mediocre one, and my brain would go, "Can I extract inspiration from it?" I'm never out of ideas. But it takes practice to train your brain to do this constantly, and I do mean constantly.
—Jesse Q. Sutanto[1]

Published in 2021 by Berkley (Penguin Random House)
295 pages, approximately 73,750 words
The author's second published novel

GENRE

Romantic Comedy

AMAZON CATEGORIES

Asian American Literature & Fiction, Humorous Fiction, Romantic Comedy

AWARDS

NPR Best Book of 2021 list

CHAPTER 20
HOW DO YOU INTRODUCE A COMPLEX PLOT?

Opening chapters are both hard to write and crucially important to a novel's success, which is one reason I'm looking closely at the first chapter of every novel I'm writing about. Novelists have to draw us into the story and get us hooked on the plot while also getting us up to speed on the characters and setting. In other words, we readers want things to start happening, but we also need to understand why they are happening and what's at stake in order for us to care. It's a tricky balancing act!

I picked Jesse Q. Sutanto's *Dial A for Aunties* in part because her ambitious double-barreled plot requires her to cover a lot of ground in her early chapters. By the end of chapter one alone, she's accomplished the following:

- Introduced us to our protagonist, Meddy, and established her core backstory conflict: She feels loyal to her mother and aunts (due, in part, to a family curse that means all the men in the family leave), but that loyalty has thwarted both her career ambitions and her romantic relationships.
- Established the supporting cast of Meddy's mother and three aunties and their complex sibling dynamics.

- Kicked off one plot: Meddy and the aunties are preparing for the biggest wedding they've ever handled in their family business; the tensions (and stakes) are high.
- Established a second plot: Meddy's mother has set her up on a blind date that is going to lead to the accidental murder that will become only one of many complications for the wedding job plot.

Sutanto manages all of this in the space of twenty pages—that's only about five thousand words! Let's see how she does it.

To start, she covers one key piece of the backstory—the family curse—in a prologue. I've discussed the pros and cons of prologues in depth in Chapter 5, but this is certainly a case where a prologue helps Sutanto accomplish her goals. Set eight years before the story begins, the prologue introduces the family curse, which goes back generations, and shows how it influences Meddy's choices—in this case, her decision to attend nearby UCLA rather than go to Columbia University, even though all of her male cousins have decamped for the East Coast as soon as they could.

The final beats of the prologue sum up Meddy's reality:[1]

> "You so lucky," Big Aunt says, for the millionth time, to Ma. "She stay with you forever. You always have companion."
>
> Is it true? Am I doomed to stay with them forever, just because I'm the only one not heartless enough to leave? I force a smile and nod benignly as they fuss about me, and I try to look forward to the rest of my life, living here in the same house with my mom and aunts.

We readers know, however, that this isn't the story of the rest of her life—otherwise we wouldn't have a novel ahead of us. Our initial story question then is this one: How does Meddy break out of these limitations she's imposed on her life?

Chapter one opens in the present day with the entire family packed into a crowded dim sum restaurant in the San Gabriel Valley, in what is clearly a familiar ritual. The setting is a savvy choice on Sutanto's part because it provides a lot of rich sensory texture for her to explore, as well as opportunities for her to show this family's complex interpersonal dynamics and linguistic and cultural makeup.

For example, the process of ordering establishes that Meddy's Mandarin is less fluent than her aunts', who also speak to one another in Indonesian, another language Meddy isn't fully fluent in. And look at this passage:

> The table being round means all the dishes are equally within reach of everyone, but Chinese family meals aren't complete without everyone serving food to everyone else, because doing so shows love and respect, which means we all need to do it in the most attention-seeking way possible. What's the point of giving Big Aunt the biggest siu mai if nobody else notices?

Do you see just how much work this passage is doing? Sutanto teaches readers unfamiliar with dim sum restaurants or Chinese culture what the norms are, works in an evocative food detail (siu mai are delicious dumplings, usually filled with pork and shrimp), and establishes that Big Aunt has the most power in the family.

Similarly, as the first plot—the big wedding job—is discussed, each character naturally reveals which aspect they are in charge of and, at the same time, a great deal about their personality and relationships with Meddy and the rest of the family. For example, Fourth Aunt is in charge of the music. She gives her report and then Sutanto stitches in a bit of background:

> Fourth Aunt's face goes from icy glare to satisfied smirk. "Of course, the band and I have been practicing night and day. People keep coming by the studio to listen to me sing, you know." There are two versions of Fourth Aunt's life story. Version one has to do with her being a celebrated child prodigy with a voice that newspapers described as "angelic" and "a national treasure." She

was well on her way to stardom, but chose to leave it all behind when all her sisters decided to move to California. Version two has her as a so-so singer who cunningly convinced her entire family to uproot themselves and move to California so she could pursue her pipe dreams of breaking out in Hollywood. One version is Fourth Aunt's; the other is Ma's.

Again, triple duty: We learn Fourth Aunt's role in the upcoming wedding, we get one possibly unreliable version of the family's immigration story, and we see the sibling rivalry between Meddy's mother and aunt.

After we learn the basics about the wedding and Sutanto reminds us again of Meddy's underlying conflict (she "desperately wants out" of the family business but "pretends to love all of it"), she sets up the next plot, which introduces some immediate drama. Meddy learns that her mother has signed up for a dating app, pretending to be her, and has set up a date for her after chatting with someone for weeks.

Meddy's initial response is horror and indignation, but then Sutanto dips further into her internal thoughts to show why she eventually agrees to go through with the date:

> But the last time I went on a date was . . .
>
> Last summer? Last fall? Christ on a cracker. Has it really been that long? And don't even get me started on the last time I got laid. As my best friend Selena likes to remind me, "Girl, you need to get some before that thing closes up shop for good." I look down at my lap, at that "thing." Why can't Selena just say "vagina"? *You're not gonna close up shop for good, are you?*
>
> Okay, I have just started talking to my vagina. Maybe Ma's right. I desperately need to go out on a date. And so what if it's been set up in the weirdest, most awkward way ever?

This is a wonderful example of how to write internal monologue that is lively, engaging, and supremely entertaining. The quick reference to Meddy's friend Selena feels natural and also establishes a useful secondary character. In addition, we see Meddy's voice coming through: her use of the phrase "Christ on a cracker" and her willingness to use the term "vagina," unlike Selena, who sidestepped it.

By the end of the chapter, readers have a number of open story questions they want to see answered, which will pull them forward into the book:

- How disastrous is this blind date going to be? (Because we can already guess it *will* be a disaster.)
- Will the wedding be a success? Will the sibling rivalries or Meddy's lack of enthusiasm cause problems?
- Will Meddy ever gain the courage to live the life she wants rather than the one her family wants for her?

In Chapter 22, I'll show you how Sutanto answers—and deflects—these story questions as the novel unfolds, but first we're going to do a close examination of a single scene.

TAKEAWAYS

- If you need to introduce a large cast of characters, find a setting that allows you to gather them all in one place and show readers the group dynamics and tension.
- Reveal key details about characters naturally through dialogue and action.
- Activating two plots at the same time can help you maintain interest and pacing by giving readers two sets of story questions they are eager to have answered.

CHAPTER 21
HOW DO YOU MAKE A DIALOGUE-FOCUSED SCENE FEEL ACTIVE?

Back in Chapter 2, I listed the components of fictional scenes—action, summary, dialogue, character description, setting, interiority, and backstory—and analyzed a scene from Ann Patchett's *The Dutch House* to see how one author used the tools available to her. In the scene I analyzed, Patchett relies heavily on summary, character description, and interiority—largely tools of telling. These tools work well for a novel that is focused on uncovering a complex history of interpersonal relationships to understand how they are impacting the characters' present lives.

Let's now apply the same technique to a more action-oriented novel, Jesse Q. Sutanto's *Dial A for Aunties*, to see how an author might use the same set of tools in a different combination. You can read my analysis of the novel's opening in Chapter 20, but to recap, we've learned that Meddy is a wedding photographer, in business with her mother and aunts. On the eve of their biggest event ever, Meddy goes on a blind date with a man her mother has set her up with by impersonating her on a dating app. The early chapters have also established that Meddy loves her mother and aunts but also wishes for more independence from them, and that she had an intense college relationship with a man named Nathan—a relationship she has never really gotten over. Chapter seven shows us the aftermath of Meddy accidentally killing her date with a Taser after he tries to assault her (no spoiler here since this plot revelation is in the book description!).

As you can tell from Figure 1 (at the end of Chapter 2), chapter seven is dominated by dialogue (40 percent) and action (25 percent), with a healthy serving of interiority (22 percent), a couple summary bridges (6 percent), and a sprinkling of backstory (4 percent) and character description (3 percent). In contrast, the scene from Ann Patchett's *The Dutch House*, which I analyzed in Chapter 2, was dominated by interiority (at 31 percent), with dialogue making up only 22 percent of the scene, and action a meager 9 percent. Compared to Patchett's backward-looking, meditative scene, Sutanto's scene is firmly grounded in the present moment. This fits their respective subjects and is solidified by their narration choices. Both novels have first-person (I) narrators, but Patchett's uses past tense while Sutanto's uses present tense.

Let's look at some of the details of how the scene unfolds and see how Sutanto is using her palette to move the plot forward and bring us closer to the characters, especially her protagonist, Meddy. As the scene opens, Meddy is sitting in her garage, the body of her date in the trunk of her car, trying to understand how she got to this moment. Suddenly, her mother is there, and we get our first bit of dialogue:

> She frowns at me. "What is it, Meddy? What's wrong?"
> I wasn't planning on telling her anything. Of course I wasn't—the last person I want to tell is Ma. She wouldn't know what to do, or say, or—
> "Ma, I killed him."

This first exchange sets up the internal conflict that fuels the whole scene. Meddy wants to keep her mother (and aunts) at arm's length but can't stop herself from accepting their comfort and help—which they are all too ready to provide. There is intergenerational conflict here, doubled or tripled by the cultural gap between Meddy and her family.

Sutanto, however, plays the conflict for laughs throughout much of the scene, adding a deeper note only occasionally. For example, after surprising Meddy by announcing she's called her aunts, who are on their way over, Ma tells her to cut up some mangoes for them, despite Meddy's protests:

"Your aunties coming over, so late at night, coming to help us get rid of body, and we don't even offer them any food? How can? Oh, we have dragon fruit, good, good. Big Aunt's favorite. Wah, got pear too. Very good. Help me peel, don't be so rude to your aunties, you will bring shame."

"Oh, right, it's the lack of fruit that'll bring shame, not the dead body in the car."

But, as happens again and again throughout the book, Ma turns out to be right, and the ritual of preparing and sharing the fruit provides a moment of comfort and bonding before the group has to confront the reality of the dead body and decide what to do next. Sutanto uses the fruit business to get the aunts into the scene and continue establishing the basics of their family dynamics.

At this point, Sutanto needs a bit of summary, after Big Aunt prompts Meddy to tell them what happened:

I don't hesitate. There's just something about Big Aunt, a mix of firm authority and motherly warmth that nobody can say no to. I'm feeling so guilty about having them rush here in the middle of the night—to help me with a dead body, no less—that I try relaying the story in Indonesian. But not even one sentence in, Second Aunt tells me my atrocious Indonesian is giving her a headache and I should just stick to English. With some relief, I tell them about my date with Jake, about how he insisted on driving me home, and the things he said.

My aunts and mother cover their mouths with horror and shake their heads.

"How could you set Meddy up with such a douchebag?" Fourth Aunt snaps at Ma.

Sutanto doesn't waste the chance here to give us more insight into Meddy's emotional state and her complex feelings about her relatives as well as the cultural and linguistic misunderstandings that led to the dead body in the trunk. Because we are getting fresh details, these few sentences of summary mixed with interiority don't slow down the scene. Very quickly we are back to dialogue and the feeling of forward momentum.

In a laugh-out-loud-funny sequence, Meddy learns that her mother had been sexting with Jake, the date, without even realizing it:

> I slam the phone down and stare at Ma. Fourth Aunt is literally lying on the floor, laughing.
>
> "What? What is it?" Big Aunt says. "He sound like very nice boy, offer to cook eggplant for you."
>
> "Right?" Ma cries, gesturing wildly. "I read that and I think, wah, this boy is so lovely, so caring for my daughter, even ask her, is she thirsty?"
>
> I bury my face in my hands. "Nooo! Ma, those emojis—the water droplets and the eggplant—they're sexual innuendos!"

But the hilarity leads to a deeper message that this family, despite their many conflicts, are fiercely loyal. It's now Meddy's mother's turn to feel guilty as she wonders if her naiveté led to Jake's death—a question that is quickly answered by the rest of the group:

> I open my mouth to answer, but my aunts beat me to it, shouting, "NO!" in unison.
>
> "So what if you say you want eat eggplant?" Second Aunt says. "Maybe one day you want eat eggplant, but then another day you don't want, is okay you change mind."
>
> "Yes, he is very bad boy, very bad," Big Aunt says.

The overall emotional arc of the scene is from a Meddy who is alone and frightened in her car, unsure of her next move, to a Meddy who is affirmed, comforted, and supported by her family. When she resumes her story and alludes to Jake's intended sexual assault once more, her aunts erupt in curse words in various languages and her mother declares, "It is good thing he already dead, otherwise I kill him." It's funny and cathartic all at once. And we know that there must be more such scenes to come because they are only at the beginning of the problems they are going to have to solve together—among them, getting rid of a dead body.

TAKEAWAYS

- The components you use to build your scenes will vary according to the plot, themes, and genre of your book, and they will likely also vary by scene. There is no magic formula.
- While different scenes and books will use more or less of some components, variety is always beneficial. Break up long sections of dialogue with action, interiority, and descriptive details to vary the pace.
- Use tension between characters to add stakes to every conversation. Make dialogue do more than just convey information. You can use subtext and interiority to show gaps between what a character is saying and what they are thinking.
- In comedic scenes, contrast a character's internal thoughts with the external situation to heighten humor and reveal their true reactions.
- Share background details or needed context via summary bridges between sections of dialogue. Sprinkle information throughout the scene rather than delivering it in one long 'info dump.'

CHAPTER 22
HOW DO YOU USE SUBPLOTS TO ADD TENSION?

SPOILER WARNING

The final act of a romance novel is particularly tricky to plot since the author needs to stoke suspense by keeping the lovers apart without doing anything that will make readers question the relationship. Even well-crafted novels can falter when an author relies on a minor misunderstanding that reasonable people could resolve quickly. (For example, Sally Thorne's otherwise excellent romance *Hating Game* suffers from this problem, in my opinion.) I believe this narrative challenge is fueling the popularity of romance subgenres like romantic suspense, paranormal romance (or romantasy), and the rom-com, all of which rely on additional plot strands to keep the lovers apart, entertain readers, and increase the suspense that will provide extra energy for the inevitable happy ending.

Jesse Q. Sutanto's rom-com *Dial A for Aunties* has four distinct plot strands, all of them with their own fireworks:

- **The dead guy plot:** The protagonist, Meddy, accidentally kills her blind date (who had it coming) early in the novel and then must spend the rest of the novel figuring out what to do with the body.
- **The romance plot:** This is a second-chance romance; part one of the novel gives us the backstory between Meddy and her college boyfriend, Nathan.
- **The wedding plot:** Meddy is a photographer, working for a family wedding business that also includes her mother and aunts. They've been hired for an enormous wedding involving two wealthy Indo Chinese families—an event that could make or break their business. This wedding turns out to be a reliable source of chaos and plot shenanigans.
- **The family plot:** The relationship between Meddy's mother and her three sisters, Meddy's aunts, is loving but also full of sibling rivalries that stoke tension. In addition, Meddy must reconcile her desire to please her family with her desire to follow her own heart.

Note that two of these plots—the romance and family plots—are primarily internal, focused on character development, while the other two are primarily external, focused on action.

Let's take a close look at how Sutanto balances these four strands and plays them against one another to keep the energy and suspense of the novel at a high pitch all the way through. Figure 7, at the end of this chapter, shows the intensity of each plot strand across the three parts of the novel. Sutanto makes it feel effortless, but one glance at the tangled threads in Figure 7 will show you just how much work it takes to balance this many plots. (We'll see a similar balancing act, solved in a different way, in Chapter 31 on Mick Herron's *The Secret Hours*.)

The first thing to notice is that the romance strand, seemingly so central to a rom-com, is the slowest to start and often gets put on the back burner, without a mention. The novel has thirty-six chapters; fifteen of them, just over 40 percent, don't touch on the romance plot at all. Nathan doesn't even appear in the novel until chapter eleven, at the very end of part one—until that point, we've only met him in four low-intensity backstory chapters, which are set seven years previously, during Meddy's time at college. Sutanto can get away with this in part because of the romance trope she has chosen. With second-chance romance, we don't need to see the lovers spend a lot of time getting to know one another to feel sure that they are meant to be together.

Sutanto compensates for that relatively slow, backward-looking start to the romance plot by providing a lot of intensity in the dead-guy plot, right through the first part of the novel—look at its soaring plot arc in Figure 7 as the other threads are just getting into gear. In addition to seeing the death itself and the reactions of Meddy and her family, which I analyzed in detail in Chapter 21, we also see them take action, deciding that they will pack the body in a cooler, leave it in Big Aunt's bakery, and figure out what to do with it after the wedding. In chapter eleven, the last chapter of part one, they discover that the cooler has instead been delivered to the island wedding venue along with the rest of their supplies.

The beginning of part two has a much more intense start than the beginning of part one, now that Sutanto finally has all of her plot strands operating. From here on out, she is able to choose which strands carry the suspense and interest of the reader. There are, predictably, various mishaps getting the body into the wedding venue, and they aren't able to dispose of it right away. Through part two, whenever the dead guy plot is on ice (sometimes literally!), the wedding plot takes center stage as we meet a new cast of characters who deliver all of the drama a wedding can bring.

If you look at part three in Figure 7, you'll see that Sutanto turns up the intensity of all four strands in the climactic final chapters of the novel—although the romance strand is essentially put on pause for four chapters while she resolves the other plot lines. This is exactly the point where another novelist might stumble into an ill-advised plot twist to create a forced misunderstanding between her lovers. Sutanto doesn't need to manufacture a new problem or diversion because her various plot strands provide plenty and she plays them like a master.

Let's look at one sequence in detail to see how she does it. Sutanto is savvy about the way she uses the three-act structure, even giving playful titles to the three parts: "Girl Meets Boy," "Girl Finds Boy," "Girl Gets Boy." The part breaks are also places where she positions key events in the romance plot. Part one ends as Meddy realizes Nathan is one of the owners of the resort where the wedding is being held; part two ends with Meddy forcing herself to pretend to Nathan that the dead guy in her hotel room is a quick fling; and the epilogue is, of course, our happily ever after.

But a focus only on the three-act structure would cause us to miss the crucial pivot-point Sutanto has placed in chapter nineteen, right around the middle of the novel. After the revelations of chapters eleven to fourteen, Sutanto dials down the intensity for a few chapters. We've met the bride by now, the beautiful Jacqueline, and learned that the groom and groomsmen are all still drunk after the rehearsal dinner the night before—the first of what will be many problems for this ill-starred wedding.

However, Jacqueline's maid of honor, Maureen, comforts her and quickly whips the groom and groomsmen into shape. Meddy and her family have safely stashed the dead body in Meddy's hotel room and have a plan to get rid of it later, so that aspect of the plot seems to be waning in intensity too. Sutanto draws our attention to the inherent drama of the penjemputan ceremony, which requires the groom and groomsmen to pass tests set by the bridesmaids in order to see the bride, and then the tea ceremony, during which the bridal couple are showered with over-the-top gifts.

Everything seems back on track as Meddy returns to her room in chapter nineteen to confront a new but seemingly small problem: Someone keeps calling the dead guy's phone. Meddy works up the nerve to use his fingerprint to unlock the phone and that's when our two external plot strands intersect. It's the maid of honor, Maureen, who keeps calling, and we learn in the next chapter that she and the dead guy, whose name is Ah Guan, had planned to steal the pricey haul from the tea ceremony. When Maureen can't find Ah Guan to hand off the goods, she decides to frame Meddy—instantly ratcheting up the stakes for the whole family once again. Somehow (!) getting rid of a dead body isn't their most pressing problem any longer.

I won't reveal any more details of the plot, but I do want to call attention to the way Sutanto steadily increases the intensity of the family plot throughout the book until it is at a steady boil in part three. Unlike the romance plot, the family plot is rarely absent from the novel—there are only two chapters where it doesn't appear as an element. And while the romance plot delivers the required happy ending, it's the family plot that generates Meddy's character arc and enables the happy ending. Ultimately, Meddy must confront the problems in her relationships with her mother and aunts—and become a more active participant in her own life—in order to set the whole story world to rights.

TAKEAWAYS

- Adding a subplot or trope borrowed from a different genre can fix a manuscript that feels flat, boring, or slow-paced.
- Use subplots to showcase different aspects of your characters' personalities and provide opportunities for growth outside the main plot.
- Balance intense action subplots against slower-building relationship or internal subplots. Pair quieter scenes in one subplot with more intense scenes in another subplot.
- Build to the same intensity across interwoven subplots at climactic moments, like in the final chapters of the novel.
- Be strategic about using structural elements like part breaks or the midpoint for pivots, shifts, or reversals in one or more subplots.

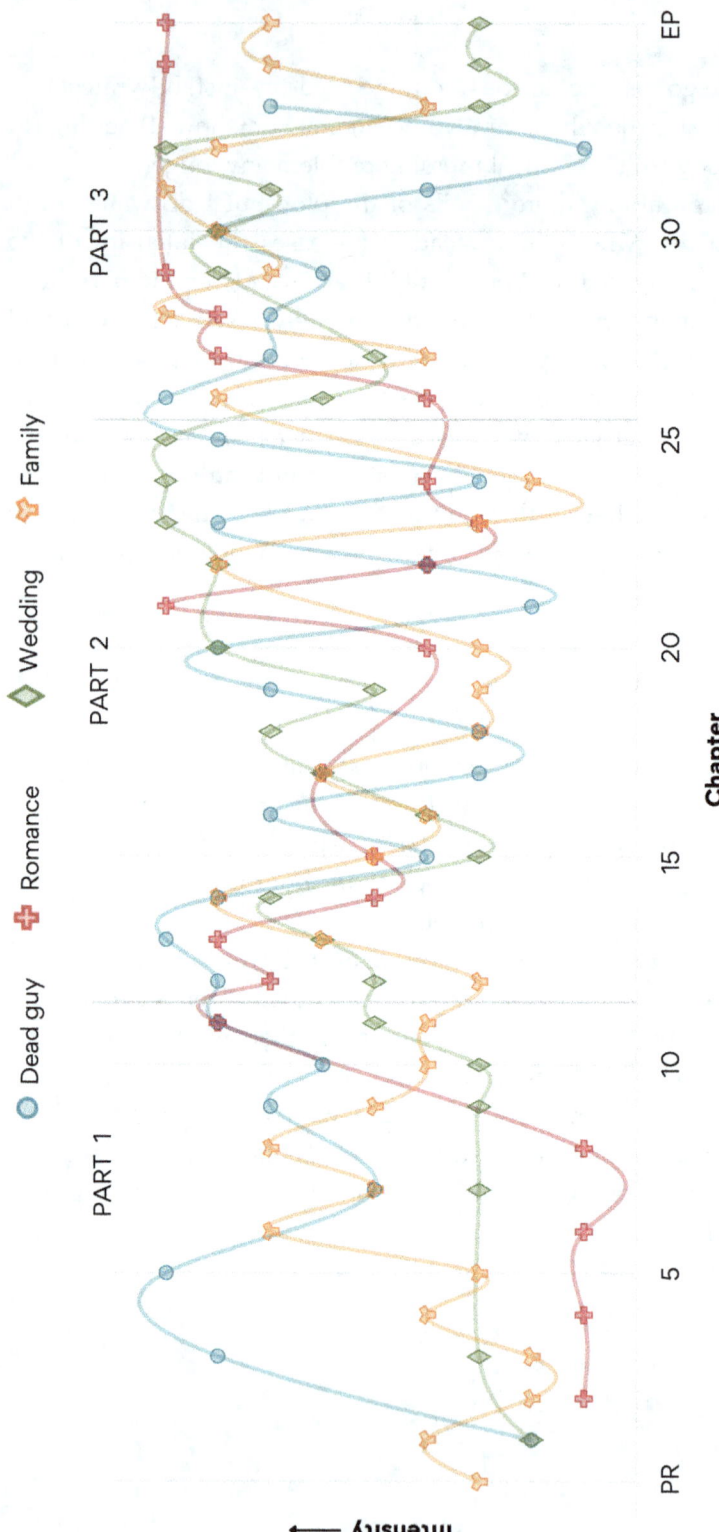

Figure 7: Subplots in *Dial A for Aunties*. Multiple subplots provide steady tension because they can ramp up and down at different times.

BLACK SUN,
BY REBECCA ROANHORSE

STATS

I . . . did a draft of 95,000 words, turned it into my editor and he thought I could do better. I took it back, broke it down to its bones and re-wrote the entire thing.
—Rebecca Roanhorse[1]

Published in 2020 by Saga Press (Simon & Schuster)
450 pages, approximately 112,500 words
The author's fifth published novel

GENRE

Epic Fantasy

AMAZON CATEGORIES

Native American Literature, Historical Fantasy, Epic Fantasy

AWARDS

Nominated for the Nebula and Hugo Awards, winner of the Alex Award

CHAPTER 23
HOW DO YOU LURE READERS INTO AN EPIC FANTASY WORLD?

The opening of a fantasy or science-fiction novel requires extra thought because, in addition to introducing the characters and kicking off the plot, writers must acclimate readers to a whole new world. In this chapter I'll do a careful analysis of the opening of Rebecca Roanhorse's *Black Sun* to show you exactly how she pulls us into her story world and makes us want to know more about how it works and what's at stake.

Our initial introduction to the setting comes in the form of two maps. The first shows us the land of Meridian, curving around the Crescent Sea, with labels for the Obregi Mountains and a number of what we can assume are cities.[1] The second is a close-up map of the City of Tova, one of the places named on the main map. The city is divided into a number of distinct regions, rather like New York City; each region is labeled with a name, and many of them are also associated with a specific clan.

The beginning of N. K. Jemisin's *The City We Became* also has an opening illustration (see my analysis in Chapter 4), but that book is urban fantasy, meaning that it is set in a real-world location, though one operating under unfamiliar rules. Jemisin's map hints at those differences and also gives clues about important details.

Similarly, Roanhorse's map provides both visual iconography and linguistic taxonomies that help set the tone. On the Meridian map we can see icons that look like pyramids, others that look like spears, and a sun marking the location of Tova. In the corner lurks a feathered serpent figure that may remind readers of depictions of the Aztec god Quetzalcoatl. The names on the City of Tova map provide clues about what is considered important in this world. Clans, for example, are named for birds, and in the center of the city is a small island labeled "Sun Rock."

If you include a map, you can't count on readers looking at it before beginning the novel, but you can rely on it to be a back-up tool for readers who want to check a place name or reorient themselves to the broad landscape of the novel at some point during their reading. Do you need to include a map if you are writing fantasy or sci-fi? If the scope or landscape of your novel is fairly self-contained—for example, if it takes place only in a single city—then you likely don't need one. However, if your novel world has an epic scope or a lot of place names, readers will appreciate having a map. Fortunately there are online tools that make creating such a map relatively easy and inexpensive.[2]

Following the map and the title page (which also features a bird), we get a list of "The People of the Meridian." Like the map, this list will be skipped by some readers, but they may come back to it later to remind themselves of which characters are grouped together or belong to a specific place. Just a brief skim, however, gives us a sense of the kinds of people and relationships the novel will include. We see familiar labels like "priest," "merchant," "healer," "servant," "tutor," "sailor." Note how this collection of terms implies an historical rather than a futurist fantasy world. (Consider, for example, the assumptions you would make about this set of labels: "entrepreneur," "doctor," "waiter," "teacher," "astronaut.") The list also reinforces the importance of birds and the sun, with some characters identified as sun priests and others identified as giant crows or as members of clans associated with birds.

Next, we encounter a passage from *The Florentine Codex* addressed to "you," which has the effect of drawing us into the novel. Here are the first and last lines:

You are the substitute, the surrogate of Tloque Nahuaque, the lord of the near and far . . . .

[You] are his wild beast, you are his eater of people, you are his judge.

This evocative passage sets our expectations for the stakes and themes of the novel: life and death, certainly, and possibly power and loyalty.

Do you see how much texture Roanhorse has provided even before we get to the first chapter? Again, the broader the scope of your novel and the less familiar your fantasy world, the more of these preliminary pieces you should consider including. Readers will draw intuitive assumptions from details they don't yet understand and also know where to go to get reoriented.

We're now at chapter one, but we have two more elements before we reach the opening sentence. First, we get a time stamp: "The Obregi Mountains, Year 315 of the Sun (10 Years before Convergence)." We're starting to narrow our focus now, from that big-picture Meridian map to one specific mountain range. The time stamp, again, tells us what is important in this story world. The sun is central, and there is a key event called "Convergence" that we now know is significant. By way of comparison, think about the way the BC (Before Christ) date label centers Christianity. (For a longer discussion of time stamps, see Chapter 14.)

To give you a sense of the work fantasy writers must do, consider how many assumptions we bring to a time stamp like "San Francisco, Summer of 1968." We know that San Francisco is a city in the United States, a wealthy and powerful nation that was, in 1968, fighting an unpopular war across the globe in Vietnam. The large number of readers who know about the "Summer of Love" in San Francisco know that we might see hippies, musicians, and protests pop up in the novel. Fantasy writers must fill in those associations from scratch, sentence by sentence. Roanhorse starts this work in the epigraph to the chapter, which comes after the time stamp:

 O Sun! You cast cruel shadow

> Black char for flesh, the tint of feathers
> Have you forsaken mercy?

The ominous tone and the plaintive question about mercy make us wonder about what calamities this year 315 has witnessed, and once again reinforces the centrality of the sun in this fantasy world. The sun is both the name of the epoch and the caster of "cruel shadow."

Before we get to the first sentence of the novel, I want to give one practical piece of advice about time stamps, having helped a number of writers fine-tune these for their novels. In most cases, you'll want to set a marker and then move forward in time because (unless time works differently in your world) you can rely on familiar units like days, weeks, and years. In that case, the initial marker can be almost anything or be left out altogether. You could include only a place name, for example, before the first chapter and then tag the second chapter "Five years later." If you do have big time jumps, especially if they go both backward and forward in time, using a key event as a marker, like Roanhorse does here with "Convergence," will help readers understand how different pieces of the plot fit together.

Now—at last!—the opening paragraph. Here it is in full:

> Today he would become a god. His mother had told him so.

These two short sentences ring out like a cathedral bell tolling a death. They may be grammatically simple, but they are narratively complex. Our first story question is a weighty one: What does it mean that he will become a god? Does one have to die in this story world to become a god? Does this "he," apparently our protagonist, know what becoming a god entails? The second sentence, citing his mother as the source of this knowledge (as well as the simple grammar) implies that he might not know—that he might be quite young. Notice as well how many time structures are contained in these two sentences: "Today" signals that we are in the present, but the verb "would become" is in the future. Will he indeed become a god today? The next sentence is focused on a past moment when his mother "had told" him of this future prediction. Has she told him just a moment ago? Or has she been telling him of this prophecy throughout his childhood? Past, present, and future are all mixed together in this opening paragraph.

Let's move forward one more step to the next paragraph and a half:

"Drink this," she said, handing him a cup. The cup was long and thin and filled with a pale creamy liquid. When he sniffed it, he smelled the orange flowers that grew in looping tendrils outside his window, the ones with the honey centers. But he also smelled the earthy sweetness of the bell-shaped flowers she cultivated in her courtyard garden, the one he was never allowed to play in. And he knew there were things he could not smell in the drink, secret things, things that came from the bag his mother wore around her neck, that whitened the tips of her fingers and his own tongue.

"Drink it now, Serapio," she said, resting a hand briefly against his cheek. "It's better to drink it cold. And I've put more sweet in it this time, so you can keep it down better."

With that proffered cup, we are suddenly in a live scene, anchored in the "today" of the first sentence. And it's a scene that is familiar to us, that could take place in our world—a mother hands her son something to drink. Roanhorse focuses on sensory details in the next few sentences, continuing to ease us into this unfamiliar world via smell and sight memories we might identify with. Only at the end of the paragraph do we get another nibble of story: The mother cultivates "secret things" that she guards carefully and has put into the drink.

It's not until the third paragraph of the novel, in the dialogue line spoken by the mother, that we get our protagonist's name. This choice has a way, paradoxically, of deepening the reader's connection to the protagonist. Consider how the first line would read differently if Roanhorse had used his name in the first sentence: "Today Serapio would become a god." A name is an external identifier—a way that others think of us. Roanhorse is showing us Serapio thinking of himself and so "he" is the better choice. It's also part of the author's strategy of slowly, steadily parceling out new information.

The second part of the mother's dialogue line, about keeping the drink down, adds another note of menace to the scene. How strong, how dangerous must this drink be if the boy's body has rejected it in the past? A couple paragraphs later, however, the drink is the least of our concerns because the mother warns the boy he must finish every drop, "Else it won't be enough to numb the pain," and he obeys, while looking nervously at the cords, the bone needle, and the gut thread he knows she will use on him.

Only now, when we know that something painful is going to happen to the boy and that it is the mother who will inflict this pain, does Roanhorse slow the scene a bit to provide more details about the world. Serapio notices his mother's collar of crow feathers with dyed-red tips, and she tells him, "Your father thought he could forbid me to wear this . . . . But [he] doesn't understand that this is the way of my ancestors, and their ancestors before them. He cannot stop a Carrion Crow woman from dressing to honor the crow god, particularly on a day as sacred as today." She tells him that his father's people, the Obregi, "fear many things they do not understand." Serapio has only ever known the Obregi, he reflects, but his mother has told him she is preparing him to return to her people, the Carrion Crow clan in the city of Tova.

Do you see how Roanhorse makes this backstory and world-building context count? What could motivate a mother to hurt her son? The high stakes of the scene heighten our desire to find the answers, and it is the backstory and the story world that provide them. Without the motivation to find answers, the details about the Obregi and the Carrion Crow clans and their various beliefs would seem dry and boring. At this point we return to the live scene, to the mother using that cord and needle and thread as the sun is darkened by a shadow we recognize as an eclipse, but the mother, and now Serapio, believe to be the crow god eating the sun.

Even a reader flipping quickly through the preliminary materials would have subliminally noticed how important the sun is in this story world: the "black sun" of the title, the sun symbol on the map to mark

Tova, the sun priest in the character list, the epoch of the sun in the time stamp, and the apostrophized sun in the chapter epigraph. If the crow god eats the sun and thus "holds sway over the world," as his mother puts it, this must be an important moment indeed in the world of the story. Roanhorse dramatizes that importance—*shows* it—rather than tells it in this opening chapter.

TAKEAWAYS

- Use elements such as maps and character lists to orient your reader if your novel features a complex fantasy world and a large cast of characters.
- Use time stamps at the beginning of chapters to keep readers oriented if your novel jumps around in time.
- When introducing a new story world, begin with something that is familiar and weave in new details gradually.

CHAPTER 24
HOW DO YOU INTEGRATE WORLD-BUILDING INTO SCENES?

A crucial skill that fantasy and sci-fi writers must master is how to deliver setting details in a way that feels seamless and natural rather than like an info dump. In this chapter, I'm going to break down the second chapter of Rebecca Roanhorse's epic fantasy novel *Black Sun* to show you exactly how she does it. Note that all writers can use these tips for how to seamlessly deliver the setting details that will make their fictional worlds come to life.

As discussed in Chapter 23, the first chapter of the novel sets up a crucial piece of plot backstory but delivers only a few details about the story world. In chapter two, we jump forward in time ten years, and the true action of the novel starts. This is also the chapter where Roanhorse does the most intensive work to establish the rules and conventions of her story world.

In this chapter, I'm going to list every piece of information we glean about the world of the novel, almost as if I were writing an encyclopedia entry about the society she depicts, then I'll show you how she delivers each piece as part of a scene that keeps us wanting to read further.

NOVEL STUDY

1. The continent of Meridian is a crescent-shaped landmass curving around the Crescent Sea. Its three main cities are Hokaia, its military center; Tova, the religious center; and Cuecola, the commercial capital.
2. Cuecola is a walled city, with both narrow streets and wide avenues. Housing ranges from modest thatch-roofed homes to multistory stone mansions. Ceremonial and communal spaces include pyramids, tombs, market squares, and a royal ball court.
3. Cuecola is home to a class-based society stratified by both wealth and power. Ranks include slaves, servants, the poor, the common citizens, the merchant lords, the nobility, the House of Seven, and royalty. In principle, the same laws apply to all classes, but the upper classes use power and bribery to get their way.
4. Kuharan is a small farming community outside Cuecola, governed by the same laws and customs as the city but with more conservative leanings.
5. Cuecola has a tropical climate. Flora and fauna include papayas, palm, cactus (fermented for beer), corn, anise, chachalaca birds, and jaguars.
6. Cuecola is a conservative society, by twenty-first-century Western standards: Skirts are more socially acceptable than trousers for women, and homosexuality is a capital offense.
7. Meridian is a maritime society, with different cities and regions connected by ships sailing the Crescent Sea, though traffic comes to a standstill in the late fall and winter due to fierce storms. The journey by ship from Cuecola to Tova commonly takes thirty days. The captain of a fast ship can earn enough in twelve years to be able to retire.
8. This is a pre-industrial society: There is no mention of factories, electricity, guns, or engines. Clothing is sewn to order by hand.
9. Typical dress in Cuecola for common women includes a skirt and a huipil (a garment commonly worn in Mexico and Central America). Sashes are worn to mark rank or

occupation. Noblemen wear their hair long, tied back in a high bun, and it is common for them to wear a lot of jewelry. A loincloth and cape is a typical nobleman's dress.
10. Jaguars are important animals in Cuecola. The city's pyramids are decorated with jaguar-headed stele, and a nobleman can bear the title of "White Jaguar."
11. The Teek are a people from another land. Their eyes are bright blue, gray, or, in rare cases, a shifting kaleidoscope of jewel colors.
12. There is at least one form of magic in this world, a "Song" wielded by the Teeks and used to control others as well as some aspects of the natural world. Non-Teeks are afraid of their magic.
13. Body parts are commonly sold or stolen in Meridian. In particular, Teek bones are considered good luck charms and multi-colored Teek eyes are sometimes collected and worn as jewelry.
14. Tova is built atop a high cliff and is away from the Crescent Sea, though it is linked to the sea by the river Tovasheh. It is the home of the Sun Priest and the Watchers, who keep the calendar.

A lot of information, right? There are some interesting details here, but it's all pretty dry. What's missing is a reason for us to care, and that's what Roanhorse provides in her story. Let's walk through the chapter in order now, and I'll show you how Roanhorse weaves in all of the details above.

We start with a zoomed-out view of the city of Cuecola and its surrounding villages. It's dawn, and fruit sellers are walking "through the narrow streets and wide avenues alike, past the modest oval-shaped, thatch-roofed homes of the common citizens and up through the more lavish multistoried stone mansions of the merchant lords," calling out their wares. All of the details in item 2 are covered but are anchored in a specific place and time: dawn in Cuecola. We know we are about to be in a scene and, by the end of the paragraph, we meet our point-of-view character for this chapter, Xiala.

Once we do, the reader is focused on Xiala's predicament. She wakes to find herself in jail—and not for the first time. This time, however, it appears she has done something serious enough that she is in real trouble. After that first big chunk of information in the opening paragraph, the world-building details come in small snippets over the next few pages and emerge naturally from context.

For example, we get a sense for the climate and the flora and fauna (item 5) as Xiala wakes up and processes what she can hear ("the rustle of the wind through the palms and the familiar cries of chachalacas waking in their nests") and smell ("freshly pulped papaya" and the reek of "body odor and fermented cactus beer"). We learn about typical Cuecolan dress for women (items 6 and 9) by seeing what Xiala is wearing as she scans herself for something she can use to make noise to alert the guard to let her out.

A short dialogue exchange with the guard reveals a bit of the social order (item 3) as Xiala demands to be let out, saying she has a ship waiting for her, and the guard mocks her: "Oh, a ship? You a sailor, then? No, no, a captain? Wait, a merchant lord himself! One of the House of Seven." This progression in ranks makes it clear that the House of Seven is some kind of mark of power and prestige.

The next shift in the scene is when the tupile, the prison constable, shows up with a man dressed as a nobleman (item 9), his long hair in a "high bun" and jewelry on his neck, ears, and wrists. Note that Roanhorse is leaning on familiar structures and words, like "merchant lords." Aside from the proper nouns for characters and places, "House of Seven" and "tupile" are the only unfamiliar terms we've encountered thus far. Other terms, like "cantina" and "huipil," are drawn from Spanish and so will be familiar to some readers. They also do the double duty of telling us (along with details like the climate and the flora and fauna) what kind of culture this one is analogous to. We know more than we realize and can make reasonable assumptions about how this society might work.

The interplay between the tupile, the nobleman, and Xiala confirms what we already suspect. The tupile asserts that this is a culture in which everyone—aristocrat or slave—must obey the laws (item 3). But

Xiala knows that he is swayed by the power of Lord Balam, the nobleman, who adds a bribe to his persuasion.

Roanhorse pulls us through the scene with story questions: Why is Xiala imprisoned? And then why does Lord Balam intervene to have her released? The conversation between the two characters as they walk back to the center of Cuecola after her release provide the answers, and those answers reveal more about the world. Xiala got drunk after some kind of confrontation with a merchant lord who double-crossed her. A beautiful woman in the cantina took her home to Kuharan, the small town where she was imprisoned, but their sexual encounter is interrupted by the arrival of the woman's husband, who has Xiala arrested after she punches him (items 4 and 6).

Xiala at first wonders if this nobleman—who introduces himself as "Lord Balam of the House of Seven, Merchant Lord of Cuecola, Patron of the Crescent Sea, White Jaguar by Birthright" (item 10)—is after one of her bones (item 13) or eyes, which have the rare Teek coloration (item 11). She's prepared to use her Song magic in self-defense if she has to (item 12).

It turns out, however, he has a quest he wants her to undertake. He offers to make her captain of a ship for a term of twelve years, paying her a salary and percentage of trading profits, if she will transport an Obregi man to the city of Tova in twenty days or less. On the one hand, Xiala reflects that this deal would allow her to retire at the end of the term. On the other hand, it is a long journey, typically requiring thirty days, and the Crescent Sea is stormy at this time of year (items 7, 14, and 1). Roanhorse relies on readers' excitement at recognizing a familiar fantasy trope and the suspense around whether or not Xiala will say yes to give her the space to also illuminate us about the geography and other details of this world.

TAKEAWAYS

- Spend time building out the principles and details and structures of your story setting, then look for opportunities in each scene to reveal those details.

- Give readers information as they need it to form opinions about a choice facing the character or to make sense of what is happening in that moment rather than giving them information they don't need to know until much later in the novel.
- Balance new information and concepts with familiar activities and relationships that operate similarly in your fantasy world and our world.
- If you can't find the right moment for a specific detail, ask yourself whether it's something readers need to know. Perhaps it's just something that you as the writer needed to know in order to write the scene.

CHAPTER 25
HOW DO YOU USE TIME JUMPS TO CREATE SUSPENSE?

SPOILER WARNING

As we've discussed in previous chapters on Rebecca Roanhorse's *Black Sun*, opening a fantasy novel poses extra challenges because authors must introduce readers to the story world alongside the characters and their stakes. Roanhorse raises the bar even higher by using four different point-of-view characters to tell her story, which means that she must also teach us about the conflicts, goals, motivations, and stakes for each one. How does she build all of that groundwork for the story while delivering enough action to keep readers interested?

One solution comes from the way she handles time in the novel.

Figure 8, at the end of the chapter, shows the chronology of the novel and identifies which chapters are narrated by which point-of-view character. *Black Sun* is a long, complex novel, so I'm not going to walk you through the details of the plot. But a top-level view will reveal some familiar tropes and plot strategies that will allow you to understand Roanhorse's artistic choices and apply them to your own work—no matter what genre you write in.

As you can see from a quick glance at Figure 8, most of the action occurs over a twenty-day period leading up to the day of Convergence, with our point-of-view characters trading off narration duties in a somewhat regular cadence. However, Roanhorse's strategic departures from this pattern are the key to understanding how the novel works. We're going to look at four aspects of the chronology of *Black Sun*: the opening, Serapio's backstory chapters, the introduction of Okoa's POV strand, and the ending.

Let's start, of course, with the opening. As Figure 8 shows, the first three chapters take us to three distinct points in time:

- Chapter one, POV Serapio, 10 years before Convergence: Serapio's mother blinds him, whispers his secret name in his ear, then commits suicide during the solar eclipse.
- Chapter two, POV Xiala, 20 days before Convergence: Xiala begins a journey to bring Serapio to the city of Tova before Convergence.
- Chapter three, POV Naranpa, day of Convergence: Naranpa, Sun Priest in the city of Tova, is pulled from the river; she is conscious but believed to be dead.

In the space of these three chapters, Roanhorse gives us a balanced tripod of present (Xiala beginning her journey), past (Serapio's blinding), and future (whatever calamity befalls Naranpa). All readers are familiar with journey narratives, so we can immediately use that storyline to ground ourselves. Roanhorse uses time stamps (as discussed in more detail in Chapter 23) to orient us in time; we know that Convergence must be the climax of the story, and we know from the beginning of each of these three chapters where we are in relationship to it. The time stamps also activate another story intuition, telling us that Serapio's past must have something to do with Naranpa's future; Xiala's journey then represents the steady narrative line sailing across the chapters to connect these two moments in time on the day of Convergence. This clever opening helps us understand the structure of the complex plot and stokes suspense for what is to come.

Now let's look at how Serapio's backstory chapters operate and why Roanhorse positions them where she does. While Xiala and Serapio both have eleven POV chapters, almost half of Serapio's chapters pull us backward into the past. There is a particularly long stretch in the middle of the novel, from chapters eighteen to twenty-nine, where we lose touch with Serapio's present-day POV altogether. However, Xiala has four POV chapters in that section, so we see Serapio from the outside, if not the inside, and we know he is steadily moving toward the end point of his journey. We learn in the final chapters of the novel that our initial intuition is correct. Serapio's appearance at Convergence is the event that irrevocably changes this story world, moving us from one epoch to another. We can't fully understand why and how he achieves this shattering change without seeing him come to comprehend it himself over time—and that's the purpose of the backstory chapters. We need to see him learning about the power he ultimately unleashes, and we need to have some empathy for the reasons he chooses to unleash it.

It's quite likely that Roanhorse wrote those backstory chapters sequentially, and they may have even been grouped together originally as part one in an earlier draft of the novel. Keeping those chapters together and allowing the story to unfold in chronological order would still achieve the goal of showing readers how and why Serapio fulfills his destiny on the day of Convergence. However, starting the novel with this set of chapters would have dampened the suspense of the opening. The four additional backstory chapters skip forward years at a time, showing us Serapio being taught by a series of tutors and learning, from them and from himself, the extent of his powers, his family history, and his future. It's a classic coming-of-age narrative and by that last backstory chapter, set five months before Convergence, we know the end of Serapio's story: Whatever force he is destined to unleash on the day of Convergence will consume him too. Instead of grouping these backstory chapters together and giving us a coming-of-age narrative *followed by* a journey narrative, Roanhorse mixes them by manipulating the order in which the reader encounters these story threads. She places the last backstory chapter, in which Serapio (and the reader) fully understands his destiny, in the last third of the novel, a hundred pages from the end, where it can become part of the suspenseful climax rather than the end of one narrative strand that saps suspense from the next.

Naranpa, the Sun Priest, is Serapio's inverse. While Serapio's chapters often pull readers backward in time, Naranpa's chapters usually shove us further forward. When we see the past through her eyes, as we do in chapter three, it's in the form of embedded memories rather than standalone backstory or flashback. Roanhorse never lets us get too far away from Naranpa's present-day stakes, which are always quite high. In chapters nine, ten, and fourteen, we see her encountering a number of challenges: a thwarted attempt to assassinate her, the unexpected death of the powerful matron of the Carrion Crow clan, and attacks on her power by the priestly Watchers, a group she, as Sun Priest, supposedly wields power over. Naranpa has the least understanding and agency of the POV characters; in fact, she is so often wrong in her assessment of other people that her bad guesses sometimes serve as red herrings, which heightens the suspense for readers. At the same time, her motives are generally admirable, which makes us hope that one of these times she'll be right or be able to achieve her vision for the city of Tova.

We aren't introduced to our fourth POV character—Okoa, the son of the dead matron of the Carrion Crow clan—until chapter fifteen. Roanhorse uses Okoa's POV to show us just how wrong Naranpa has been. For example, the matron did not die in her sleep, as was reported to Naranpa, but was found in the river, a presumed suicide—though Okoa has his doubts about that assumption as well. I suspect that Roanhorse wrote more chapters for Okoa, likely showing us more of his storyline reaching further back in time, that were cut for this final version. Those chapters might have given us more context, but they wouldn't have led to any plot fireworks. Instead, Roanhorse waits to introduce this POV character until the moment he can also travel to Tova and start influencing the unfolding plot. Whatever backstory we need to understand his motivations is, like with Naranpa and Xiala's story strands, given in brief passages of memory and flashback.

When we finally reach the long-awaited day of Convergence in the final chapters of the novel, Roanhorse moves carefully between points of view as the day unfolds in order to maximize the drama and suspense. Let me give you a high-level tour, just as I did for the opening of the novel:

- Chapter thirty-six, POV Naranpa, day of Convergence: As usual, Naranpa is the first character to show us the climactic day of Convergence. This chapter finally connects to her seeming death in chapter two, showing us how she ended up in the river.
- Chapter thirty-seven, POV Serapio, night before Convergence: Here Roanhorse moves *backward* in time once again with Serapio to show us Serapio positioning himself on Sun Rock, where we know the Convergence ceremony is due to be held. This chapter is positioned here to stoke reader suspense.
- Chapter thirty-eight, POV Okoa, day of Convergence: Again, Okoa is the character who sees the entire plot landscape clearly and explains it to the reader.
- Chapter thirty-nine, POV Serapio, soon after: This is the climax of the novel, in which we see Serapio's destiny come to final fruition.
- Chapter forty, POV Xiala, soon after: Xiala is an observer figure, showing readers the immediate aftermath of the climax from a different viewpoint.
- Chapter forty-one, POV Zataya, soon after: Roanhorse adds a new POV character for a single chapter, showing us another view of chapter two—Zataya is the witch who pulls Naranpa out of the river.

- Chapter forty-two, POV Okoa, soon after: Okoa continues his role as the narrative guide, in this case bringing the various strands of the plot to a resolution.

I want you to notice two things about Roanhorse's choices at the end of the novel. First, she presents the events in the order she wants *readers* to experience them, not in chronological order or in the order characters experience them. It can feel unnatural to mix chronology in this way, but as long as you use time stamps or other clear markers, your readers will willingly follow you backward and forward in time. Second, Roanhorse establishes early in her novel that each POV character has a specific role, making it easier for her to decide which character should reveal which slice of story. Serapio is the main protagonist, whose actions have the biggest plot consequences. Xiala is the well-placed observer, as well as an outsider whose motives sometimes run counter to those of other characters. Naranpa is a source of chaos and tension, as well as a focus for the reader's sympathy. Okoa is the explainer and resolver. Each of these narrative roles gets a turn to do their work as Roanhorse moves through their points of view in the final chapters.

The overarching lesson? It's your job as the writer to control how the reader experiences the story—and you have more latitude than you might think. As we saw in Chapter 6 on *The City We Became*, you don't have to distribute POV chapters fairly, like cookies to preschoolers. And, as we'll see again in Chapter 31 on Mick Herron's thriller *The Secret Hours*, you don't have to tell your story in chronological order. If you handle your materials with self-assurance, readers will follow where you guide them and won't even notice your behind-the-scenes machinations.

TAKEAWAYS

- Think about the reader's experience of your plot to help you determine the best order in which to narrate the events of your novel.

- Introduce new point-of-view characters only at the point where they are going to affect the events of the plot—not before.
- To maximize suspense, show the most dramatic events from the POV of the character who has the highest stakes in the outcome.
- As the climax nears, toggle between POVs more rapidly to build a multi-perspective crescendo. Be strategic about the order so each revelation builds on the previous one.

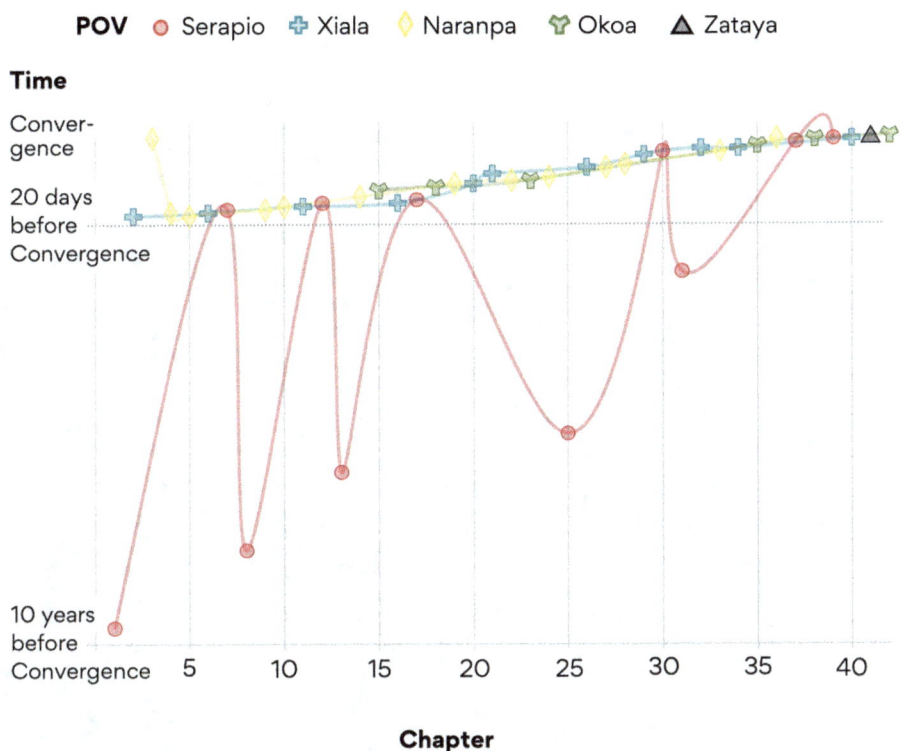

Figure 8: Chronology of *Black Sun*. The first three chapters build suspense by mixing chronology, while periodic backstory chapters explain motivations.

THE MARRIAGE PORTRAIT, BY MAGGIE O'FARRELL

STATS

I have a vague idea of where the story is going to go, but I do believe in the kind of sense of the unconscious or the instinctive. You're relying on your instincts for quite a lot, especially things like grammar or tense—I will often leave the story to find itself.
—Maggie O'Farrell[1]

Published in 2022 by Knopf (Penguin Random House)
333 pages, approximately 83,250 words
The author's ninth published novel

GENRE

Historical Fiction

AMAZON CATEGORIES

Renaissance Literary Criticism, Renaissance Historical Fiction, Literary Fiction

AWARDS

Finalist for Women's Prize for Fiction, Reese Witherspoon Book Club Pick

CHAPTER 26
WHAT CAN VERBS DO FOR YOU?

One of the challenges of writing historical fiction is that readers may already know the broad contours of your plot. Authors can sidestep that challenge by picking an obscure subject, as we saw Lauren Groff do in *Matrix*. Or they can embrace the challenge, making it part of the pleasure of the book—like watching Houdini escape from the box (or not!) while bound and blindfolded.

That's the option Maggie O'Farrell chooses in her novel *The Marriage Portrait*, which is about Lucrezia di Cosimo de' Medici. The transfixing portrait of Lucrezia, featured in the novel's cover design, not to mention her relationship to the notorious Medici family, has made her story fairly well-known, but O'Farrell makes sure all of her readers know it before the novel begins.

The historical note before the first chapter tells us:

> In 1560, fifteen-year-old Lucrezia di Cosimo de' Medici left Florence to begin her married life with Alfonso II d'Este, Duke of Ferrara.
>
> Less than a year later, she would be dead.
>
> The official cause of her death was given as "putrid

fever," but it was rumoured that she had been murdered by her husband.

We know, then, the end of Lucrezia's story: dead at sixteen. But notice that O'Farrell positions the information in the middle of the note, ending instead with a mystery: Did her husband murder her?

In chapter one, O'Farrell seems to sweep away that mystery as well, taking us almost immediately to the moment Lucrezia realizes her husband plans to kill her. Here's the opening paragraph:

> Lucrezia is taking her seat at the long dining table, which is polished to a watery gleam and spread with dishes, inverted cups, a woven circlet of fir. Her husband is sitting down, not in his customary place at the opposite end but next to her, close enough that she could rest her head on his shoulder, should she wish; he is unfolding his napkin and straightening a knife and moving the candle towards them both when it comes to her with a peculiar clarity, as if some coloured glass has been put in front of her eyes, or perhaps removed from them, that he intends to kill her.

Notice what O'Farrell is doing with her verb tenses in this passage. Not only is she writing in present tense, she's using progressive verb forms: "is taking," "is sitting down," "is unfolding." The progressive is used to show an ongoing action, one that is unfinished. O'Farrell puts the reader *inside* this moment with Lucrezia, with no gap between what she is experiencing and what we are seeing.

Here's how the passage would read if it were written in the simple past tense instead:

> Lucrezia took her seat at the long dining table, which was polished to a watery gleam and spread with dishes, inverted cups, a woven circlet of fir. Her husband sat down, not in his customary place at the opposite end but

next to her, close enough that she could rest her head on his shoulder, should she wish; he unfolded his napkin and straightened a knife and moved the candle towards them both when it came to her with a peculiar clarity, as if some coloured glass had been put in front of her eyes, or perhaps removed from them, that he intended to kill her.

See how we feel more distant from her in this version? In particular, notice how that specific moment of her realizing her husband plans to murder her stands out less. In the original, that's the moment the progressive verb form resolves into the simple present: "he **is unfolding** . . . he **is straightening** . . . he **intends** to kill her." Like many writing 'rules,' the advice to avoid gerunds, those -ing words, is counterproductive when taken to extremes. The progressive form exists for a reason, and you can see it at work here.

After the first paragraph, we get some flashes of backstory as Lucrezia thinks about their journey to this remote hunting lodge:

 But this is no hunting lodge, is what Lucrezia had wanted to say when they reached their destination: a high-walled edifice of dark stone, flanked on one side by dense forest and on the other by a twisting meander of the Po river. She would have liked to turn in her saddle and ask, why have you brought me here?

In this passage too O'Farrell marshals torturous verb tenses and moods to make us feel Lucrezia's constraints. She "had wanted to say"; she "would have liked to turn." She cannot, does not do either one. Not even the backstory is told in simple past tense.

If we know that Lucrezia dies not very long after this scene, and if we are now convinced, as she is, that her husband murders her, what mystery is left? Lucrezia herself takes us directly to that question at the end of the chapter: "How will he do it?" She imagines a few possibilities, sure that her husband would be capable of any of them. Here are the final words of the chapter:

She sets down her cup; she lifts her chin; she turns her eyes on to her husband, Alfonso, Duke of Ferrara, and wonders what will happen next.

After all of those complex verb forms, the verbs in this paragraph ring out with the clarity of church bells: "sets," "lifts," "turns."

That last clause, she "wonders what will happen next," is a clear challenge—and enticement—to the reader: Here is this self-possessed girl—still a girl at sixteen—calmly contemplating the man she is convinced will murder her and wondering what will happen next. O'Farrell has managed to move the suspense from the basics—will she live or die? who murders her?—to the specifics: How will it happen? And what will Lucrezia's experience be in the weeks, days, or perhaps mere moments before her murder?

Do you want to keep reading? I do.

TAKEAWAYS

- If your novel retells a familiar story, you can shift your reader's curiosity about *what* happens to questions about *how* and *why* it happens, and how your POV character or characters experienced the events, focusing on emotional truths rather than historical facts.
- Give us deep access to your POV characters' interior thoughts and emotions if writing about a familiar historical figure. Take advantage of dramatic irony; the reader might know more about what happens to a historical figure than a character yet knows in the world of the story.
- Your verb choices can help you control narrative distance. Use progressive verb forms ("-ing") to create an immersive, in-the-moment feel. Shift to simple present tense for key realizations to maximize their impact.

CHAPTER 27
HOW DO YOU CONTROL OMNISCIENT NARRATION?

As I discussed in Chapter 12, I'm seeing signs that omniscient narration may be coming back into vogue, and Maggie O'Farrell's novel *The Marriage Portrait* gives us another example to dig into. Omniscient point of view is when a narrator enters the mind of any character in a scene, as opposed to limited point of view, in which we have access to the internal experience of only one character at a time.

O'Farrell's flavor of omniscient narration is less experimental than Groff's, but it still feels fresher than the tactics used by nineteenth-century authors, who tended to keep us outside characters, even when describing feelings—like a museum docent explaining the themes of a piece of art.

I started my last chapter on omniscient narration with a contrasting example from George Eliot's *Middlemarch*. Eliot also wrote a book set, like *The Marriage Portrait*, in Renaissance Florence—the deservedly obscure *Romola* (1863). Here's the beginning of chapter five, in which we meet the title character:

> The Via de' Bardi, a street noted in the history of Florence, lies in Oltrarno, or that portion of the city

which clothes the southern bank of the river. . . . its left-hand buildings flanking the river and making on their northern side a length of quaint, irregularly-pierced façade, of which the waters give a softened loving reflection as the sun begins to decline towards the western heights. But quaint as these buildings are, some of them seem to the historical memory a too modern substitute for the famous houses of the Bardi family, destroyed by popular rage in the middle of the fourteenth century.

The implied narrator is a resident of the nineteenth century, not the fourteenth, just like the implied reader. Eliot is taking us to Via de' Bardi, in other words, and describing what is there in the 1860s before telling us what was there much earlier, a hundred years before the characters she is about to introduce. We then get a long paragraph describing the history of the Bardi family (author footnote included!) before, finally, the narrator takes us inside one specific house on Via de' Bardi, where we meet Bardo and his daughter Romola.

After some description of the room and the inhabitants, and a quick snippet of dialogue about a book, we get our first glimpse at thought and feeling in the following passage:

As Romola said this, a fine ear would have detected in her clear voice and distinct utterance, a faint suggestion of weariness struggling with habitual patience. But as she approached her father and saw his arms stretched out a little with nervous excitement to seize the volume, her hazel eyes filled with pity; she hastened to lay the book on his lap, and knelt down by him, looking up at him as if she believed that the love in her face must surely make its way through the dark obstruction that shut out everything else. At that moment the doubtful attractiveness of Romola's face, in which pride and passion seemed to be quivering in the balance with native refinement and intelligence, was transfigured to the most lovable womanliness by mingled pity and affection: it was evident that the deepest fount of feeling within her had not yet wrought its way to the less changeful features, and only found its outlet through her eyes.

Let's try not to combust with rage at the "lovable womanliness," angel-in-the-house ideology Eliot is engaging here and instead notice the way our narrator turns emotion into something that can be perceived by an external observer, but only one with a "fine ear" and a keen gaze. We aren't taken directly inside Romola's mind as she feels pity and love, pride and passion. Instead, our narrator is telling us about them. In a way, we are inside our narrator's mind as they perceive this young woman.

O'Farrell, by contrast, makes her own omniscient narrator so lightweight as to seem transparent. We seem to see directly into the minds of her characters ourselves, and I think that's one of the tricks to making omniscient narration feel fresh. Let's take a closer look at how she does it and also how she keeps the reader grounded, so we never feel disoriented when we shift from one character's point of view to another.

I discussed the opening of *The Marriage Portrait* in detail in Chapter 26. That chapter takes us quite deeply inside the point of view of Lucrezia, establishing her as the protagonist of the book. Chapter two moves backward in time, settling into the point of view of Lucrezia's mother, Eleonora, to tell us about Lucrezia's conception and early childhood. Lucrezia was a difficult baby and then a stubborn, disobedient child; at the end of the chapter, we see her at age fifteen, bursting into her mother's room and shouting that she will not wear the bridal dress that was originally made for her deceased older sister—the one whose place she's taking in the arranged marriage to the Duke of Ferrara. This outburst is summarized from Eleonora's point of view, and the chapter closes with this remarkable passage:

> Eleonora's mind, as she sets down her stylus, raises herself from her desk and walks through the archway towards her daughter, fixes once more on Lucrezia's

conception, the way her eyes had passed over the maps of ancient lands, had been focused on strange and wild seas, filled with dragons and monsters, beset by winds that might blow a ship far off course. What a mistake for her to make! How she has been haunted by it, punished for it!

At the other end of the room, Eleonora sees her daughter's angular, tear-streaked face open like a flower with hope and expectation. Here is my mother, Eleonora knows she is thinking. Perhaps she will save me, from the dress, from the marriage. Perhaps all will be well.

Notice how O'Farrell explicitly takes us inside Eleonora's mind as she contemplates the moment of her daughter's conception (which we saw dramatized earlier in the chapter). By the end of that paragraph we get a couple of sentences that sound almost like direct transcriptions of thoughts she is having as she crosses the room to her daughter. And then in the next paragraph, Eleonora effectively takes over the narrator role: She is the one seeing and interpreting her daughter's emotions and thoughts as they are written across her face. The role Eliot gave to her omniscient narrator in *Romola* is given to another character in *The Marriage Portrait*.

By the end of chapter two, O'Farrell has trained her readers to expect that they will see Lucrezia from both the inside and the outside, and that she will be dipping into the points of view of multiple characters. In chapter three, she establishes that she will sometimes change the point-of-view character in the middle of a scene. Let's see how she does it.

The chapter opens in a very traditional omniscient style—zoomed out, setting the scene before establishing the focal point for the narration:

A foreign dignitary arrived in Florence, presenting the Grand Duke with a painting of a tiger. Cosimo was very taken with the gift and it wasn't long before he expressed a desire to own one of these vicious, singular beasts. He kept a menagerie in the basement of his *palazzo*, for the diversion of visitors, and he felt that a tiger would be an excellent addition to his collection.

He gave an order to his *consigliere ducale*, Vitelli, that a tiger must be found, captured and brought to Florence. Vitelli, who had foreseen such an outcome ever since the painting arrived at court, heaved a deep and private sigh, duly making a note in his ledger. He hoped that the Grand Duke might be persuaded against the plan or even forget it.

This passage is not so different in technique from the one I quoted from *Romola*, but O'Farrell moves much faster than Eliot to establish her POV character, Vitelli, and takes us much more deeply inside his thoughts. Cosimo, of course, does not forget about the tiger, as Vitelli had hoped. We experience Vitelli's discomfort as Cosimo, swishing around the sword he is strapping on, expresses his disappointment that the basement pen prepared for the tiger is still empty and issues this veiled threat: "Such a pity that it lies empty. Something—or someone—will have to occupy it." Vitelli broods for a moment, then gets to work procuring a tiger.

Next come two paragraphs that take us away from Vitelli's point of view:

The Grand Duke's peculiar fancy for a tiger was communicated to an emissary, and then an ambassador, a sea captain, a silk merchant, an adviser to a sultan, a viceroy, a spice trader, an under-secretary in a maharajah's palace, the maharajah's cousin, the maharajah himself, his wife, his son, then back to the under-secretary, and on to a band of soldiers, then the villagers in a remote part of Bengal.

Captured, netted and tied to a pole, the tiger journeyed from its place of heat and rain and foliage. It spent weeks and months at sea, below deck, in a dank and salt-crusted hold, before being delivered to the dockside in

Livorno. From there, it was conveyed inland in a wooden cage lashed to a cart, pulled by six terrified mules.

Do you notice the way the passive voice—"was communicated"—moves us out of Vitelli's mind and creates a bridge for us to be, in the next paragraph, not inside the mind of the tiger but at least up close to its experience? (Like gerunds, passive voice is, at times, necessary or even preferable!)

O'Farrell then brings us back to Vitelli, who arranges for the convoy to wait to enter Florence until the dead of night to avoid causing a scene. Vitelli imagines a worst-case scenario worthy of the chronically anxious: "What if the animal became enraged and perhaps burst its bonds? It could run amok through the streets, devouring children and citizens. Better, Vitelli decided, to wait for the dim hours after midnight: no one would hear them; no one would ever find out."

And precisely here, O'Farrell changes the narrative focus to the young Lucrezia. No one would find out . . .

Except for little Lucrezia, tucked into a bed with both her sisters in a room under the eaves of the *palazzo* roof. Lucrezia of the solemn gaze and pale, wispy hair—incongruously so, for all her siblings had the sleek, fox-dark colouring of their Spanish mamma. Lucrezia, who was slight and small for her age . . . . Lucrezia, who always had trouble sleeping.

She, alone, heard the tigress's cry as the cart entered the *palazzo* gates: a low, hollow call, like wind funnelled through a pipe. It severed the night with its mournful pitch—once, twice—before dying away in a hoarse rumble.

Lucrezia sat up in bed, as abruptly as if she had been stuck with a needle. What was that noise, the unfamiliar cry that had reached down into her dream and shaken her awake? She turned her head one way, she turned it the other.

Notice that O'Farrell starts from the outside before working inward, getting us used to this new focus for the narrative point of view. We get some physical description of Lucrezia and details about where she is in the house. We're not inside Lucrezia's thoughts at this point: the description of the tiger's mournful cry is not written in the voice of a child. But note the tone shift in that last paragraph. The question has the effect of moving us inside Lucrezia's mind, as does the simpler, repeating language of the head turning. O'Farrell then keeps her narration focused through Lucrezia through the end of the scene, following her as she creeps down a hidden staircase to witness the hissing, caged tigress being pulled into the courtyard and then deeper into the palazzo.

Omniscient narration is full of pitfalls for writers and readers. If it is used poorly, readers will feel disoriented or disconnected from your characters, unable to deeply inhabit their thoughts and feelings or understand their motivations. But when used carefully, omniscient narration can unlock a whole new layer of access to characters whose inner voices we might not otherwise hear.

TAKEAWAYS

- Make omniscient narration feel fresh by focusing it through your characters rather than relying on a nineteenth-century style guide narrator who hovers above the action.
- Use distance to control your reader's experience if using omniscient narration—draw back and focus on external setting details or summary before moving deeply inside another character's mind.
- Similarly, use passive voice to create a moment of distance to separate POV characters in the same scene.

CHAPTER 28
HOW DO YOU MAKE A NOVEL FEEL HISTORICAL?

L et's get the simple answers out of the way first: A historical novel needs a historical setting, of course. When does "now" end and "history" begin? The general rule of thumb in the publishing industry seems to peg that moment at roughly fifty years before the present day. In practice the dividing line doesn't matter much. Emma Cline's 2016 novel *The Girls*, set in 1969, wasn't marketed as historical fiction, for example. If you are writing a novel set in the middle of the twentieth century and want to call it historical fiction, then go for it. If that label doesn't make sense to you, then don't use it.

Now, on to the more interesting questions: How do you make a novel feel historical? How do you achieve the magic trick of transporting the reader to a different time? Let's look at a chapter from Maggie O'Farrell's *The Marriage Portrait* to see how she achieves it.

To start, O'Farrell relies on her chapter title, "The Duchess Lucrezia on Her Wedding Day," and time stamp, "Palazzo, Florence, 1560," to deliver the basic facts about our setting. We're in Lucrezia's chamber, which is crowded with servants preparing her for the wedding. O'Farrell focuses first on a familiar detail, one modern readers recognize: the wedding bouquet.

Lilies stand tall in a vase on the mantel, their stems offering up blooms as if for scrutiny. The air moving in and out of her is heavy with their scent. When she'd woken, just after dawn, the buds had been closed but now the full complexity of their petals and stamens is open for all to see. The sweet, cloying smell of them fills her chest, leaves it, fills it again. A rust-red shadow of pollen encircles the base of the vase.

We could say a lot about the symbolism of these flowers—the way this almost cloistered girl of fifteen is being prepared for scrutiny now that she is deemed sexually mature, the rust-red pollen reminding us of the menstrual blood Lucrezia's nurse managed to hide for many months, thus delaying the wedding. But what I want you to notice in the passage is how deeply O'Farrell takes us inside Lucrezia's mind and body, lingering on the "sweet, cloying smell" she is breathing in and out.

This bodily connection continues as O'Farrell drops more details into the scene: "Someone else lifts Lucrezia's arm and places bracelets on it, pushes earrings through her lobes, fastens her betrothal ruby about her neck. Lucrezia is the only motionless being. She sits at the centre of this activity, a reed caught in the eddy of a stream." The jewelry provides us something to visualize but, like the flowers, this snippet of scene also conveys that Lucrezia is passive, trapped, without agency.

We've heard a lot about the wedding dress already: that Lucrezia's mother Eleonora had chosen the blue silk and gold brocade; that it was made for Lucrezia's dead sister, Maria, who was to have married the duke; that Lucrezia had initially refused to wear it, perhaps as a way of refusing the marriage, but that Eleonora had insisted on both dress and marriage.

Once again, O'Farrell brings those details to bear on Lucrezia's body, taking us inside her skin so we can experience the profound dissociation she feels in this dress:

The gown rustles and slides around her, speaking a glossolalia all of its own, the silk moving against the rougher nap of the underskirts, the bone supports of the bodice straining and squealing against their coverings, the cuffs scuffing and chafing the skin of her wrists, the stiffened collar hooking and nibbling at her nape, the hip supports creaking like the rigging of a ship. It is a symphony, an orchestra of fabrics, and Lucrezia would like to cover her ears, to stop them with her palms, but she cannot.

Lucrezia's comfort, her taste, her wishes are all completely irrelevant. O'Farrell needs us to see the cultural and historical framework symbolized by the wedding dress so we can understand this world and her protagonist. Lucrezia did not get to say yes to the dress (or to the groom, for that matter). She has been preparing for her wedding surrounded by servants, who are hurrying to follow orders, not by loving friends and relatives.

Returning to our scene, Lucrezia is led out into the piazza, where she is met by a huge wave of sound that momentarily staggers her—a crowd staring and shouting and calling her name. She is hoisted into a high, open carriage alongside her parents, which will take them to Santa Maria Novella, where she will be married. Let's look at one more passage to see how O'Farrell weaves in historical details.

 "Do you see," Eleonora says, "these people, Lucrezia? How they love us."

Lucrezia looks at her mother, who holds a handkerchief aloft; its lace edges flutter prettily in the warm air; Eleonora smiles out of the carriage. Cosimo sits with a straight spine, his head high; he doesn't smile but every now and again inclines his chin in a regal nod. Lucrezia sees a metallic glint at the neck of his *camicia* and realises that even today he is wearing chainmail beneath his clothes: she has heard he never leaves the *palazzo* without it, so sure is he that an attempt will be made on his life. She turns her head one way, then the other, fearing an assassin might burst from the crowd. But the faces of the Florentines lining the street are blurred by motion, daubs of paint dissolving in water.

"They do, Mamma," Lucrezia says.

This crowd scene makes for a grand visual—we can see these three figures perched aloft above the roaring crowd, their silks and jewels gleaming in the sunlight. But O'Farrell isn't satisfied with just that evocative setting detail. Instead she turns this set piece into a lesson: Cosimo's grip on power is, in fact, tenuous and Eleonora is modeling for Lucrezia how to smoothly deny the truth, showing nothing but a glossy surface for the world to see.

One last note on this passage: notice the two italicized Italian words? O'Farrell doesn't lean much on language to establish historical feel. She avoids anachronisms, but she doesn't attempt to capture sixteenth-century speech or lard her pages with Italian words or phrases. When she does use Italian words, they are simple nouns whose meanings can be deciphered from context. I assume that O'Farrell's choice to use italics for non-English words is a deliberate one, since many writers are now choosing not to, and I think it underscores that she is not relying on the feel of her language to pull readers into the setting.[1] She's doing that instead through her intense, deep point-of-view narration, our bodily identification with Lucrezia.

TAKEAWAYS

- Make sure that historical details are not just set dressing but rather connect to deeper thematic or metaphorical meanings that illuminate your characters.
- Use sensory and bodily details to immerse readers deeply in a historical character's perspective and constraints.
- Limit use of period language and non-English words to occasional touchstones decipherable from context.

THE SECRET HOURS,
BY MICK HERRON

STATS

[The Secret Hours] opens . . . with a lengthy chase sequence, which is a bit more frantic than my usual openings. I wanted to drag the reader along—make them feel they'd been hijacked, almost.
—Mick Herron[1]

Published in 2023 by Soho Crime (Soho Press)
365 pages, approximately 91,250 words
The author's sixteenth published novel

GENRE

Spy Thriller

AMAZON CATEGORIES

Conspiracy Thrillers, Espionage Thrillers, Political Thrillers

AWARDS

Shortlisted for the British Book Award and CWA Gold Dagger Award

CHAPTER 29
HOW DO YOU INTRODUCE MULTIPLE PLOT STRANDS?

Mick Herron's spy thriller *The Secret Hours* has a complicated plot structure, a large cast of characters, and a storyline that stretches across thirty years. I'll walk you through the chronology and plot structure in Chapter 31; in this chapter, I'll show you how Herron uses part divisions to help readers understand the structure of the novel and to introduce three different sets of interrelated characters and story questions.

Like most novels, *The Secret Hours* does not have a table of contents, so we don't see the part titles before we start the book—we encounter them, like everything else in the novel, exactly when Herron wants us to see them. The first words of the novel, in fact, are the first part division: "Part One: Devon, Soon." The innocuous "soon," which many readers, in a hurry to start the story, won't even notice, thrusts us into the future, dangling us over an empty abyss. If what we are about to see is "Soon," when is "now," exactly?

If readers wonder about this question, Herron distracts us from it with a showstopper opening, starting with an audacious first sentence: "The worst smell in the world is dead badger." We bought this novel expecting spies and instead we get dead badgers in Devon? The first sentence is in present tense, but it declares a universal truth, not pegged to a specific time—just like Jane Austen's famous opening to *Pride and Prejudice*: "It is a truth universally acknowledged, that a single man in possession of a good fortune, must be in want of a wife."

The second sentence doesn't seem to get us closer to the spies: "He'd encountered it on his morning walk down a green lane; had caught the odour without seeing the corpse, but had guessed what it was before returning later with a shovel." Notice we don't even have a name for this narrator yet (another reminder that you can parcel out details slowly), nor do we quite understand where we are in time. This second sentence is in past perfect—often called the past of the past—telling us only that our narrator is remembering something that happened before his present moment. He encountered the badger one morning; sometime "later" he tried to bury it. Finding he can't, Max (we get his name in the fifth sentence) decides to avoid the spot for a while in the hopes that someone else will deal with it. However, that expected future—in which a farmer or even nature could take care of the problem over the course of weeks—never arrives because in the last sentence of the paragraph, the spy narrative finally kicks into gear: "Which was why he wasn't sure the badger would still be there a couple of nights later, when he was running for his life."

Now we're alert! Why is he running for his life? And why is he wondering about something as trivial as a dead badger in this moment? It takes the whole book for the first question to be answered; we learn the answer to the second question later in the chapter. But before we can get back to the badger—literally and figuratively—Herron has to rewind the story again, to the moment when Max, "not so much struggling with insomnia as letting it do its worst," hears an intruder entering his kitchen window. His response tells us a lot about him: Rather than panic, he dresses quietly and tries to remember the location of his flight kit. This intrusion is an eventuality he has trained and prepared for, we understand via these small details and hints. We also learn more about the identity he's assumed for the past twenty years as he quietly slips down the stairs.

In the middle of a long paragraph packed with details, Max nonchalantly disables the intruder with a poker and climbs out a side window. Herron is deliberately restrained in his description of this action, in his language as well as in its placement:

> Whether Max would have jabbed her so hard at the base of the skull with the poker, then slammed her head on the floor when she fell had he known it was a woman beneath the break-in gear was something he could ponder at leisure, if he survived the night.

Notice the verb tenses here: "would have jabbed" and "had he known." This is the conditional tense, which has the effect of making the action seem hypothetical. The traditional tools to make this action punchier would be to use short paragraphs and strong verbs: "He jabbed her hard at the base of the skull…" Instead, the emphasis of the sentence is on that last clause: "if he survived the night." Herron is still building the suspense here.

The original intruder is joined by assistants and that's when Max starts his run, cutting across a dark field in the hope that will slow them down—a hope that dwindles when he realizes one of his pursuers is on a motorcycle. This moment, not the moment with the poker, is the one Herron has been writing toward. As soon as Max realizes the motorcycle is behind him, we get these two sentences: "Time grows elastic at moments of stress. Apparently science supported this proposition, though for Max it was lived experience: the ever-slowing thud of his feet hitting the ground, the speeding up of the racket behind him."

He makes a plan for his next move if he can just make it across the field. And then we get this showstopper of a passage:

> But all of that was in the future, which was arriving too slowly, unless you were riding a motorbike across a rough-toned field, spitting stony soil behind you. The light grew brighter, and Max tried to run faster, as if it were a near-death experience he was hoping to avoid. Sixty-three years old. It was true it was the oldest he'd ever been; at the same time, it wasn't like seventy. Eighty.

> But time would take care of that, if it ever got back to behaving itself, and the bright headlight was swallowing everything now, clutching Max in its beam: he could see his own shadow rising up before him like a giant. In a fairy tale, it would turn and smite his pursuers; pound them into the soil. The motorbike was all but upon him; he could feel its breath on his arse. Then the gate materialised out of nowhere: he gripped its top and hurled himself over, hitting the ground like a beanbag. He'd be feeling that tomorrow, if tomorrow ever came.

What I'm going to draw your attention to repeatedly throughout my analysis of this book is just how good Herron is at distinctive description. I'm sure I could easily find ten scenes of people being chased by a man on a motorcycle and none of them would sound like this one. What's the magic here? I see three things:

First, theme: As you'll see in later chapters, time is an important theme in *The Secret Hours* (oh, look there, a time reference in the title itself!), and Herron has a lot to say about the lived experience of time—the way some moments feel long and others short; the way some memories are buried and others stay with us; the many ways in which the past can reach out and change the direction of the future. Note that both the first sentence ("Time grows elastic at moments of stress") and the last ("if tomorrow ever came") are related to this theme. Writers often weave theme statements into quieter moments of a novel—into conversations, for example, or the sometimes hushed and portentous final lines of a chapter. But what Herron's showing you here is that you can also work them into the most suspenseful moments of a scene.

Second, interiority: Herron pays a lot of attention to the inner workings of his characters' minds and seems always to be asking himself, "What would be going through this character's mind in these specific circumstances?" What is Max thinking about, in this too-slow run across a field? He's thinking about his specific plan to make it to a three-way junction up ahead, but the suspense of that will be over in just another page. In contrast, his meditation on age and aging—his concession that he's no longer young, his consolation that he's not yet elderly, and his recognition that even escaping this situation does not mean he can outrun death forever—will continue to resonate throughout the novel. And, as a fifty-year-old, I can relate to this particular mix of feelings about age and aging, even though I've never been chased across a field by a motorcycle.

Third, figurative language: Another quality that makes Herron such a good writer is that he seems allergic to cliché. A first draft of this passage might have described the motorcycle "roaring"—a description that is now so familiar for motor vehicles that we no longer even recognize it as a metaphor. To make the metaphor fresh, Herron goes back to its roots. What roars? A lion. Without using the term roar, how else can he summon the metaphorical energy of a beast ready to pounce and devour? Herron redirects this energy to the motorcycle's headlight, which is "clutching" and "swallowing," and then to the motorbike itself, "its breath on his arse." (This specific flavor of figurative language is called personification—giving human qualities to an inanimate object.)

There's one more bit of figurative language that may also relate back to Herron's close attention to interiority: He's really thought about what Max can see as he runs across the dark field, pursued closely now by the motorcycle with its bright headlight, and that's his shadow stretching out in front of him "like a giant." Max imagines the giant attacking his pursuers, and the strong verb forms here—"smite" and "pound"—set up the fast rhythm of the climax, as he grips the gate and hurls himself over.

The lesson here is that when you are writing a suspenseful scene, you don't always need to go faster—to strip down the sentences, increase the paragraph breaks and white space, and speed up the action. Done correctly, going deeper—slowing down, paying attention to the point-of-view character's sensory experiences, psychology, emotions—can be just as effective at building tension and interest for readers.

After Max gets away, just twenty-five pages into the book, we come to part two, titled "Monochrome, Then & Now." We know Max has escaped, but we also know he's on the run, and we are curious about who he was in the past and why he's being hunted now. The lingering suspense of part one gives Herron the leeway to deliver a quieter opening to part two, in which he needs to accomplish a lot of set-up work for the overall plot of the novel. And, unlike the inherent interest of a man running for his life, part two focuses on the mundane world of bureaucrats and government agencies, with only political rivalries to provide spice.

Here's the first sentence of part two:

> As everyone in the know knew, and many on the fringes guessed, the establishment of the Monochrome inquiry —announced with less fanfare than the then PM's mini-break at Peppa Pig World—was intended to leave the Service rattled.

We are in the hands of an omniscient narrator here rather than a specific character, but it's an omniscient narrator with a distinctive voice. This narrator is a little world-weary (most certainly, one of those "in the know") and a realist if not a pessimist, a set of attitudes that find an outlet in sarcasm and humor. It's an Austenian voice, in other words. Remember the first line of *Pride and Prejudice* I quoted above? Here's the second:

> However little known the feelings or views of such a man may be on his first entering a neighbourhood, this truth is so well fixed in the minds of the surrounding families, that he is considered as the rightful property of some one or other of their daughters.

Both of these narrators are telling us what was intended or assumed, and then implying that these intentions or assumptions are going to be tested.

Also, like the Austen sentence I just quoted, Herron's sentence happens to be in passive voice, which you may not have even noticed due to the effectiveness of that savage little Peppa Pig barb: "the establishment of the Monochrome inquiry . . . *was intended* to leave the Service rattled" (my emphasis). Herron uses passive voice here to build suspense for the story questions he's just introduced. Who established the inquiry and why? We get the answer only at the end of this page-and-a-half long paragraph packed with details. The Monochrome inquiry is the prime minister's revenge against the Security Service for the political scandal that cost him his position as foreign secretary under the previous prime minister.

We then follow the news of the inquiry as it "circulates Westminster" and starts to generate reactions within the Service:

> This can't be serious, was the verdict from below decks.
> "The guv'nor will have him on toast," was an opinion generally held. "He's just emptied his kettle on a basket of rattlesnakes."

The reaction of that "guv'nor"—First Desk of the Service, whose point of view we enter but whose name we never get—is what the omniscient narrator is gradually leading us to. First we see her from the outside: "in First Desk's office, with its frostable glass wall overlooking the boys and girls on the hub, the reaction was curiously muted." Then from her current assistant, Erin Grey's, point of view: "she did not, in the view of the young woman who was her administrative assistant that season, seem unduly worried by the prospect."

After a few turns of dialogue between Erin and First Desk, we move to the point of view of First Desk, learning two pieces of consequential information: That a former First Desk was a Russian spy, and that this First Desk, despite her stated confidence that the Monochrome inquiry will go nowhere, has a "nagging awareness that, times without number, what started out an inconsequential piece of mischief could gather quiet momentum" and decides to prepare a contingency plan. "She was First Desk, after all. Contingency plans were what she did." Unspoken, but hovering between the lines, is the motivation that explains so many of First Desk's actions throughout the novel. Most of her contingency plans are to protect the public or those in power; this contingency plan is to protect the power of the security services.

The next chapter brings us forward two years, presumably to "now." In separate scenes, we are introduced to Griselda Fleet and Malcolm Kyle, two low-level government bureaucrats who have been tapped to conduct the Monochrome inquiry. Both Griselda and Malcolm are POV characters, and we are given a lot of access to their backstories and motivations; we understand that they, like Max, are going to be primary actors in whatever plot is still unfolding before us. Part two is not all set-up, however; Herron introduces two shots of story suspense. First, we see a short scene with a new POV character, codenamed Ratty, which reveals there is a mole on the Monochrome panel—a group that includes several politicians and the pompous Sir Winston as titular head, in addition to the bureaucrats Griselda and Malcolm. Second, at the end of part two, by which point the Monochrome inquiry has stretched on for almost two fruitless years, Malcolm discovers that a classified file has been snuck into his shopping cart at the grocery store one evening. After Malcolm and Griselda decide to photocopy the file, distribute it to the panel, and call a witness, we get these final lines, linking us up once again to the "soon" of part one:

 That was the night before the night the team came for Max Janáček, invading his Devon fastness.
The worst smell in the world is dead badger.

Part three of the novel, titled "London, Now," does indeed bring us back to Max's story thread. But part four, titled "Berlin, Then," marks the third opening of the novel. And this one could conceivably have been the spot Herron started the novel, because it takes us further back in time than we've gone yet, to 1994. In Chapter 31, I'll examine the structure and chronology of the novel in more detail so we can decode why Herron didn't start the book here, but right now let's examine it as one last opening:

All witness #137 knew, as she explained to herself afterwards, was the instruction she'd been given: IR3, –2, 10.15 A.M. Which, decoded, meant Interview Room Three, second floor down. The time was self-explanatory. And the agenda would be lifecraft, she assumed.

In contrast to the beginning of part two, in this opening we seem to be fully embedded in the point of view of a single character—the witness who has been called before the Monochrome panel to answer questions about the file that was slipped to Malcolm—but there are hints, even here in this first sentence, that the POV isn't quite as straightforward as it looks. For example, we don't know her name, only her classification as "witness #137." (Later in the scene, she tells the story of being handed her new "workname," Alison North, before being sent to the field office in Berlin.) The first sentence also hints at the multiple narrative layers at play. The phrase "explained to herself afterwards" suggests that memory is at work here. In other words, we aren't getting direct access to the woman about to be renamed 'Alison North' in 1994; we are getting access to a remembered version of this person, filtered by whoever she is in the "now" time of the inquiry. And who that person is remains a mystery until quite late in the novel.

As we learned in Chapter 25 on the chronology of *Black Sun*, your choice about how to open your novel should be based on the experience you want your reader to have, not on the chronology of your plot or your desire as a writer to showcase a favorite character or moment. Consider which moment will pull readers into the story and figure out a way to start there. *The Secret Hours* shows us that each new part break offers a moment to begin your story again from a different moment in time with the focus on a new set of characters or a new strand of the plot.

TAKEAWAYS

- Use part breaks to signal the overall structure of your novel to readers and to make big jumps in time or shifts in point of view.

- Don't be afraid to work theme statements into the most fast-paced, suspenseful moments of your novel.
- Use figurative language to avoid or freshen up clichés. (A cliché is just figurative language that has become stale through repetition).
- Use passive voice to stoke suspense about who is responsible for the action of a sentence.

CHAPTER 30
HOW DO YOU WRITE AN ACTION SCENE?

SPOILER WARNING

As you can see from Chapter 29, Mick Herron uses his multiple plot strands and point-of-view characters strategically to generate interest in one strand that will pull readers forward through the quieter set-up work needed for another strand. We'll look at the full structure of the novel in Chapter 31, and I'll show you how all of this strategic weaving adds up to a complex, richly layered, and satisfying ending. But first, let's take a closer look at a single scene, doing another scene analysis like those we've done for *The Dutch House* (Chapter 2) and *Dial A for Aunties* (Chapter 21). Our *Dutch House* chapter was dominated by interiority, *Dial A* by dialogue; for *The Secret*

Hours, I've picked an action-focused scene so we can look at tricks and techniques for effective action writing.

Looking at our scene composition graphs for each novel (Figure 1, at the end of Chapter 2) shows us that the *Secret Hours* scene is more similar to the *Dial A* scene than to the *Dutch House* scene; the triad of dialogue, action, and interiority dominate both novels—79 percent in *Secret Hours* and 87 percent in *Dial A* (the triad constitutes only 63 percent of the *Dutch House* scene). Interestingly, the *Dial A* scene has a higher percentage of action, at 25 percent compared to the *Secret Hours* scene's 19 percent. However, the action in *Dial A* tends to be quiet, woven into the scene to support the dialogue—a laugh, a look, a shudder. The action in the *Secret Hours* scene, as we shall see, is of the show-stopping variety. Note that I've deliberately chosen scenes from these three novels that have different compositions. It's likely I could find a scene in each of these novels with similar percentages. We're also not trying to identify an ideal percentage of elements because that's going to vary depending on the goals and components of your scene.

Let's get into the details now and see what we find. For my analysis, I've chosen scene thirty-five of the novel (near the end of part three), which follows Max, the retired spy whose flight from his rural Devon cottage starts the novel. Before the scene starts, he's made his way to London and made contact with Shelley, the Security Service staffer assigned to see to his needs. Shelley, however, is milking a leg injury in hopes of a settlement and has turned his case over to a colleague, John Bachelor. Max's single interaction with Bachelor has taught him that the man is certainly an alcoholic and possibly also corrupt enough to "sell his job for the price of a round." Shelley discovers that a recent break-in at the office would have revealed that Bachelor was Max's support person and would have known his whereabouts—confirming Max's theory that Bachelor will be able to tell him who is after him.

So the scene primes us to expect a certain kind of action—a confrontation between Max and Bachelor—and the first line promises the scene will deliver it: "Finding Bachelor hadn't been the most demanding task." Notice the verb tense here: *hadn't been* rather than *wasn't*. Herron's use of the past perfect signals that we are going to see what happens after Max finds Bachelor, but first we are going to see something that happened before it. Readers are going to have to be patient, in other words, while Herron takes a short tangent away from that confrontation to do two things: give further background about the relationship between Max and Shelley, and ring the bell of one of his themes once more.

A previous scene between them has established that Shelley isn't thrilled to see Max and only agrees to help him when he threatens to tell her husband of their one-night stand. After getting the information about the office break-in, Max leans on her one more time to get Bachelor's address. Shelley agrees but notes, "I'm starting to feel like this is a lot to pay for one stray shag." The exchange is entertaining in its own right, but also sets up a clever little reversal we'll see later in the scene. The theme statement is prompted by Max using a smartphone to look up Bachelor's address. Shelley asks why he isn't using the less-traceable Nokia brick he'd had in Devon. Max's answer comes only via interiority:

> It was one thing to play the Luddite while beheading dandelions with a stick, another to deny yourself an advantage while on the run. . . . Besides, there were always loose threads. You could build an identity out of whole cloth, but as soon as you put it on you noticed how the sleeves rode up, how it was already wearing away at the elbows.

We are reminded that we do not yet know who Max was and what he might have done to be the object of a pursuit. Herron is also reminding us to be alert—that we might not know the real identity of any of the characters we've met so far, including the bureaucrats Griselda and Malcolm, either one of whom might be the mole on the Monochrome panel.

Max leaves Shelley's apartment, and Herron uses a mixture of action, interiority, and setting detail to finish this tangent loop and get us back to the point where the chapter began, with this bit of summary: "In the end, he was seven pubs into his odyssey when he tracked him down." Note that this tangent technique is an excellent one to use during revision if you find a scene that isn't quite pulling its weight but still contains a few key moments you want to include in the novel. Spool forward to the moment just before the next really dramatic event is going to begin and see if there is a way to pause the scene at that point and embed a short retrospective tangent, just as Herron does here.

Next, Herron freezes Max in place outside the pub to do some more scene-setting. We get a sentence of description: "The Fox and Bucket was on a corner, with tables outside for smokers, and dusty windows through which passers-by could see what they were missing, which included a row of booths against the far wall, each with a big wooden table, a curved banquette and a sconce with a bulb shaped like a burning candle." And then John Bachelor comes into view: "In one of these sat John Bachelor, holding a pint glass in a way that suggested it was all that was keeping him upright." That sentence alone tells us a whole story about John, but Herron provides more character description: "Max had met him only once, but had no difficulty recognising him: his appearance, even through a dusty window, was of a man nearing the end of his rope, and not an especially reliable rope at that. You wouldn't want to try hanging yourself with it." Note that Herron is leaning on metaphor rather than physical description. Describing John, for example, as "a man in his mid-fifties with the pronounced belly and unfocused gaze of an alcoholic" is perhaps more visual but less arresting—and certainly less characteristic of Max. In other words, Max's assessment of John tells us just as much about Max himself: how astute he is and also how attuned he is to the ways other people can betray you.

There's one more person in the scene for Max to assess—a pub denizen we've met in a previous scene from John's point of view. John has dubbed him 'Sparky' and describes him this way: "He wasn't a big man but didn't need to be, what with the dead eyes, and the way sparks kept popping from his ears, unless they were an optical illusion caused by poorly filtered aggression." Max, when he sits down at their table, also notes that "the aggressive force field around [John's] companion fizzed and sparked"—the assessment suggesting that Max and John view the world similarly, even if they are about to be at odds with one another.

After getting rid of Sparky, Max can get down to the business of finding out whom John has betrayed him to. But the expected confrontation, when it comes, is less dramatic than we expected. Bachelor is indeed a drunk, but apparently a drunk with ethics. Together the two men deduce that John's phone—containing Max's address—was accessed one night when he was blackout drunk. At this point, John excuses himself to go to the bathroom and Herron tantalizes us with a tiny glimpse into Max's past identity: "Faint music drifted across from the pub's other room. For no sane reason, memory threw up a different dive in a different country, and a ragamuffin jazz trio playing something haunting." If readers are disappointed at the quiet resolution of the much-delayed confrontation between Max and John, they won't have much time to feel it because at this point the scene shifts again.

Just as the memory leaves Max's mind, he sees a woman enter the pub and recognizes her as the intruder he hit with a poker two nights before. Another man, whom Max recognizes to be "a professional," warns away the other patrons in the bar and stops to pay off Sparky. Max clocked Sparky's aggression but didn't consider the possibility he was serving as a lookout; Max will continue to be surprised by people he thought he understood as the scene progresses.

The remainder of the scene is an entertaining and intense fight, with perhaps more verbal than physical sparring. The two action sequences are narrated in long paragraphs, running counter to the usual advice that writing short, snappy paragraphs can increase the sense of pace in an action-oriented scene. So what's Herron up to here and what are the effects? Let's look at these two paragraphs in detail to find out.

After some dialogue between Max and the woman—angry on her part and teasing, sarcastic on Max's part—Max realizes he has no choice but to go with them. Here's our first action sequence:

> She led the way, Max behind her, and her companion bringing up the rear; a procession that got them halfway

to the door before John Bachelor appeared from the gents, hurling a plastic swing-bin which hit the man full on the head. He staggered into Max, who stuck a foot between his legs and shoulder-shoved him. While he was hitting the floor, the woman was reaching inside her loose-fitting jacket. *Taser,* Max remembered. He was having one of those slow-time moments whose only use is as a conversation-starter afterwards. *She's going for a Taser.* He grabbed for her arm but she danced backwards, easily evading him. *Once upon a time,* his stupid brain informed him, *you could have scooped up a nice heavy ashtray from a table and crowned her with it.* Best on offer now was a single-stem vase from which a plastic flower poked.

The surprising, satisfying appearance of Bachelor kicks off the action. Notice the way Herron uses progressive verb forms to establish that multiple actions are happening at the same time: "hurling," "hitting," "reaching." (We also saw this verb form at work in Chapter 26.) Surprisingly, it's a bit of interiority, not action, that is delivered in a short, punchy sentence: "*Taser,* Max remembered." But another memory, one from the past that doesn't help him, is what occupies his attention—the thought of the heavy ashtrays that likely were on the tables of the dive bar he was thinking about just before this burst of action began. Herron is taking the opportunity to ring the bell of another of his themes—the way the past continually reaches into the present and future, refusing to let us go—and he does so in the midst of one of the most exciting, suspenseful scenes in the book.

The woman, as it happens, does not have a Taser in her pocket but "a baton that untelescoped with a flick of her wrist: a three-foot-long switch." Max can't resist taunting her once more: "What is this, a bad movie?" Now, as the man Bachelor knocked out is getting back onto his feet, we get our second action sequence:

She flicked [the switch] in his direction, and he felt a stinging sensation on his cheek. Resisted the temptation to raise a hand to its source, but felt his heart racing, and had an impulse to laugh even as the door behind the woman opened, allowing him to grin at the newcomer. "Nice timing." She wasn't fooled and didn't look round, which suited Max because he wasn't bluffing. Shelley McVie's cane came down heavily on the woman's head, splitting in two on contact. The light in the woman's eyes went out, came back on again, and then sort of popped, and she sat down heavily. When Max looked round, Bachelor had picked up a chair, and was either hiding behind it or working out how to use it in a fight, while the man who'd just got to his feet was prepping himself for action. To speed things up, Max smacked his elbow into the man's temple, and when he hit the floor again, Bachelor hit him with the chair, unless he just dropped it. But give him the benefit.

The whole passage is organized around a second deeply satisfying twist: Shelley appearing on the scene and putting her sham cane to a real use. Notice how Herron actually slows the action down in those first few sentences of the passage. In between the first action of the woman hitting Max with her switch and Shelley hitting the woman with her cane are sixty words of interiority as we see what Max is feeling—his cheek stinging, his heart racing—and what he is thinking —his impulse to laugh, his refusal to bluff. These last responses are perhaps as surprising as Shelley's appearance on the scene and, once again, tell us more about Max than about anything else in the scene. Underneath his assumed identity as a "Luddite . . . beheading dandelions with a stick" is the unfiltered, rash, impassioned person he must once have been—those sleeves of his assumed identity riding up, as he notes in the passage we examined earlier, to reveal his true identity.

Similarly, under the pressure of events, both Bachelor and Shelley show us that they have more loyalty to the Service—and their duty to protect Max—than we'd been led to expect. On the surface, Herron delivers dramatic action and surprising twists in this scene, but underneath the external intensity he also delivers a dose of emotional resonance that increases the reader's engagement with Max. Shelley might feel pressured by Max, who might feel betrayed by Bachelor, who might be exactly the weak link First Desk believes him to be. And yet, this scene makes us see that all of these variously flawed characters might be fighting on the same side of whatever battle is afoot in this novel. Max doesn't know quite what that battle is yet, nor do readers, but we'll find out together when we look at the structure of the whole novel in the next chapter.

TAKEAWAYS

- Use the promised drama of an action scene to work in important theme statements or embed plot clues ahead of the fireworks.
- Action sequences don't have to be fast; slowing down can be an effective way to increase our emotional engagement with a point-of-view character.
- Employ interiority during action scenes to slow down the pace and increase tension, using brief flashes of memory or past experiences to add depth to a character's reactions in intense situations.
- When possible, use action sequences to deliver more than just drama; character insights, theme resonances, and even memories can all be woven in.

CHAPTER 31
HOW DO YOU ADD TENSION TO A QUIET PLOT?

SPOILER WARNING

The Secret Hour may be the most narratively and structurally complex novel I've examined in this book, so it's fitting that we're ending with it. Consider the two other novels similar in genre we've looked at: *The Searcher* by Tana French and *The Last Thing He Told Me* by Laura Dave. *The Searcher* has a single point-of-view character and a straight (and quite limited) timeline; readers learn things only as the protagonist-narrator Cal learns things. *The Last Thing He Told Me* has flashback chapters, but they are short and limited in scope, and Dave gives us access only to protagonist-narrator Hannah's point of view. *The Secret Hour*, by contrast, has ten different narrators (in addition to an omniscient narrator) and a timespan of over thirty years.

If we compare the premise of each of these novels, we also find a stark contrast. While it has a slow start, the premise of *The Searcher* is clear and compelling. Teenager Brendan Reddy has disappeared, and the residents of his tiny Irish village of Ardnakelty seem uninterested in finding out what happened to him. *The Last Thing He Told Me* has a similar premise. Tech entrepreneur Owen Michaels has disappeared; his wife, left with a bag of cash and a note telling her to protect Owen's daughter, must find out why. These are easy-to-understand hooks with life-and-death stakes—typical for mysteries and thrillers. While *The Secret Hours* starts out with an exciting chase scene, the question of who is pursuing Max Janáček and why isn't actually the central premise of the plot, just one offshoot of it. The true premise connects the past plot strands of the novel to the present and isn't fully visible until the last third of the novel. A former member of the East German Stasi secret police has changed his identity and is now trying to win the contract to manage background checks for UK government jobs with security clearances (details so boring I literally just had to look them up again even though I've now read the novel twice).

I doubt that Herron intentionally set out to solve the problem of how to make a seemingly boring plot exciting. It's clear from interviews that what really interested him is the question of how the past reaches into the present in unexpected ways; as we've seen, this becomes one of the central themes of *The Secret Hour*.[1] Specifically, he was drawn to Berlin of the early 1990s, just after the end of the Cold War, and long chunks of the narrative take us to those years, following a subplot premise: A naive young security service agent is sent to gather intel on the activities of a fellow agent in the Berlin office who seems to be running an off-the-books operation to get revenge for the killing of a spy embedded in the Stasi. This is a more compelling premise, in many ways, but setting the novel entirely in the 1990s wouldn't allow Herron to explore the interplay between past and present that really interests him. Herron has to find a way to make this decades-old history matter in the present; to do so, he embeds it in a power struggle between the Security Service and the prime minister.

That boring bureaucratic matter of the vetting contract is actually part of a broader attempt to rein in the power of the Security Service, under the guise of privatization and cost-cutting.

Cleverly, Herron increases the drama and intensity of the novel by splitting these two poles of the book into four separate plot strands, each with their own constellation of characters for readers to follow. In each case, one plot strand is suspenseful, with life-or-death stakes, while the other is slower moving but more central.

Past reaching into the present

- **Max:** After living a quiet life for decades, a retired spy code-named Max Janáček is being pursued by someone threatened by his knowledge of the past.
- **Berlin:** A former Security Service agent who was given the workname Alison North testifies in front of the Monochrome panel about an ill-starred, off-the-books operation in the Berlin office in the 1990s.

Power struggle between First Desk and prime minister

- **Contract:** A rich man with a mysterious past (who turns out to be a former Stasi agent) tries to win a contract to privatize the vetting and security clearances for the Security Service.
- **Monochrome:** The prime minister initiates the Monochrome inquiry to look into past wrongdoing by the Security Service.

The Max thread and the contract thread represent active battlegrounds with live and important stakes, whereas the Berlin thread and the Monochrome thread are primarily backward-looking and have lower stakes. What Herron shows us here is a very clever solution to the problem of how to enliven a dull or lifeless plot. If this is a problem you are facing, ask yourself if there are characters or plot pieces that could be spun off into their own strands to represent different aspects of your overall premise or plot set-up. My guess is that, in the case of *The Secret Hours*, Herron first sketched out the basics of Alison's story in Berlin. He was able to give it present-day stakes by making it the focus on the Monochrome inquiry and bringing her in to testify in front of the panel—in essence, providing an excuse for her to tell this story of the past in the present. However, an appearance before a government panel doesn't exactly come with high stakes—and that's where the Max plot comes in. Max is an important but, ultimately, secondary figure in Alison's story, but by making him the protagonist and narrator of his own plot thread, Herron finds a way to make that past-focused strand generate present-day life-or-death stakes.

The lesson here for writers is to spend time asking what kinds of stories and situations your plot components can generate, especially if you are starting from a premise that you fear may be too quiet for reader expectations for your genre or for the kind of story you want to tell. What threads can you tease out and light on fire, allowing readers to enjoy the dramatic blaze until the thread finally sets your primary plot ablaze? Which characters could be spun off into their own plot thread with higher stakes? Teasing out different threads and thinking about how to maximize the drama within them might lead you to a subplot or surprise twist that could enliven your book.

Now that we have a handle on the overall structure of the novel, let's look more closely at how Herron weaves these four plot threads together. We looked at the opening of each of the four plot strands in Chapter 29, so here I'll focus on the climax and ending of each strand. All of them are complex, with multiple point-of-view and secondary characters, and it takes Herron two-thirds of the novel (parts one through four) to set up all of the plot strands and get each poised to hit their interwoven climaxes in the third act of the novel (parts five through seven). Every step of the way, Herron uses his storytelling tools to control the pacing and intensity of the novel, as well as when and how readers get information. The novel does not have a predictable structure or pattern of chapter breaks or point-of-view shifts; instead, Herron has his hand on the instrument panel at all times, ready to use omniscient narration, point-of-view handoffs, time jumps, and scene, chapter, or part breaks whenever they are needed.

Figure 9 (at the end of the chapter) charts the external and internal intensity of the four plot strands within each part of the novel. The size of the circles corresponds to page count; for example, in the external plot, you can see that the Berlin thread dominates parts four and six, while the Monochrome thread dominates part two. Herron uses part breaks to keep the reader oriented in time, but when grouped together they also fit nicely into the standard three-act structure: parts one and two make up act one, parts three and four make up act two, and parts five through seven make up our climactic act three—just where we'd expect to find the most intense external action.

The first thing to note is how important the Max thread is for the stakes, pacing, and intensity of the external plot. Without Max, we lose the punch of action that pulls us into the book, as well as the scene I analyzed in Chapter 30 in which he confronts John Bachelor and has to elude his pursuers once again. The high stakes of that scene are especially welcome after a comparatively quiet series of chapters focused on laying the groundwork for the Monochrome plot thread.

You can also see from Figure 9 that Max plays an important role in the climax of both the external and internal plots. By part six, readers have enough information to guess that the man known to us as Max is the man Alison North has been referring to as "Otis," whose name is on the classified folder smuggled to the Monochrome panel by way of Malcolm's grocery cart. A very alert reader might have made the connection in part four, when Alison recalls a night at a club that matches the details of the snippet of memory Herron embeds in the fight scene I analyzed in Chapter 30.

In the climax of the novel, Max is waiting outside a restaurant for a man named Carl Singer, who owns the agency employing the group pursuing him. Max intends to find out who hired Singer's group; what he finds instead when Singer leaves the restaurant is that he'd been dining with Karl Schenker, the ex-Stasi agent who killed Max's sister back in the 1990s. (He's also the man who, under a new identity, is trying to get the Security Service vetting contract.) Max is crossing the road to confront him when agents acting on the orders of First Desk scoop him up before he reaches Schenker, bringing him back to the Regent's Park headquarters. There we see an emotional reunion between Max and Alison, who haven't seen one another since Alison lost her legs in the bomb planted in Max's car—probably by Schenker and intended for Max.

By contrast, the contract thread starts out low in intensity, in both the external and internal plots, only exploding into energy and action during the climax of the novel. We know that First Desk is opposed to the entire idea of the vetting contract—for her it represents an important loss of power and resources and a diminishment of the Security Service overall. Even before knowing his real identity, she blocks Fabian de Vries (aka Karl Schenker) from winning it because she was suspicious of his murky past and his financial hold on the former prime minister, among other powerful figures. By the climax of the novel, she has put together all the pieces of the puzzle: Schenker/DeVries executed one MI5 agent and gravely wounded another, has paid a mole on the Monochrome inquiry (leading to his pursuit of Max, who could expose his past), and, after being told he wouldn't get the vetting contract, has already established Carl Singer as a virtual proxy. In the last burst of action in the novel, First Desk eliminates him with a maneuver that even DeVries, a very experienced and ruthless operator himself, does not see coming. The contract thread turns out to be unexpectedly riveting—it allows the past to reach out and make trouble in the present—but it's also complex and relies on surprise twists Herron wants to keep hidden until the end.

As we've seen, Herron uses the excitement of the Max thread to compensate for the delayed gratification of the contract thread. However, he also has two more threads to work with—those focused on the Monochrome inquiry and the testimony they elicit from Alison, which becomes the Berlin thread. The Monochrome thread is used primarily as a plot delivery vehicle. It provides an audience for the Berlin thread, so readers can experience those events through Alison's point of view, but also try to put the puzzle pieces together, alongside Malcolm and Griselda, the POV characters for the Monochrome thread. And the appearance of the Otis file before the panel is ultimately what prompts Schenker to go after Max, as we've seen. But

Herron also uses the Monochrome thread as comedic relief, like his hilarious skewering of the pompous Sir Winston, the titular head of the panel. And, although the stakes are not life or death, the thread does provide a punch of external intensity when Malcolm and Griselda decide to proceed with Alison's testimony even after the inquiry is officially halted, as well as a punch of internal intensity when that testimony reveals one of the most closely guarded secrets of the Security Service—that a former First Desk was a Russian spy.

Finally, the Berlin thread operates structurally much like the contract thread, starting slowly and reaching a high level of intensity only in the last third of the novel. In this thread, the highest intensity comes in the internal plot; the external events are still echoing in the present action of the novel, but their active impact is muted, except in the internal emotional engagement of Alison and her listeners as she recounts the events—the betrayals and double betrayals and unexpected shows of loyalty—that led to the life-altering injury she suffered.

The internal plot of the Berlin thread is also a place where Herron can most clearly articulate the theme of the novel. One of those spots comes near the end. Alison has finished her testimony and left the Monochrome offices, but instead of going home she heads to Regent's Park, where, we learn for the first time, she is the longtime archivist for the Security Service. As she journeys through the wet London streets, she recalls the day her assistant, Erin, started the research that ultimately led her to uncover Karl Schenker's identity and pass the Otis file to the Monochrome inquiry so the secret could be revealed. Erin's purpose in doing so is the same as First Desk's—to prevent the Security Service from losing power—and Alison asks her why she's so devoted to the present. Erin's answer, recalled at this point in the novel, rings out with bell-like clarity: "Because it's only the present for a moment. In the long run, it's all history." And past history, as we've seen, retains the power to reach into the present. All stories, Herron is saying, are ultimately circular rather than linear, leading us back to ourselves rather than to some newer, more enlightened plane of existence.

The Secret Hours is an excellent novel to learn from because Herron knows exactly how and when he wants readers to get specific pieces of information, and he manipulates the chronology of the story and uses various narrative tools to accomplish it. When I work with writers who are struggling with plot structure, I often find that they are either surveying the story up on high, from the creator's perspective, or in the trenches, aligned with one or more of the point-of-view characters. Rather than see their story holistically or partially, writers at the revision stage need to see it sequentially—from the *reader's* point of view. You've imagined this story and now you have to, in a sense, forget everything you know about it in order to view it like a reader.

TAKEAWAYS

- Brainstorm subplots or characters that could be spun off from your main plot to increase the tension or stakes, or provide a surprise twist or interesting point of view.
- Use omniscient narration, point-of-view handoffs, time jumps, and scene, chapter, or part breaks to control pacing as well as when and how readers get plot details.
- During the revision stage, try to put aside what *you* know about the story and imagine how it will unfold for the *reader*.

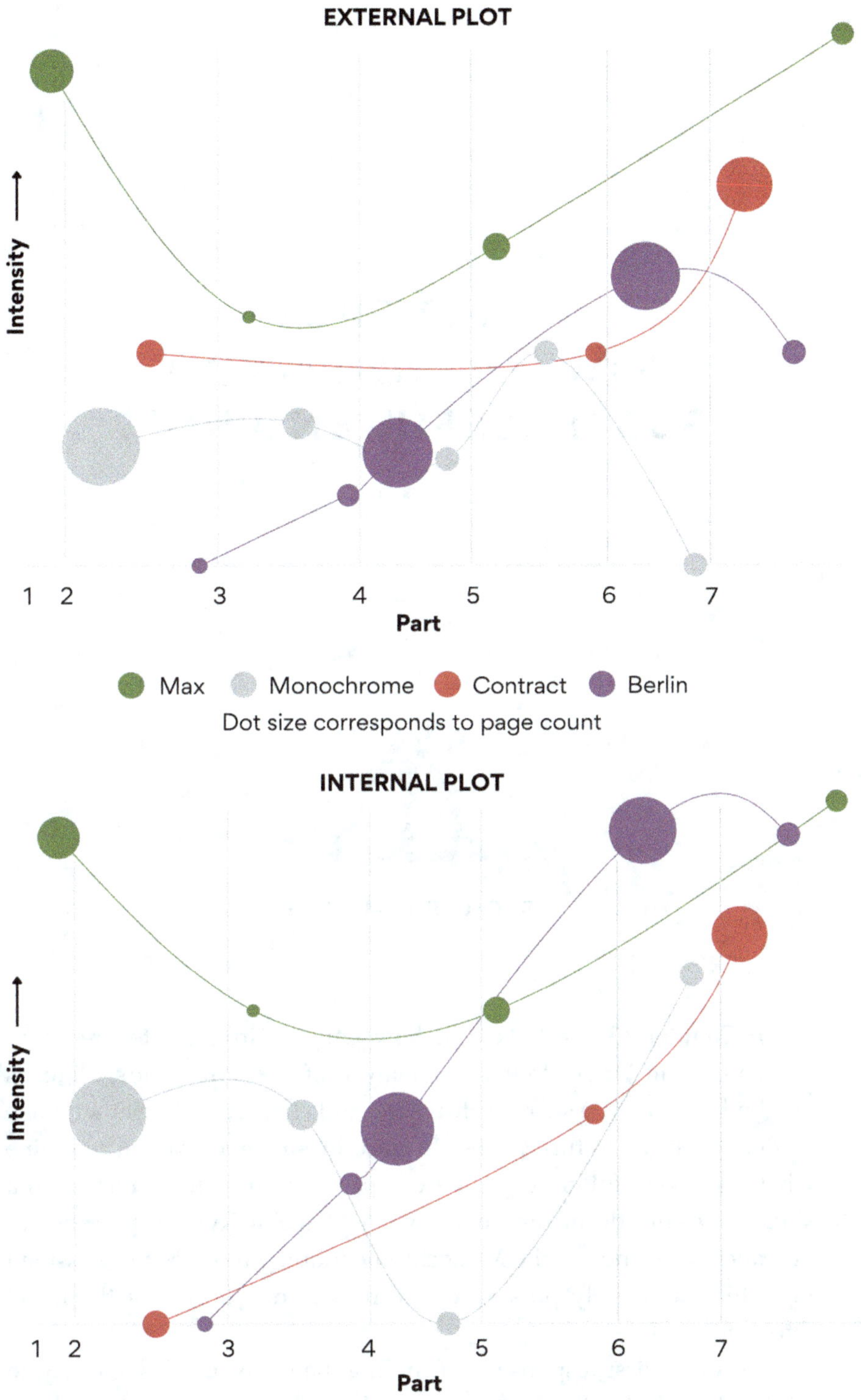

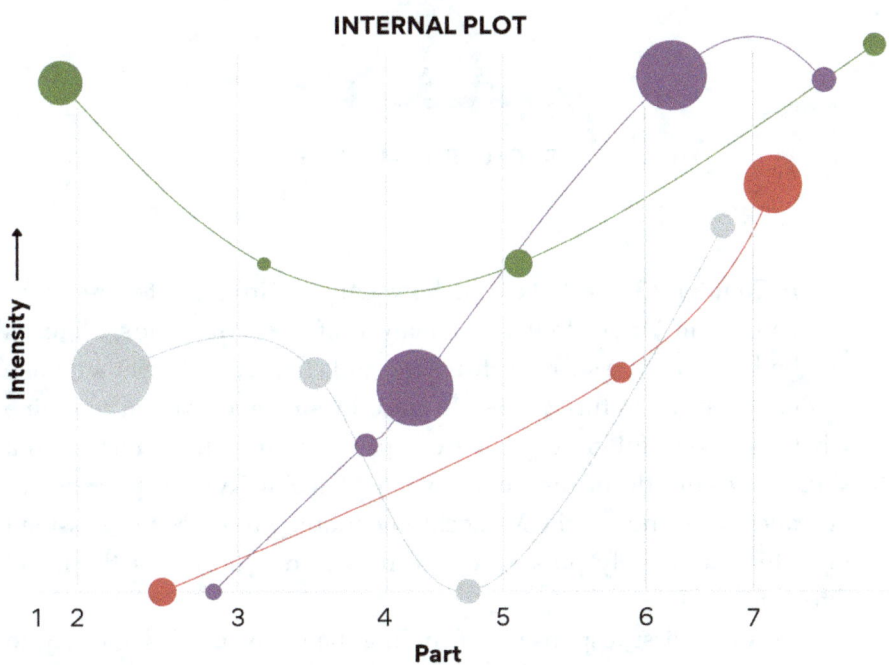

Figure 9: Internal versus external plots of *The Secret Hours*. A fast-start, high-intensity subplot balances a lower-intensity, slow-build subplot.

CHAPTER 32
HOW DO YOU WRITE SUSPENSEFUL ENDINGS?

SPOILER WARNING

In Chapter 13, we looked at how Lauren Groff created resonant endings in *Matrix*. In this last analysis of *The Secret Hours*, I'll focus on how to write suspenseful scene and chapter endings that make readers continue to turn pages. To start, let's take a moment to define what a suspenseful ending is by comparing two endings related to a single key episode in the novel, when Malcolm Kyle, a government bureaucrat assigned to the Monochrome inquiry, receives the classified file which ultimately puts all of the present-day events of the novel into motion.

Malcolm's first response after finding the file is, understandably, to panic. Used to having his problems solved by others, he decides to consult his former boss, surprising her during her breakfast in the gardens behind the Savoy Hotel. Not only does his boss sneer at the flowers he's impulsively bought her and refuse to help him, she also reveals that he won't be returning to his old job when the inquiry is over, as he'd thought, but sent to labor in obscurity in the provinces. The scene ends on an appropriately elegiac note:

> He looked back once, after walking off in the opposite direction, but she'd already disappeared into the February morning. The freesias, though, still lay on the bench, as if marking the place where someone, who had been of importance to someone else, had died.

This is a good example of a resonant ending. Herron has finished off this scene; it's a complete episode, and we don't expect to get any more information from it than we've already received. The simile at the end does not stoke curiosity; instead it highlights a significant step on Malcolm's character arc. He realizes now that his own notion of himself as the "second-highest achiever of his year's intake" was incorrect.

In contrast, let's jump back to the scene in which Malcolm receives the classified file, which is the first cliff-hanger of the novel. The scene starts off quietly. Herron, knowing he is going to end the scene with a bang, takes the opportunity to give us some character background. The scene is set in a grocery store, and as Malcolm shops, we learn that "he never went anywhere without a list," that he has a "sense of dread when the credit card bill dropped into his inbox," and that he'd been voted out of the shared house he'd moved into after graduating. (Notice that all of these details *show* rather than *tell*: Herron lets readers make their own deductions rather than informing us that Malcolm is fastidious, poor, and unlikeable.) Then, a bit of seemingly mundane action: Malcolm collides with a woman's full trolley and helps clean up the mess. He goes to the self-service checkout, and there Herron serves up the last line of the chapter: "Under the bag of oranges, he found the envelope."

Clever, right? The surprise ending is enhanced by the seeming ordinariness of what comes before it. For a cliff-hanger like this to be successful, we need to have enough context to understand that it is significant. In this case, we already know that Malcolm is a member of a government panel tasked with examining classified files, but that First Desk has effectively blocked them from getting their hands on any. So we have good reason to suspect the envelope contains a juicy secret of some sort.

The white space of the scene break gives the suspense a moment to build—and to build even further when, in this case, we realize Herron has flipped to another plot thread and we are going to have to wait to find out what's in the envelope for at least a few more pages. Be careful not to make readers wait too long, however. It's fine to follow a cliff-hanger with a few scenes focused on other plot strands or POV characters, but you must immediately address the cliff-hanger when you return to the same story strand.

Picking up the scene immediately after a break is also quite effective. In that case, it's best to use a chapter break rather than a scene break so the cliff-hanger has more time and space to linger. The most dramatic cliff-hanger in *The Secret Hours*—the revelation that the Monochrome witness Alison was injured by a car bomb in Berlin—is left to hang over both a chapter break and a part break. Like the grocery store cliff-hanger, Herron delivers it in a single short sentence, though this one is given extra resonance with figurative language. We are deep in flashback when the cliff-hanger comes, following along with Alison in 1994 when she sits down in Otis's car and turns the key in the ignition: "In the bright moment that followed, her life divided in two."

In *The Secret Hours*, the Max thread is the one that has the most cliff-hangers, like the one that immediately precedes the scene where Max confronts his official Security Service handler, John Bachelor, which I analyzed in depth in Chapter 30. Herron uses a structure very similar to Malcolm's grocery store scene, showing us Bachelor steadily drinking his way into oblivion and wondering how his life has gone wrong. Here are the last two paragraphs of the scene:

> Beer in hand, the world was slightly better. Which wasn't to say there weren't plenty of ways it could still spin out of orbit.
>
> "Hello, John," said Max Janáček, looming out of nowhere. "How've you been?"

The question is innocuous, but we know this is the prelude to a confrontation because previous chapters have prepped us on the background and the stakes. Max believes that, one way or another, Bachelor can get him closer to answering the question of who is trying to capture him. Our own curiosity about that answer (and eagerness to know what form this confrontation takes) pulls us onward into the book.

Note that you don't want to overuse cliff-hangers. They are a showy, noticeable technique and lose their effectiveness if repeated too often. However, in addition to the resonator endings I discussed in Chapter 13, you can also use surprise endings, which work similarly to cliff-hangers but have lower stakes. A wonderful example, also involving Max, occurs a few scenes before the one we just examined. First Desk, who has been alerted that Max was the target of an attempted abduction, calls Shelley, his former handler, to see if she's heard from him. This is our first glimpse of Shelley, and we have no reason to disbelieve her when she declares she hasn't. Here are the last paragraphs of the scene:

> Reluctant as Shelley was to allow her boss the last word, it's always satisfying to disconnect first, so that's what she did.
>
> Putting away her phone, she said, "Well, didn't take her long, did it?"
>
> Max nodded thoughtfully.

The stakes are lower here because we can guess that Max is there to get Shelley's help rather than confront her—in other words, we don't expect a dramatic action scene on the other side of that scene break—but the surprise is still effective.

You can also end a scene with an action that allows readers to fill in a gap by inference rather than having to show a scene that won't move the plot forward. Here's an example from near the end of the novel. Alison has just been reunited in the present with the man who was Otis and is now Max in a basement room at Regent's Park, the headquarters of the Security Service. She's already been interviewed by First Desk and refused to tell her how she'd recognized Karl Schenker, but she says she'll tell Max, knowing that First Desk will be listening in. Here are the final lines of the scene, at the end of that conversation:

> They [Max/Otis and Alison/Molly] shared a smile, and for a moment they were back in their old lives, the ones that had turned out to belong to other people, or at any rate, to no longer belong to them.
> "So what happens now?"
> "Oh, I expect we'll find out," Molly said, even as the door was opening, and First Desk coming in.

There are only a couple dozen pages left in the book and we know there is at least one more suspenseful scene still to come—Karl Schenker will be dealt with one way or another. We don't see Molly find out what happens to him, but we know she will. We don't need to see the conversation between First Desk, Max, and Alison because Herron has already resolved the Max and Berlin plots via this reunion, and whatever First Desk has to say to them won't move the plot forward. Readers are just as eager as Max and Alison to find out what happens next, but whatever First Desk has entered the room to say is not how he wants to reveal it. We can imagine the conversation during that brief pause of the scene break before Herron hurries us forward to find out what does happen next.

TAKEAWAYS

- Ending a scene on a cliff-hanger gives you the opportunity to open the scene more quietly, perhaps establishing critical character details or backstory.

- Surprise endings are like cliff-hangers but with lower stakes.
- Especially at the end of the novel, you can end a scene with an action that allows readers to infer that a low-stakes, low-intensity scene has occurred without having to include it in the novel.

CONCLUSION: HOW DO YOU READ A NOVEL?

Download your free templates and worksheets:
www.thebluegarret.com/novel-study-downloads

I know from my ten years of working with authors that writing craft is something that can be studied, practiced, and learned. And there are so many ways to learn these days. In addition to the traditional MFA programs, writers can find online classes, podcasts, and craft books like this one. But even with all of these options, I still think that reading widely and carefully is the best—and certainly the most pleasurable—way to learn how to improve your own writing. You also get to customize your curriculum to focus exactly on what you want to learn and who you want to learn from.

Any reading is valuable, whether you are lounging on a beach or sitting in a library with a pencil in hand to take notes, but in this final chapter I'll show you how you can supercharge your reading to get the most benefit from it. I'll give you templates, methods, and questions you can apply to novels in your genre to uncover the craft tools your own favorite writers are using to make the books you love.

Remember: Good writing isn't produced by magic, it's produced by craft. When you understand how a skilled novelist structures plots, shapes characters, constructs scenes, and crafts sentences, you'll be able, with practice, to use these same tools on your own materials. You'll discover that there are more tools and techniques than even the most comprehensive craft guide can catalogue. Eventually, you'll find yourself inventing your own new techniques, contributing to the ever-evolving style changes that make novels novel and keep readers enthralled.

CHOOSE YOUR BOOKS

You can use this reading strategy as a one-off exercise to apply to a novel you especially admire and want to learn from, but you can also make a broader plan that will give you an excellent grounding in your chosen genre. In that case, I'd recommend choosing several recent books (published within the last two or three years) in the genre or subgenre you are writing in, plus one or two in a very different kind of genre, preferably one that is unfamiliar to you. You could also spend a few minutes thinking about which specific writing techniques (like dialogue or point of view or plotting) you want to learn about and then seek out books that showcase those techniques. Scan your bookshelves or ebook library for titles you'd love to reread. Or go to a library or bookstore and be guided by chance, browsing covers and dipping into book descriptions and first chapters until you find a novel that seems promising.

While you can certainly learn from books you dislike or books that aren't well crafted, the process won't be nearly as much fun as studying books you truly love. Don't create an impressive list full of books you *think* you should read but don't actually enjoy. If you start a book and hate it, cross it off your list and go on to the next—perhaps just taking the time to understand exactly why you hate it because that is instructive too.

READ AND TRACK

How you approach this part of the process will depend on how your brain works and on how much time and patience you have. As with your reading list, be honest with yourself and don't keep forcing yourself to do something you hate. (I have endless patience for reading and extremely limited patience for many other things; you might be wired differently.) I'll outline a few possible approaches; try them out and follow the one that works best for your circumstances and inclinations, or mix and match to create your own approach. The goal in all of these approaches is to get to know the novel well enough to see its underlying structures and then do some targeted analysis to understand how the author is using specific craft tools to achieve the effects you are interested in learning about.

A minimalist approach simply involves multiple readings. Read through a first time just for pleasure, or give yourself a head start by choosing a book you've already read once. (Audio works very well for a first reading and allows time-pressed folks to multitask!) Try to do a second reading soon after you do the first, so the structures and details of the story are still relatively fresh in your mind. Then head to the questions in the next section and answer those that interest you. Come back to the novel to do targeted rereading of a scene or section if you want to study a specific technique.

If you want to give yourself a bit more data to work with, then highlight or take notes on anything that jumps out at you as you read, especially during a second read-through. This might be an especially beautiful sentence or a plot surprise or a scene you want to come back and analyze in greater detail. If you are reading on paper, you can take notes right on the book (think of these as your study textbooks!) or you can use sticky notes and tabs or copy material and observations into a notebook or computer file. If you are reading an ebook, you can use your app or device's highlighting and note feature. Take the time to export your notes at the end and save them on your computer. If you are reading on paper and want to get an immediate visual sense of the structure of the book, you can use different colored markers to color the edges of chapter and part breaks or mark them with sticky notes.

Your notes will help you answer the questions in the next section and will also guide you to specific aspects of the book that you want to study further.

The maximalist approach involves filling out a story spreadsheet to capture important information about each scene. (You can download my story spreadsheet template at this link: www.thebluegarret.com/novel-study-downloads.) You don't need to fill in every column for every book, though it's instructive to do so at least once. For books you've already read once, you'll have a sense for which elements are important to track and you might come up with your own categories.

Finally, any of these approaches work beautifully as a group project. Gather together a group of readers and use the questions in the next section as discussion prompts. Different readers will notice different aspects of the book, so you'll learn more than you would by reading solo. You can even divide and conquer the story spreadsheet, which makes the work much less tedious.

STUDY AND ANALYZE

Here's the fun part where you get to start uncovering the tools and techniques the author is using. Once you've read and reread your chosen novel and done whatever level of note-taking and tracking works for you, move through my suggested questions. I've grouped them in categories so you can focus on those you are most interested in. You can write out your answers or just think through them one by one. Additional follow-up questions you can add to each:

- How does this apply to my manuscript?
- Do I want to try something similar?
- Or does this technique or strategy or result point me toward a different path that might work better for my book?

As with the previous section, choose the approach that works best for you. Stop after the overview questions if the exercise starts to feel tedious and move on to another book before returning to a new set of questions. (I certainly did not answer all thirty-nine questions in this list for every novel I studied!)

Another technique to try is to reread a single scene you enjoyed, then flip back to these questions and answer one that seems especially relevant to that scene. Then dip back into the novel, reread, and repeat. You'll become faster at answering these questions each time through and, even better, you'll start spotting the answers *as you read*. Just like building physical muscle during exercise, doing this kind of reading and analysis will build your writing and revising muscles.

You can also download these questions in worksheet format from my website: www.thebluegarret.com/novel-study-downloads.

Overview

(1) Before you dive into your analysis, write down the top three things you love about this novel: What made you want to read it again? What made it a satisfying and immersive reading experience?

(2) Now skim over the categories below and try to connect your favorite elements to specific craft choices the author made. If you are only going to answer a few questions for this novel, focus on those categories. For example, if you loved the protagonist, you might work through the questions on character development and point of view. If you loved the pacing of the novel, then take a look at the questions in the plot structure and scene sections.

(3) Is there anything you didn't like about the novel or didn't think was as successful as it could have been? As with the previous question, can you connect those weak spots to specific craft tools from the categories below?

(4) How is this novel related to other novels in the genre? Are there any elements that make it stand out? Does it use familiar tropes in the genre and, if so, how does the novelist put their own twist on that trope?

(5) Are there specific techniques this author uses that you can apply to your own work? Anything you want to experiment with? Anything you want to avoid?

Plot structure

(6) How does the author use part, chapter, and/or scene breaks to control pacing? Do they use breaks to change POVs or move forward or backward in time?

(7) Are there any subplots? How do they interact with and support the main plot? What functions do they serve?

(8) Is the story told in chronological order? If not, where are the time jumps located? How would reading the story in chronological order affect the way you experience it? How does the writer signal that they are moving backward or forward in time?

(9) Categorize each scene on your story spreadsheet according to intensity and identify key plot points or structural elements like part breaks. Compare the visual structure of the book you produce to the experience of reading it. Where does the author place the most intense scenes? How does the novel's plot structure compare to plot templates or beat sheets you are familiar with?

(10) If you've tracked open and closed story questions (and/or, for a mystery, clues and red herrings) on your story spreadsheet, note the rhythms and patterns the novelist uses. What's the relationship between closed questions and open ones? Are there story questions that are never closed? How did the rhythm of open and closed questions impact your reading experience?

Openings

(11) Take a look at the cover and any other front matter, like an epigraph or illustration. What signals do they send? What mood do

they convey? How is the title related to the content or themes of the book? What attracted you to the cover or title of this book when you first picked it up?

(12) How does the opening work? List the first 10 things (big or little, emotional or physical) you learn about the protagonist. Why did the novelist choose these details? Where does the author position details like the protagonist's name or appearance?

(13) How does the author introduce the protagonist's main conflict or goal?

(14) What made you want to keep reading or stop reading? What questions were you curious about as a reader?

(15) Does the novel have a prologue? If so, what is its function? How else could the author have delivered the crucial elements of the prologue? If the novel doesn't have a prologue, imagine what material might have been included in one. Do you think that would have been an effective strategy?

Scenes

(16) Pick at least one scene and categorize every sentence, using these categories: action, summary, dialogue, character description, setting, interiority, and backstory. What do you see? Which parts of the scene feel fast and which feel slow? Which components are used to convey the purpose of the scene or the deeper themes? Which components would you consider showing and which would you consider telling? Are there any of these components you feel you need to use more or less in your own current manuscript?

(17) Compare two scenes with different qualities—for example, an action-focused scene and a scene with a lot of interiority. What kinds of techniques does the author use in each one?

Character development

(18) What are the key moments in the protagonist's character arc? Is there an inciting incident that gets the action going? Is there an all-is-lost moment where it seems the protagonist is going to fail to achieve their goal? Where are those moments placed in the novel?

(19) How does the author reveal character traits through actions and decisions rather than direct description?

(20) How do secondary characters function in the novel? What are their purposes? How do they contribute to the protagonist's development?

Backstory

(21) How does the writer handle backstory in the novel? Are there past events that provide the key to understanding the protagonist's motivations and choices? If so, how do you learn about these events? Where does the novelist provide hints about these events and where do they do a deeper dive or flashback?

(22) How does the author integrate backstory without slowing down the plot and pacing?

Point of view

(23) Does the novelist use third-person (he/she) or first-person (I) narration? Is the narration in past tense (she said) or present tense (she says)? How do these choices affect the way you experience the story?

(24) If there are multiple point-of-view characters, how does the author differentiate their voices? How much page time does each narrator get?

Interiority

(25) Are there moments where interiority is used to create tension or dramatic irony? For example, are there places in the novel where the reader knows something the point-of-view character does not? Or spots where one character has information another character in the scene doesn't have?

(26) If there is a film or TV version of the novel, watch that and take notes on the differences. Find a scene that is similar in both media and reread the novel version again, noting especially how the novelist uses interiority (thoughts, feelings, memories, internal reactions) and how that is translated to the visual version. The differences will give you insights about how and when to use interiority in your own work—and what you might do if you want to externalize it instead.

Setting

(27) Without looking at the novel, list the first ten details or words that come to mind when you think about the novel's setting. Now reread the first three chapters and list the setting details that jump out at you. Are there specific details that conjure up a larger world? Do any of these details echo larger themes in the novel?

(28) How does the author use sensory details to bring the setting to life?

(29) How does the setting influence the characters and plot?

Dialogue

(30) How does the novelist differentiate the voices of different characters? If they use dialect or non-English languages, which kinds of words do they choose to change?

(31) How does the author use dialogue tags and action tags?

(32) How does the author weave setting details, action, and interior thoughts, feelings, and memories into the spaces around dialogue lines?

Sentences

(33) Take a close look at any sentences you highlighted. What makes them stand out? How does the writer use tools like syntax (word order), verb tense, and sentence length?

(34) How does the author use sentence structure to control pacing or direct the reader's attention to specific moments?

(35) How does the author use figurative language like metaphor and simile?

Endings

(36) On the scene level, compare cliff-hanger endings with resonant endings to see how the author uses each technique. Why and when do they choose one kind of ending over another?

(37) On the story level, how does the author resolve the various plot strands of the novel? Are there any story questions that are left open?

Theme

(38) How does the author introduce and develop the main themes throughout the novel? When was the first moment you glimpsed one of the themes?

(39) Are there any symbols or motifs that the author uses to reinforce the themes?

MAKE THESE TOOLS YOUR OWN

Now that you have all of these rich insights about the tools and techniques used in the novel you studied, what do you do with them? How do you apply them to your own work?

To start, let's address a common anxiety that explains why many writers *don't* read much fiction—they worry that they will be overly influenced by another writer's style or even inadvertently stray into plagiarism. I understand the fear since an accusation of plagiarism can ruin a promising career. However, in the realm of fiction, I can't think of a single case in which an author has unintentionally plagiarized the work of another. When we've seen cases of plagiarism crop up, they've been egregious and deliberate.

Remember too that the purpose of your novel study is to uncover tools and techniques. You aren't looking at a finely crafted desk and then building your own desk using the original as a model. Instead, you are looking at how each piece was made and with what tools. How do these hinges work? What kind of polish creates this rich finish on the surface? Did the woodworker use a drill, a saw, or a hammer to create that curving line?

For example, if you've identified a symbol or motif an author uses to convey the theme of their novel, it's unlikely those exact symbols or motifs would work for your book. Instead, use them as a model and go back to the themes of your own novel and brainstorm a list of symbols or motifs that fit it—or go back to your manuscript to look for them because they are likely already present in some form.

Not all tools and techniques will be suited for your book. However, realizing a specific tool won't work might put you on the track of a tool that *will* work, or perhaps give you the creative inspiration to invent a new one.

Above all, I hope your novel study will encourage you to think about your own work strategically and confidently, knowing that you can analyze and improve it. I hope that on days when your brain feels slow and your ideas seem dull, you'll be able to reach for one of the tools or techniques you've identified and be able to start working, without waiting for the unpredictable magic of creative inspiration to strike. I hope that your novel study will make you feel more knowledgeable about your tools, so you'll feel more confident in wielding them and better able to take those creative leaps that *feel* like magic—but are actually craft.

MORE NOVEL STUDY

The Novel Study project isn't over! If you want to read fresh new installments, sign up for my newsletter, which goes out every other week:

> www.thebluegarret.com/newsletter

If you found the book valuable and want to support my work, please leave a review on Goodreads or your favorite online retailer, which helps other readers find the book.

I love talking to groups of writers and readers! If you'd like me come talk to your book club or writer's group, either virtually or in person, take a look at my speaking page and get in touch:

> www.thebluegarret.com/speaking

NOTES

INTRODUCTION

1. Stephen King, *On Writing: A Memoir of the Craft (Reissue)* (Scribner, 2000), 57, 210.
2. King, *On Writing*, 146.
3. Jessica Page Morrell, *Thanks, but This Isn't for Us: A (Sort of) Compassionate Guide to Why Your Writing Is Being Rejected* (Jeremy Tarcher/Penguin, 2009), 322.

STATS

1. Belinda Luscombe, "Ann Patchett Explains Why She Had to Totally Rewrite Her New Novel *The Dutch House* And Her Problem with Villains," *Time*, September 26, 2019, https://time.com/5686818/ann-patchett-the-dutch-house-interview.

2. WHAT ARE THE COMPONENTS OF A SCENE?

1. Lisa Cron, *Wired for Story: The Writer's Guide to Using Brain Science to Hook Readers from the Very First Sentence* (Ten Speed Press, 2012), 152.

3. HOW DO YOU USE CHRONOLOGY FOR MAXIMUM EFFECT?

1. Susan Bell, *The Artful Edit: On the Practice of Editing Yourself* (W.W. Norton, 2007), 141.
2. Ann Patchett, interviewed by Mary Laura Philpott, Lit Hub, September 23, 2019, https://lithub.com/ann-patchett-discusses-her-new-novel-the-dutch-house.

STATS

1. N. K. Jemisin, "Book Renovation," author website (blog), posted February 7, 2022, https://nkjemisin.com/2022/02/book-renovation.

4. WHAT DOES YOUR COVER AND FRONT MATTER SAY?

1. Use Amazon's 'Read Sample' or 'Look Inside' feature to get a peek at the map if you don't have a copy of the novel in front of you.

NOTES

5. SHOULD YOUR NOVEL HAVE A PROLOGUE?

1. N. K. Jemisin, "The City Born Great," *Reactor Mag*, September 28, 2016, https://www.tor.com/2016/09/28/the-city-born-great.
2. Walt Whitman, "I Sing the Body Electric," Poetry Foundation, https://www.poetryfoundation.org/poems/45472/i-sing-the-body-electric.

6. HOW DO YOU BALANCE MULTIPLE POINTS OF VIEW?

1. Second person (you) is used occasionally, but it's an advanced choice! If you want to take a look at an example, check out Tommy Orange's 2018 novel *There There*.
2. John Truby, *The Anatomy of Story: 22 Steps to Becoming a Master Storyteller* (Farrar, Straus and Giroux, 2008), 32.
3. See Emma Darwin's in-depth blog post "Ten Ways to Move Point-of-View" on how to use this technique successfully. Posted November 23, 2014, https://emmadarwin.typepad.com/thisitchofwriting/2014/11/ten-ways-to-move-point-of-view-and-dont-let-the-self-appointed-experts-tell-you-otherwise.html.

STATS

1. Mindy Carlson, "Tana French," *The Big Thrill*, March 15, 2024, https://www.thebigthrill.org/2024/03/tana-french.

7. HOW DO YOU OPEN A MYSTERY NOVEL?

1. The term "filter words" was coined by John Gardner in *The Art of Fiction*. As readers of my previous book, *All the Words*, may remember, I think this concept is one of the few nuggets of wisdom in a book that is otherwise pompous, dated, and full of casual misogyny. You can read my full review in *All the Words* or on my blog: https://www.thebluegarret.com/blog/art-of-fiction-gardner-review.

8. HOW DO YOU USE DIALOGUE TO REVEAL CHARACTER?

1. The organization Writing the Other regularly offers an online class on how to use dialect effectively and wisely: https://writingtheother.com.

10. DOES YOUR PLOT NEED TO FOLLOW A SET STRUCTURE?

1. For non-Western story structures, see *Craft in the Real World* by Matthew Salesses. For non-arc shapes, check out Jane Alison's thought-provoking book *Meander, Spiral, Explode*.
2. In *Story Grid*, Shawn Coyne discusses how forcing characters to choose between two

NOTES

bad choices (or, the opposite, between two irreconcilable goods) can add tension and focus to your plotting. See chapters 44 and 45.

STATS

1. Lauren Groff, interviewed by Dave Miller, June 1, 2021, *Think Out Loud*, Oregon Public Broadcasting, transcript and audio, https://www.opb.org/article/2023/01/17/author-lauren-groff-on-her-novel-matrix.

STATS

1. JoAnn Yao, "Q&A with Casey McQuiston, *I Kissed Shara Wheeler*," We Need Diverse Books blog, May 2, 2022, https://diversebooks.org/qa-with-casey-mcquiston-i-kissed-shara-wheeler.

14. HOW DO YOU HOOK A READER BEFORE THE FIRST SENTENCE?

1. Elizabeth A. Harris, "'I Just Want Something That's Gay and Happy': L.G.B.T.Q. Romance Is Booming, *New York Times Magazine*, March 30, 2022, https://www.nytimes.com/2022/03/30/books/lgbtq-romance-novels.html.

STATS

1. "Author Laura Dave Discusses Her Newest Novel, *The Last Thing He Told Me*," *Library Journal*, March 15, 2021, https://www.libraryjournal.com/story/author-laura-dave-discusses-her-newest-novel-the-last-thing-he-told-me-lj210315.

STATS

1. "Q&A with Jesse Q. Sutanto: *Dial A for Aunties*," Read More Co. blog, August 9, 2021, https://www.readmoreco.com/blogs/authors-interviews/q-a-with-jesse-q-sutanto.

20. HOW DO YOU INTRODUCE A COMPLEX PLOT?

1. Sutanto includes a long author's note at the beginning of the novel explaining her own family's complex linguistic heritage, their mixed fluencies in Indonesian, Mandarin, and English: "Some of the aunties in *Dial A for Aunties* speak the sort of broken English that my parents' generation does. . . . I'm aware while writing this that I'm straddling a very fine line between authenticity and stereotype, and it's my hope that this book defies the latter." See Chapter 8 for a discussion of dialect.

NOTES

STATS

1. "'Sometimes People Have Trouble Imagining Indigenous People In The Future': Author Rebecca Roanhorse On New Book 'Black Sun,'" CBS News interview, October 28, 2020, https://www.cbsnews.com/losangeles/news/rebecca-roanhorse-black-sun.

23. HOW DO YOU LURE READERS INTO AN EPIC FANTASY WORLD?

1. In the ebook and paperback editions, both maps are positioned at the front of the novel. In the (quite beautiful) hardcover edition, the maps are incorporated as the front and back endpapers. Use Amazon's 'Read Sample' or 'Look Inside' feature to get a peek at the maps if you don't have a copy of the novel in front of you.
2. Online map-making platform Inkarnate (www.inkarnate.com) is popular among self-published fantasy authors. Many authors also hire graphic designers to create custom maps. If you are traditionally published, your publisher might include a map as part of the design package for the book.

STATS

1. Zlata Rodionova, "Maggie O'Farrell Shares Insights into Her Own Writing Process at GH Live," *Good Housekeeping*, November 11, 2023, https://www.goodhousekeeping.com/uk/lifestyle/a45810566/maggie-ofarrell-writing-process.

28. HOW DO YOU MAKE A NOVEL FEEL HISTORICAL?

1. See my blog post "How to avoid errors in historical fiction" for tips, https://www.thebluegarret.com/blog/how-to-avoid-errors-in-historical-fiction. On the question of italicizing non-English words, see Thu-Huong Ha's article "Bilingual authors are challenging the practice of italicizing non-English words," published in *Quartz*, June 24, 2018, https://qz.com/quartzy/1310228/bilingual-authors-are-challenging-the-practice-of-italicizing-non-english-words.

STATS

1. Carole V. Bell, "To Mick Herron, Failure Is More Interesting Than Success," *BookPage*, September 2023, https://www.bookpage.com/interviews/to-mick-herron-failure-is-more-interesting-than-success.

31. HOW DO YOU ADD TENSION TO A QUIET PLOT?

1. "Mick Herron on his new book, The Secret Hours," John Murray Books YouTube channel, August 21, 2023, https://youtu.be/lMtmdfIPiRk.

TAKEAWAYS AND TOPIC INDEX

BACKSTORY

- Consider using time jumps to reveal backstory gradually, allowing readers to piece together the past alongside the characters. (Ch 3)
- Provide only the amount of backstory you need in order to make each POV character's motivations clear—a character with a flatter arc needs less backstory. (Ch 6)
- Position backstory strategically to heighten suspense or provide context for key revelations in the plot. (Ch 10)
- Use a snippet of recalled dialogue to liven up a backstory recollection. (Ch 15)
- Provide enough backstory for readers to care about your characters and understand how their arcs might develop, but make sure there is also something happening in the "front story" of the scene, like an action or decision or goal. (Ch 18)
- One way to use backstory is to give readers access to information the point-of-view character might not remember, creating dramatic irony. (Ch 19)

TAKEAWAYS AND TOPIC INDEX

CHARACTER DEVELOPMENT

- Show the why: Rather than telling the reader how a character feels, show us *why* they feel this way. (Ch 2)
- Use a character's reactions to past events to reveal their growth or stagnation over time, demonstrating how their history shapes their present actions and decisions. (Ch 3)
- When developing multiple point-of-view characters, ensure each has a distinct voice, perspective, and character arc that contributes uniquely to the overall narrative. (Ch 6)
- What your point-of-view character notices—and doesn't notice—can reveal just as much about that character as it does about whatever they are observing. (Ch 9)
- If you need to introduce a large cast of characters, find a setting that allows you to gather them all in one place and show readers the group dynamics and tension. (Ch 20)
- Reveal key details about characters naturally through dialogue and action. (Ch 20)
- Use subplots to showcase different aspects of your characters' personalities and provide opportunities for growth outside the main plot. (Ch 22)

DIALOGUE

- Look for places you can either strip off or enrich dialogue tags (for example, "he says"). (Ch 8)
- Rely mostly on word choice and syntax to give dialogue a historical or regional flavor. Use non-standard spellings sparingly, and be alert to the power dynamics involved in those choices. (Ch 8)
- Take advantage of the space in between dialogue lines to deliver a snippet of character description, backstory, or interiority. (Ch 8)
- Use subtext—the difference between the surface meaning of dialogue and the feelings underneath—as a way to show the

stakes of a conversation or the tension in the relationship between the speakers. (Ch 8)
- Consider using reported speech to give the sense of a community's reaction to an event. If it makes sense for your narration style, you can filter this speech through the point of view of your narrator. (Ch 15)
- Use the white space around dialogue to reveal details about the character speaking. Bracketing those details between two dialogue lines keeps the pace lively. (Ch 15)
- Use dialogue lines to sneakily hint at important facts about a character rather than revealing them directly. (Ch 15)
- If you are using a limited, close narration style, you can allow your point-of-view character to take over the white space in another character's dialogue paragraph with their own thoughts and reactions. (Ch 15)
- Use tension between characters to add stakes to every conversation. Make dialogue do more than just convey information. You can use subtext and interiority to show gaps between what a character is saying and what they are thinking. (Ch 21)
- Share background details or needed context via summary bridges between sections of dialogue. Sprinkle information throughout the scene rather than delivering it in one long 'info dump.' (Ch 21)

ENDINGS

- Use your ending to not only resolve plot threads but also reinforce your central themes. (Ch 13)
- The falling action or resolution of the novel (everything after the climax) is your opportunity to reveal what it all meant—why you wrote the novel and what you want readers to take away with them. (Ch 13)
- Ending a scene on a cliff-hanger gives you the opportunity to open the scene more quietly, perhaps establishing critical character details or backstory. (Ch 32)

- Surprise endings are like cliff-hangers but with lower stakes. (Ch 32)
- Especially at the end of the novel, you can end a scene with an action that allows readers to infer that a low-stakes, low-intensity scene has occurred without having to include it in the novel. (Ch 32)

INTERIORITY

- Anchor summaries or extended internal reflections to the present moment by occasional references to an easy-to-understand action, like making a meal. (Ch 7)
- Use interiority to reveal a character's biases or preconceptions, showing how these influence their interpretations of events and other characters. (Ch 10)
- Use techniques like interiority, filtering, and physical reaction to build suspense and maximize the drama of a climactic moment. (Ch 18)
- You can deliver the primary story questions to your reader by using interiority to show what your point-of-view character is asking. (Ch 19)
- In comedic scenes, contrast a character's internal thoughts with the external situation to heighten humor and reveal their true reactions. (Ch 21)
- Employ interiority during action scenes to slow down the pace and increase tension, using brief flashes of memory or past experiences to add depth to a character's reactions in intense situations. (30)

OPENINGS

- Use your first lines to make readers curious (who is Andrea?) rather than establish basic information (the narrator's name). (Ch 1)

TAKEAWAYS AND TOPIC INDEX

- Don't reveal too much in your opening paragraphs: Give your readers space and time to make guesses you later confirm. (Ch 1)
- Spend time playing around with your title. What would be the effect of including a verb? Adding a pronoun? Changing the tense or shifting to a different pronoun? (Ch 4)
- Use a map or frontispiece illustration to drop hints or to illuminate contrasts or connections between story or setting elements. (Ch 4)
- Inject suspense and action—not just atmospherics—into the prologue, if you include one. (Ch 5)
- Save important backstory information for later in the novel, after we've met your protagonist and understand their current problem and what's at stake. (Ch 5)
- Dramatize the novel's premise through a mini-story that functions as the prologue. (Ch 5)
- Make sure that your first chapter launches 'live' story questions—questions your characters don't know the answers to—in addition to backstory questions. (Ch 7)
- Don't feel like you need to tell readers everything at once—start with the familiar ("village"), then add specifics ("Ardnakelty") later. (Ch 7)
- If you include a content warning, make sure it matches the tone of the novel and the voice of your primary narrator. (Ch 14)
- The job of your first chapter isn't to tell readers everything they need to know about your protagonist or story world; its job is to hook readers so they will keep reading. (Ch 14)
- Hook readers by jumping straight into a dramatic situation, withholding key details, twisting familiar genre tropes, and establishing a strong narrative voice to help readers identify with a protagonist narrator. (Ch 14)
- If your reader already knows the hook of your novel, use that foreknowledge to create dramatic irony and build anticipation, while delivering important backstory information. (Ch 17)

- Use familiar, well-loved tropes that are common in your genre but find ways to tweak them, especially if you open the novel with one. (Ch 17)
- If you include a prologue in a thriller, mystery, or suspense novel, use it to generate new questions in the reader's mind, beyond those already created in the book description. (Ch 17)

PLOT STRUCTURE

- Decide *when* in time to locate the story's narrator. Use chronology jumps to raise questions, control what you reveal and hide, and provide additional layers of meaning with the benefit of hindsight. (Ch 3)
- Experiment with chronology jumps during revision, not drafting, once you thoroughly know the characters and events. (Ch 3)
- Use a spreadsheet or notecards or a graph to see your chronology visually and experiment with mixing it up. (Ch 3)
- Build momentum and suspense by answering one part of a story question but leaving another part open. If you answer a *who* question, leave open a *how* or *why* follow-up question to pull readers forward. (Ch 7)
- Use plot templates as a way to generate ideas or to spot missing pieces, but don't feel that you need to cram your plot into a template that wasn't designed for it. (Ch 10)
- Map out and study novels in your genre so you can see a variety of approaches. Then go back to your own novel and do the same mapping. What stands out now? (Ch 10)
- Use structure to help you decide where to place key plot moments or important pivot points. (Ch 10)
- Vary the intensity of your internal and external plots—they can ebb and flow at different times to create a range of effects. (Ch 10)

TAKEAWAYS AND TOPIC INDEX

- Time stamps keep readers oriented in place and time, but they can also be used to build suspense by establishing a timeline and ticking clock. (Ch 14)
- Use beat sheets and story templates for inspiration or to diagnose plot problems or gaps, not as a set of rigid rules. (Ch 19)
- Offer readers new story questions as your novel unfolds. If your story is organized in three acts, the primary story questions should change for each act. (Ch 19)
- Activating two plots at the same time can help you maintain interest and pacing by giving readers two sets of story questions they are eager to have answered. (Ch 20)
- Adding a subplot or trope borrowed from a different genre can fix a manuscript that feels flat, boring, or slow-paced. (Ch 22)
- Balance intense action subplots against slower-building relationship or internal subplots. Pair quieter scenes in one subplot with more intense scenes in another subplot. (Ch 22)
- Build to the same intensity across interwoven subplots at climactic moments, like in the final chapters of the novel. (Ch 22)
- Be strategic about using structural elements like part breaks or the midpoint for pivots, shifts, or reversals in one or more subplots. (Ch 22)
- Use elements such as maps and character lists to orient your reader if your novel features a complex fantasy world and a large cast of characters. (Ch 23)
- Use time stamps at the beginning of chapters to keep readers oriented if your novel jumps around in time. (Ch 23)
- Think about the reader's experience of your plot to help you determine the best order in which to narrate the events of your novel. (Ch 25)
- Use part breaks to signal the overall structure of your novel to readers and to make big jumps in time or shifts in point of view. (Ch 29)

- Brainstorm subplots or characters that could be spun off from your main plot to increase the tension or stakes, or provide a surprise twist or interesting point of view. (Ch 31)
- Use omniscient narration, point-of-view handoffs, time jumps, and scene, chapter, or part breaks to control pacing as well as when and how readers get plot details. (Ch 31)
- During the revision stage, try to put aside what *you* know about the story and imagine how it will unfold for the *reader*. (Ch 31)

POINT OF VIEW

- Use your POV choices to control the distance between reader and narrator(s), as well as the pacing and suspense of specific scenes. (Ch 6)
- Choose a narration style that underscores your theme. Jemisin's multiple voices emphasize her message that healthy cities function by housing many different voices and perspectives. (Ch 6)
- When developing multiple point-of-view characters, ensure each has a distinct voice, perspective, and character arc that contributes uniquely to the overall narrative. (Ch 6)
- You don't need to give each POV character equal page time: Choose the balance based on the needs of your plot and theme. (Ch 6)
- Use scene or chapter breaks to move between narrators, or carefully (and rarely!) do a POV handoff within a scene. (Ch 6)
- Be deliberate about your point-of-view choices. Know why you are making your overall choice, as well as the effects of choices in individual scenes. (Ch 12)
- Establish omniscient narration early by providing details your point-of-view character or protagonist cannot know. (Ch 12)
- To make omniscient narration feel fresh, give readers close

TAKEAWAYS AND TOPIC INDEX

access to the protagonist, moving away only for select moments. (Ch 12)
- Use filter words to identify whose experiences and thoughts we are seeing when using omniscient narration. (Ch 12)
- Incorporate pieces of 'primary evidence' (letters or other materials) from your story world to illuminate other POVs in a single-POV novel. (Ch 16)
- Introduce new point-of-view characters only at the point where they are going to affect the events of the plot—not before. (Ch 25)
- To maximize suspense, show the most dramatic events from the POV of the character who has the highest stakes in the outcome. (Ch 25)
- As the climax nears, toggle between POVs more rapidly to build a multi-perspective crescendo. Be strategic about the order so each revelation builds on the previous one. (Ch 25)
- When writing historical fiction, give us deep access to your POV characters' interior thoughts and emotions. Take advantage of dramatic irony; the reader might know more about what happens to a historical figure than a character yet knows in the world of the story. (Ch 26)
- Make omniscient narration feel fresh by focusing it through your characters rather than relying on a nineteenth-century style guide narrator who hovers above the action. (Ch 27)
- Use distance to control your reader's experience if using omniscient narration—draw back and focus on external setting details or summary before moving deeply inside another character's mind. (Ch 27)
- If using omniscient narration, use passive voice to create a moment of distance to separate POV characters in the same scene. (Ch 27)

SCENES

- Use the mix of components (action, dialogue, interiority, etc.)

best for *your* specific scenes—there is no ideal mixture that works for every scene. (Ch 2)
- Make sure your scene has a purpose and that at least one character is changed in some way by the end of the scene. (Ch 2)
- Compress less important details of a scene using summary. (Ch 2)
- Stretch out the most important moments of your scene, using setting details and interiority, in addition to action and dialogue. (Ch 2)
- Position long sections of summary, character description, or backstory immediately before or after more dynamic action sections to vary the pacing of the scene. (Ch 2)
- Be deliberate about where you place surprises or new information within a scene. Placing the surprise at the end is a guaranteed method to keep readers turning pages, but vary the rhythm—don't end every scene with a cliff-hanger. (Ch 18)
- If you've ended a previous chapter on a cliff-hanger, you don't have to resolve it at the beginning of the next chapter as long as you start the scene in a place that makes readers believe they'll get to the revelation soon. (Ch 18)
- The components you use to build your scenes will vary according to the plot, themes, and genre of your book, and they will likely also vary by scene. There is no magic formula. (Ch 21)
- While different scenes and books will use more or less of some components, variety is always beneficial. Break up long sections of dialogue with action, interiority, and descriptive details to vary the pace. (Ch 21)
- Use the promised drama of an action scene to work in important theme statements or embed plot clues ahead of the fireworks. (Ch 30)
- Action sequences don't have to be fast; slowing down can be an effective way to increase our emotional engagement with a point-of-view character. (Ch 30)

- When possible, use action sequences to deliver more than just drama; character insights, theme resonances, and even memories can all be woven in. (Ch 30)

SENTENCES

- Use grammar and syntax to direct your readers' attention where you want it. Sentence fragments can build suspense as readers wait for a sentence anchored by a verb. (Ch 7)
- Structure sentences to control the pacing of revelations, using longer, more complex sentences to build tension before delivering key information in short, punchy sentences. (Ch 18)
- Your verb choices can help you control narrative distance. Use progressive verb forms ("-ing") to create an immersive, in-the-moment feel. Shift to simple present tense for key realizations to maximize their impact. (Ch 26)
- Limit use of period language and non-English words to occasional touchstones decipherable from context. (Ch 28)
- Use figurative language to avoid or freshen up clichés. (A cliché is just figurative language that has become stale through repetition). (Ch 29)
- Use passive voice to stoke suspense about who is responsible for the action of a sentence. (Ch 29)

SETTING

- Make setting details do double duty, like evoke a theme of the novel or reveal backstory. (Ch 1)
- Be alert to the connotations of words when writing description and use them to establish mood. (Ch 9)
- Description is a place to pull out all of your specialized writer tools, like simile, metaphor, and personification. (Ch 9)

TAKEAWAYS AND TOPIC INDEX

- Weave snippets of description in between more active aspects of a scene—between a series of actions or in the white spaces of dialogue lines. (Ch 9)
- Use description to foreshadow future plot developments or character arcs. (Ch 9)
- Chapter and scene openings are opportunities for description that also establishes setting, date, and time. (Ch 9)
- Tie setting description to action: Make sure that your characters are moving, interacting, remembering, not just staying in place to be described. (Ch 11)
- You likely need fewer details than you think to establish the historical feel of a book, but make sure those details are both specific and vivid. (A falcon is a memorable detail!) (Ch 11)
- Intersperse historical or fantasy details with familiar ones, like descriptions of time, nature, human emotions. (Ch 11)
- When introducing a new story world, begin with something that is familiar and weave in new details gradually. (Ch 23)
- Spend time building out the principles and details and structures of your story setting, then look for opportunities in each scene to reveal those details. (Ch 24)
- Give readers information as they need it to form opinions about a choice facing the character or to make sense of what is happening in that moment rather than giving them information they don't need to know until much later in the novel. (Ch 24)
- Balance new information and concepts with familiar activities and relationships that operate similarly in your fantasy world and our world. (Ch 24)
- If you can't find the right moment for a specific detail, ask yourself whether it's something readers need to know. Perhaps it's just something that you as the writer needed to know in order to write the scene. (Ch 24)
- Make sure that historical details are not just set dressing but rather connect to deeper thematic or metaphorical meanings that illuminate your characters. (Ch 28)

- Use sensory and bodily details to immerse readers deeply in a historical character's perspective and constraints. (Ch 28)

THEME

- Introduce your theme subtly in the opening chapters through symbolic details, character actions, or setting descriptions, allowing readers to gradually recognize the underlying ideas. (Ch 1)
- Consider how your novel's title and cover design can introduce your themes before the reader even begins the story. (Ch 4)
- Choose an epigraph (if you include one) that connects to the themes of your novel—think of your book as joining a conversation started by the work you quote from. (Ch 4)
- Use metaphor and setting to suggest the theme and mood of the story. (Ch 7)
- Don't be afraid to work theme statements into the most fast-paced, suspenseful moments of your novel. (Ch 29)

ACKNOWLEDGMENTS

I published my first book, *All the Words*, in February 2020, just a few weeks before the world shut down. Even though *Novel Study* is a natural progression from that first book, it took me almost two years to start writing it.

Looking back, I can see that without the intellectual companionship and encouragement I gained from some virtual classes and communities I joined during the pandemic, it would have taken me much longer to get started again. Thank you, especially, to my wonderful Ruby community; to my journey group (still going strong!), Vivian and Lucy; and my accountability partner and fellow dreamer Katey.

I'm also lucky to have a strong group of smart and nurturing editing colleagues who have become lifelines for me in a profession that can be lonely if you let it. Thank you to Rachel, Tanya, Antonn, Kristen, Nicole, Andy, and Genevieve for all of the support, encouragement, and companionship.

This book benefited tremendously from the careful, thorough feedback of my beta readers. Thank you to Paul, Francesca, Michelle, Lori, Susan, Ted, Alyssa, and Roy for the time and care you put into your comments.

And, finally, thank you to my family—Rehmi, Sam, Gracie, Danna, and Karen—for always believing that I can do anything I set out to achieve, and making sure I have the time and support to actually get it done. And thank you to my friend family—Rachel and Dave, Tara, Ryan, and Rachel—for all of the joy, laughter, good food, and honesty.

Kristen Tate
September 2024

ABOUT THE AUTHOR

Kristen Tate has been a freelance book editor for a decade, helping authors transform their work from rough draft to finished book. She has a PhD in English from Columbia University, with a focus on publishing history. She is also the author of *All the Words: A Year of Reading About Writing* and writes a regular newsletter full of craft advice and encouragement for authors. She lives in San Francisco with her family.

facebook.com/thebluegarret
instagram.com/bluegarret
tiktok.com/@bluegarretbooks

ALSO BY KRISTEN TATE

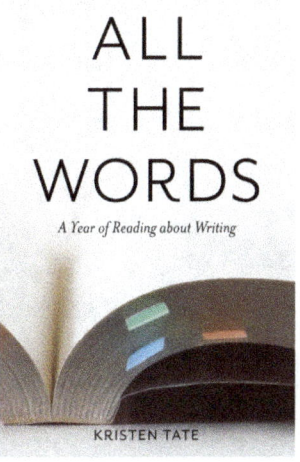

If you read one book about writing every week for a year, what would you learn?

Thanks to the self-publishing revolution and events like National Novel Writing Month, the genre of writing craft books has exploded in recent years. Book editor Kristen Tate set out to read and review one writing advice book each week for a year, from classics like E. M. Forster's *Aspects of the Novel* and Anne Lamott's *Bird by Bird* to newer works like Jane Alison's *Meander, Spiral, Explode* and Jessica Brody's *Save the Cat! Writes a Novel*.

What she discovered was a dizzying array of approaches to writing: plotters who know even the smallest details about characters before they write a word; pantsers who blithely dive right into a draft without a plan; anti-adverb crusaders and advocates for complex sentences; and, always, that the best way to learn is to read the kinds of books you want to write.

All the Words is also a meditation on the challenges and pleasures of starting and sustaining a weekly practice of reading, thinking, and writing. It's an optimistic, encouraging book that will motivate you to keep reading and, most importantly, keep writing.

www.ingramcontent.com/pod-product-compliance
Lightning Source LLC
Chambersburg PA
CBHW052133070526
44585CB00017B/1806